Zen is Eternal Life

Zen
is Eternal Life

by

RŌSHI P.T.N.H. JIYU-KENNETT

Formerly published as

Selling Water by the River

SHASTA ABBEY PRESS,
MOUNT SHASTA, CALIFORNIA 96067

Third Edition—1987
Fourth Edition—1999

Originally published in 1972 as *Selling Water by the River*.
Second edition published in 1976 as *Zen is Eternal Life*.

Front cover: The author meditating in the Meditation Hall at
Dai Hon Zan Sōjiji. Back cover: The author sweeping
leaves in the grounds of Dai Hon Zan Sōjiji.

Frontispiece: The author after her Dharma Transmission ceremony.
She received Dharma Transmission from the Very Reverend Kohō
Keidō Chisan Zenji, Chief Abbot of Dai Hon Zan Sōjiji
and Archbishop of Sōtō Zen of the Kantō Plains.

Printed in the United States of America.

ISBN 0-930066-20-0
Library of Congress Catalog Card Number: 99-072819

The TransIndic font used to print this work is available from Linguist's Software, Inc.,
PO Box 580, Edmonds, WA 98020–0580 USA tel (425) 775-1130.

*To my master, the Very Reverend Kohō Keidō Chisan Zenji,
late Chief Abbot of Sōjiji and Archbishop of the Kantō Plains.*

CONTENTS.

Book Three. The Teachings of Keizan Zenji.

PREFACE TO THE FIRST EDITION.

In 1186 military government, under Yoritomo Minamoto, was established in Japan and, with it, came one of the greatest changes ever experienced in the history of that country. Up until that time the seemingly pleasure-loving aristocracy in Kyoto had written their poems, painted pictures and sung, apparently forgetting that the peasantry existed; degeneracy appeared to be in the air. The Buddhist hierarchies had enjoyed political support in return for mysterious and beautiful ceremonies which were seemingly more or less devoid of genuine spirituality. Then, with the fall of the aristocracy, the temples and monasteries found themselves on their own, a prospect very few seemed to be able to adapt to.

Amidst all the turmoil a new spiritual force began to arise. In the year 1191, Eisai Zenji, a Japanese Buddhist priest, returned from China and established the Rinzai school of Zen: he had spent four years studying under Master Eshō. The new and vital school of Buddhism that he brought with him was like a beacon of light shining in the religious darkness of mediaeval Japan.

The *kōan* system of the Rinzai school was itself a fairly new development in the history of Zen. It was mainly through the eloquent master Daie Sōkō, in the early part of the twelfth century, that it had become widely used in China. The kōan exercise, with its shouting, kicking, crying and beating, culminating in the sudden understanding of *kenshō*, attracted the young samurai of Japan who seemed to have quickly absorbed its methods into their own discipline.

Shortly before Eisai's death, a young trainee, named Dōgen, began studying under the aged master. Upon the death of his teacher, Dōgen, who was not satisfied even with the Rinzai teachings, found it necessary to travel to China in order to further his studies. There he found the "serene reflection" type of meditation practiced by the Sōtō school of Zen and it is with these teachings, which he brought back to Japan, that this book is concerned.

Sōtō Zen followed mainly the Indian tradition and was the religion of the ordinary person, man or woman. In his writings, after his return, Dōgen proclaimed that there was no difference between the meditations of a man and a woman, a rich person and a poor one, everyone being able to find peace and freedom if he truly sought it. It is because of its apparently simple approach, the very opposite, to me, of the approach of Rinzai, that I have chosen Sōtō for myself.

Under his Chinese master, Nyojō, Dōgen learned that Sōtō masters were not bound by any one system of teaching: they preferred to use kaleidoscopic teaching methods and to allow the kōan to develop naturally in the daily life of the trainee, as his spiritual understanding ripened, rather than force his growth through the unnatural tension created by a fixed system of kōans. It was in 1227 that Dōgen returned to Japan to teach the "new" Sōtō system; so called despite the fact that Sōtō is the oldest of the three Zen schools.

During his lifetime, Dōgen realised that the time for spreading Sōtō Zen in Japan had not yet come so he spent most of his life organising small communities. It is for this reason, and this reason only, that Sōtō Zen had to wait several generations before it was to enjoy widespread acceptance in Japan under the aegis of Keizan Zenji. Anesaki tells us, in his *History of Japanese Religions*, that the times were ripe for a new and vital religion, Rinzai seemingly having, by then, degenerated into a means of artistic religious expression rather than being a source of real spiritual help for the masses who were in dire need of it.

Until the time of Keizan, Dōgen's Zen seemingly had clung to its Chinese heritage thus alienating itself from the common people of Japan. Keizan brought the old ideas of Buddhism into line with the new spirit of the times—and in so doing exemplified one of Dōgen's greatest teachings—by his insistence that Zen could survive only if it came alive for the time in which its adherents were living. To this end he, like Dōgen, taught the most advanced forms of hygiene and living habits then extant, blending them with the culture of the Japanese people and the ancient spirit of Zen so that every act of daily life became an act of religious understanding. Through this simple process Sōtō Zen spread throughout the country until today it is the second largest school of Buddhism in Japan, its teachings keeping ever in step with the times and yet retaining their original spirit.

I studied at the London Buddhist Vihara and was a lecturer at the London Buddhist Society. It was while studying Buddhist history that I discovered that all the seemingly known great Zen masters appeared before the Sōtō and Rinzai lines separated, although there were many good masters later in both lines. I spent time in Chinese temples of the Rinzai school in Malacca, Singapore and Hong Kong but felt that its teachings did not go far enough; it therefore seemed only natural that I should devote my fullest energies to pursuing the Sōtō way; after all, this had been my original intention. This I did for seven years and seven months in Japan with a three-month return visit to Malaysia during this time.

There is a Japanese saying that, whilst Rinzai is for the generals, Sōtō is for the farmers. It would appear that, whereas Rinzai Zen is much better known for its religious arts than for its genuine spiritual help for the ORDINARY man and woman, Sōtō Zen teaches the way for every living person, whether they be student, factory worker or executive, to find peace and freedom in everyday life. The farmer in his fields can apply Sōtō Zen to his daily life just as much as can the queen of England or the president of the United States; all find complete peace of spirit without the stress or strain they would experience should they try to reach the same state through the Rinzai kōan method.

Bearing these facts in mind, Sōtō Zen is ideal for the present-day religious revival in America. Both Dōgen and Keizan were far in advance of their own day and age and, in some ways, are still in advance of ours; what they wrote and taught is as applicable now as it was when they wrote it. Although the old forms of many of the ceremonies are still kept and performed intact, their meaning and spirit are abreast of the times in which we live and this vitalises them in a way no other religion, at present extant, seems to me to be able to equal.

At a time when the young are seeking a religion that means something to them personally, rather than one that requires rigid adherence to doctrine and old rules, Dōgen's insistence upon finding freedom, perfection and peace of spirit within oneself, amidst the struggle of everyday life and within the structure and times in which one lives, is as relevant as it was when he lived and it is my certain knowledge of this that has led me to place the following work before the public.

I beg the reader's pardon for the inadequacy of this book; whatever merit it has must be given to the Buddha, Dharma and Sangha; may you be peaceful and happy.

Rōshi P.T.N.H. Jiyu-Kennett

Abbess of Shasta Abbey, California, and former Foreign Guestmaster, Sōji Temple, Yokohama, Japan.

October, 1971.

PREFACE TO THE THIRD EDITION.

After seventeen years in America, much of what has been said in various places in this book, concerning Japanese temples and Japanese ways, is no longer relevant for we have found complementary equivalents that preserve the spirit of the teachings of Dōgen and Keizan whilst not being bound by their ethnic traditions. This has led us to revert to the original translation of the *Denkōroku* in this edition as well as to the original form and title of the book itself; however, for the sake of continuity, we are retaining the preface to the first edition, slightly altered, so as to make the transition from East to West easier. I believe it was Kohō Zenji's fond hope that, when Zen came to America, it would come as a pure bride, uncluttered by attachment to its former ethnic connections. After seventeen years, we now know that this is possible, but we did not wish to remove anything whatsoever from the actual writings of Dōgen and Keizan concerning Japan and the Orient so these references have remained although we now use American equivalents when teaching. This edition contains a revised glossary and index.

Rōshi P.T.N.H. Jiyu-Kennett

June, 1987.

PREFACE TO THE FOURTH EDITION.

Reverend Master Jiyu-Kennett passed away on November 6, 1996. We, her disciples, are honored to be able to bring out this fourth edition of her first book, in the spirit of continuing to make the offering of teaching which epitomized her life right to the end.

We have naturally wished to make as few changes as possible in this edition, so that first time readers will be able to see her words directly and get a true sense of both the flavor and substance of her teaching. To this end, there are only three changes of any significance between the third edition and this one. First, the cover has been redesigned so as to make the book more accessible. Second, the sections about the author and about the Order she founded have been revised to reflect events that have occurred since the third edition.

The third change has been to reorganize the chapters of Book Two so that they are grouped under the names of the volumes of Dōgen Zenji's work in which the originals are to be found. This has been done to facilitate finding other translations of the same works, as Rev. Master Jiyu-Kennett regarded the translations she worked upon as complementary to other translations. One of these moves, however, may surprise readers of previous editions of this book, and that is the move of the translation of the *Kyōjukaimon* from the section on the

teachings of Keizan Zenji to the section on the teachings of
Dōgen Zenji. This change has an interesting story behind it.
When Rev. Master Jiyu was in Japan, this text was customar-
ily referred to as "Keizan's *Kyōjukaimon*," so she naturally assumed that Keizan Zenji was its author. A few months before
her death, our translator, Rev. Hubert Nearman, reported to me
a most odd thing: in his research for another project, he had
needed to refer to the original text of the *Kyōjukaimon* and
could not find it among the collected works of Keizan but did
find it in the works of Dōgen. Intrigued by this, Rev. Master
Jiyu asked that Rev. Hubert research the matter further. Unfortunately she passed away before that research was completed, but this is what he found.

There are two versions of the text: one in Chinese, one
in Japanese. The latter is not strictly speaking a translation of
the former, but rather a reworking of the order of the characters and the addition of certain modifiers so as to make the
text comprehensible to readers of Japanese. This Japanese text
bears an inscription indicating that it was done by Keizan
Zenji, and further noting that the text itself was not original
to Dōgen but was rather Dōgen's written version of a much
older, orally transmitted, work. Since scholars have not located any Chinese source for the commentaries to the precepts
that form part of the *Kyōjukaimon*, it is likely that these are,
indeed, original writings of Dōgen.

So, what Rev. Master Jiyu knew as "Keizan's *Kyōjukaimon*" was probably the Japanese version of the text. In one
sense it does not really have an "author," belonging to oral tradition, but we felt that Rev. Master Jiyu would probably have
wanted to follow the tradition of giving primary credit for the
text to Dōgen, since he was the first to write it down and is the
probable author of the commentary: hence the change we have
made in its placement in this edition.

We offer this edition to you in the hope that it may be as useful and inspiring to you as it has been to us.

Rev. Daizui MacPhillamy
for the Order of Buddhist Contemplatives.

September, 1998.

BOOK ONE.

THE STEM
OF THE LOTUS.

All men know suffering which is as the mud in which the lotus takes its root: all men know the lotus blossom which gazes at the heavens. Few men indeed know how to nourish the root of True Religion within themselves in the mud of ignorance that surrounds them and fewer still know how to make that root flourish and grow the long stem needed in the dark water before the flower can bloom in the clear light of day. In this introduction I am attempting to show how to grow the long stem of the lotus, from the root to the blossom, for the stem of the lotus and Zen training are identical.

CHAPTER 1.

THE HISTORY OF THE BUDDHA ACCORDING TO ZEN BELIEF.

On the full-moon day of May, in 623 B.C., Prince Siddhartha Gautama, afterwards Shakyamuni Buddha, was born in Lumbini Garden, in Kapilavastu, on the borders of Nepal, His family being of the aristocratic Sakya clan or caste. His father was King Suddhodana and His mother Queen Maha Maya: seven days after His birth His mother died and His aunt, Maha Prajapati, His mother's younger sister, who was also married to King Suddhodana, became His foster mother. Asita, who was an intimate friend of the king, visited the palace to see the Child but, when the Baby was brought to him, the Child placed His feet in the ascetic Asita's matted hair. Asita, foreseeing by this action the Child's future greatness, rose from his seat and saluted Him with *gasshō* as did also the king. After this, Asita first smiled and then wept for he knew that Gautama was the Buddha that was to come and that he, owing to his own prior death and rebirth in a formless realm, could not be alive to benefit from the Buddha's superior wisdom.

On the fifth day the Child was named Siddhartha Gautama, which means "wish-fulfilled," and many learned Brahmins were invited to the palace for the naming ceremony. Among them were eight distinguished men, seven of whom, on examining the Child's characteristics, raised two fingers thus giving a double interpretation that He would be

3

either a universal monarch or a Buddha: the youngest and most learned, however, Kondanna, raised only one finger, thus firmly declaring that He would definitely retire from the world and become a Buddha.

During the ploughing festival the future Buddha had an unprecedented mental experience which served as the key to His enlightenment. This festival was arranged to encourage agriculture and both nobles and commoners, in gala dress, participated. The Child was left on a screened and canopied couch, beneath a rose-apple tree, to be watched by His nurses however, at the climax of the festival, the nurses stole away to watch and the Child, sitting cross-legged and concentrating on the inhalation and exhalation of His breathing, gained one-pointedness of mind which is the first ecstasy. The Prince was so absorbed in meditation when the nurses returned that, struck with awe, they told the king who came and saluted his son for the second time.

After an excellent education and being specially trained in the art of warfare, Gautama married His beautiful cousin, Yashodhara, both of them being sixteen years of age. Thereafter He led a luxurious life, unaware of the life of tribulation led by most people outside the palace. He had three palaces so as to be able to enjoy His life to the full; each was for a different season, hot, cold or rainy. Renunciation of luxury and pleasure was not yet within His mind.

However, His contemplative nature and boundless compassion did not allow Him to enjoy royal pleasures as others did. He knew no woe but He had a deep desire to witness the way of life of humanity in general even amidst His own comfort and prosperity.

One day He went outside the palace and saw the darker side of the life of men. First He saw a decrepit old man, then a diseased person, later a corpse and, finally, a dignified hermit.

The first three of these sights showed Him the inexorable nature of life and the universal sickness of humanity; the fourth showed Him the means of overcoming this and the way to attaining calm and peace. Thereafter, realising the uselessness of sensual pleasures and the value of renunciation, He decided to leave the world. It was after this decision that He heard of the birth of His son and, regarding the child as an impediment rather than a blessing, named him Rahula.

He now realised that the time was ripe for His departure and, after ordering Channa to saddle Kanthaka, His horse, He stood on the threshold of the princess's chamber and cast a dispassionate glance at His wife and child. His compassion dominated Him however even at the moment of His parting so that He stole away at midnight, attended only by Channa, to become a penniless wanderer at the age of twenty-nine.

After travelling for a long way He rested on the far bank of the river Neranjara and there shaved His head, giving His garments and ornaments to Channa to take back to the palace. He now adopted the simple yellow garb of an ascetic and led a life of voluntary poverty as a homeless beggar.

He commenced His search for calm and peace by studying with Arada Kalama, an ascetic of repute who, after his pupil's developing the seventh Arupa Dhyana, or the Realm of Nothingness, regarded Him as his equal. The future Buddha was not satisfied, however, with mere mental concentration so He went to Udraka Ramaputra with whom He developed the final mental stage of the Realm of Neither Perception nor Non-Perception. Since, in those days, the ancient sages could proceed no further than this in mental development, the teacher invited Him to take full charge of all his disciples.

Finding that there seemed to be no-one competent to teach Him, since all were enmeshed in ignorance, Gautama gave up looking for external help from teachers since He realised that Truth and peace are to be found within oneself and not gained from another. Thereafter He wandered in the district of Magadha arriving eventually at Uruvela. Hearing of His renunciation, Kondanna, who had foretold His destiny at His birth, and four sons of the other sages who had been present at the same time, Bhaddiya, Vappa, Mahanama and Assaji, also renounced the world and joined Him. Asceticism was practiced very severely in those days in India and Gautama practiced all forms of austerity to such an extent that His delicate body was reduced almost to a skeleton but the greater His torments the further His goal receded, their only result being exhaustion.

Then came Mara suggesting to His mind that He live a life of merit which would involve Him in sacrifices and celibacy, but the future Buddha discarded these things since sense-desires, aversion, hunger, thirst, craving, sloth, torpor, fear, doubt, distractions, obstinacy, profit, praise, honour, false-fame, the extolling of oneself and contempt of others He knew to be the weapons of Mara. Resolving that it would be better to die in the battle against such things rather than to live vanquished, He dismissed these possibilities and made firm His determination to reach Buddhahood.

It was after this decision that He abandoned self-mortification as futile and adopted the middle path for He now realised that the way to enlightenment was the one of simply sitting which He had discovered when He was a child and He therefore took food. This so disgusted the five ascetics who were with Him that they deserted Him on the spot saying He had become indulgent. After a substantial meal, offered by Sujata, He resolved just to sit.

Seated under the famous pipal tree, at Buddha Gaya, with His mind tranquil and purified, He developed the supernormal knowledge of the true way to the destruction of the passions and, comprehending things as they truly are, realised His original enlightenment exclaiming, "I was, am and will be enlightened simultaneously with the universe." He was thirty-five.

He was born human and He lived and died as a man; however, although He was human and neither deified nor immortal, He became an extraordinary man. He must not be thought of as an incarnation of Vishnu nor of any other god and His personal salvation cannot save others. "You yourselves must make the exertion; the Buddhas are only teachers," was one of His sayings and, "Remember thou must go alone; the Buddhas do but point the way," is another famous quotation. Instead of placing an unseen, almighty god over man, and making him subservient to such a belief, Shakyamuni Buddha raised the worth of mankind. Selfless service and the equality of all men and women are the corner-stones of His teaching.

CHAPTER 2.

BASIC ORIGINAL DOCTRINES ESSENTIAL TO ZEN.

Anatta (No-soul or individual self).

Apart from mind and matter which constitute this so-called being, which we know as man, there is no immortal soul, or eternal ego, with which we are either gifted or have obtained in a mysterious way from a mysterious being or force. The Buddhist doctrine of rebirth should be distinguished from the theory of re-incarnation, or that of transmigration, for Buddhism denies the existence of an unchanging or eternal soul. The forms of man or animal are merely the temporary manifestations of the life force that is common to all. "Being" is only a concept used for conventional purposes. Birth is simply the coming-into-being of a psycho-physical existence. Just as a physical state is conditioned by a preceding state as its cause, even so the coming-into-being of this psycho-physical life is conditioned by causes anterior to its birth. As one life-process is possible without a permanent thing passing from one thought-moment to another, so a series of life-processes is possible without anything to transmigrate from one life to another. This body dies; there is no less life-force; nothing transmigrates from one body to another. The future being there will be conditioned by the present life force here. A new being is neither absolutely the same as its predecessor (since the composition is not identical) nor entirely different, being the same stream of life-force which, like electric current, can be tapped when a new bulb is plugged in, so as to give light, but which is unseen, when the bulb breaks, until a new one is again plugged in. Just as with the electricity there is no lack of current when a bulb breaks, merely the necessity for a new bulb, so with rebirth there is a continuity of a life force which manifests itself in birth and seems invisible in death; just that and nothing more.

Karma.

Action or deed, either good or bad. The law of moral causation; action and reaction in the ethical realm; it includes both past and present actions. It is not fate; not predestination imposed by some mysterious power to which we must helplessly submit. It is one's own doing which reacts on one's own egocentric self so it is possible for us to direct the course of our karma. Karma is action, and *vipaka* is its reaction: thus, cause and effect. Karma, being a law in itself, needs no lawgiver; it operates in its own field without the intervention of an external, independent ruling agency. Inherent in it is the potentiality of producing its due effect: the effect already blooms in its cause. Karma, good or bad, is caused by not knowing things as they truly are, and ignorance and craving are the chief causes. "No doer is there who does the deed, nor is there one who feels the fruit;" this can be understood clearly after deep and true meditation thereon. Our will, or ego, is itself the doer of karma, and feeling is itself the reaper of the karmic fruit; apart from these mental states, there is none to sow and none to reap. Karma is not "stored" somewhere either in the consciousness or in the body; being dependent on mind and matter, it manifests itself at the opportune moment and is an individual force which is transmitted from one existence to another. Not everything is due to karma, otherwise a person would always be bad if it was his karma to be bad. Seasonal phenomena, the order of germs and seeds, the theory of cells and genes, the order of act and result, natural phenomena such as gravitation and other similar laws of nature, the order of mind and the psychic law such as the processes of consciousness and arising and perishing of consciousness are all laws in themselves. Karma, which is the third of these five universal laws, helps, with the other four, to account for diversity in the world. Karma gives hope, self-reliance, consolation and moral courage to a Buddhist; it teaches individual responsibility and explains the problem of suffering, the mystery of so-called fate and predestination in other religions and, above all, the reason for the inequality of mankind.

Rebirth.

Past karma conditions the present birth, and present karma, in combination with past karma, conditions the future birth. As stated earlier, rebirth must be distinguished from reincarnation or transmigration since an unchanging or eternal soul is non-existent; since there is no individual "I" to think, there is nothing to be reborn.

The Four Noble Truths.

Shakyamuni Buddha saw old age, disease, death (i.e. three aspects of suffering) and the priestly life when He went outside the palace. Thereafter suffering became His all-absorbing problem and He entered the priesthood in order to work on it. He discovered the answer to His problem in the Four Noble Truths and, inadvertently, enlightenment. The first of these Truths was that of the existence of suffering. Birth, decay, death, sorrow, lamentation, pain, grief, despair, not to get what one wants and existence itself as the world knows existence, are suffering; all these things are karmically acquired. The Three Characteristics, *anicca* (transiency), *dukkha* (suffering), *anatta* (no separate self), can be understood by experience but cannot be adequately explained in words; the three warnings, sickness, old age and death, must come to all and the beginning of the wheel of existence is inconceivable. The second Truth is that of the origin of suffering, which is craving, and this can be three-fold; it can be sensual, spiritual or material. Whereas the first is clear the other two need some explanation. Spiritual craving is the desire to be reborn in some state better than the one we now occupy, such as in a heaven; material is the outcome of the delusive notion of a more or less real ego which is annihilated at death and which stands in no causal relation with the time before and after death; this craving arises as a result of the senses and consciousness. The doctrine of Dependent Origination may be regarded as a detailed explanation of the second Truth. The third Truth is the extinction of suffering; thus Nirvana is possible in this life for it is the control of greed, hate and delusion. It is the constant cleansing of oneself, even after one has realised one's innate enlightenment and, before it, the dropping of all one's desires, ideas and notions which we ourselves have filled our minds with and thus created waves on the sea thereof which prevent us from seeing the moon or reflection, of our true essence clearly. When we have utterly discarded all this rubbish, we realise the realm where there is neither the solid nor the fluid, heat, motion, this world or any other world, sun or moon. In this state there is neither arising nor passing away, no standing still, no being born or dying, no foothold, development or basis; this is the end of suffering. There is an unborn, unoriginated, uncreated, unformed; if there were not, the realisation of our true nature would not be possible; we must never cease from meditation and, indeed, Shakyamuni Buddha never ceased from it either for, should we do so, then we will begin to again fill the pond of the mind with our own ideas and notions, likes and dislikes and, in so doing, hide once more the moon, or reflection, of our true essence. It is for this reason that no true trainee ever says that he has understood Buddhism; nor does he say he does not understand it; just he goes on training himself eternally, always becoming Buddha every moment of his life which turns, therefore, into every minute enlightenment or every minute Zen. He is neither conscious of it nor is he unconscious of it. He just trains in Buddhism, for the sake of Buddhism, just as Shakyamuni Buddha carried His begging bowl and wore His robe every day of His life after His understanding as well as doing His meditation. The fourth Truth is the Eightfold Path which leads to the maintaining of the cessation of suffering. Since most people indulge in one of two extremes, either sensual pleasure or self-mortification, suffering, for them, exists. Buddha avoided both extremes and found, instead, the Middle Path which leads to true peace of mind and which is called Nirvana. Since this Path is explained more fully in the "Kyōjukaimon" later on, I will simply give the names of the so-called steps here. They are:– right understanding, right thought, right speech, right action, right livelihood, right effort, right mindfulness and right concentration.

Anicca.

Impermanence, change; all things change, all life grows old, decays, being ever changing. This doctrine includes the total separation of all moments one from another and leads ultimately to the void of the *Scripture of Great Wisdom* and Dōgen's "Uji."

There are many other doctrines and beliefs in early Buddhism which arose either directly out of original Hindu teaching or some other source but the above, which are what Shakyamuni Buddha taught, are all that are <u>necessary</u> for the study of Zen. Some of these other teachings can help to clarify some of the difficulties that may seem to appear in the foregoing doctrines. If the reader has difficulties in clarifying the foregoing he should visit or telephone one of the Abbeys or Priories of our Order.

CHAPTER 3.

THE GROWTH OF ZEN FROM BASIC HINAYANA DOCTRINE.

Zen has been called a Transmission outside the Scriptures and this is true but this does not mean that the Scriptures are to be ignored, especially by the very beginner who knows nothing of Buddhism for, in order to understand Zen, I believe one must possess a thorough knowledge of the basic teachings given in the previous chapter as well as be aware at least of a brief history of Shakyamuni Buddha and the way in which His teachings grew and were expanded into what is now called Mahayana Zen. Therefore I am now presuming that the reader has thoroughly examined the previous chapters and, upon this knowledge, we can now build our study of how I understand Zen thought to have grown.

Remember that although some Zen scholars DID attempt to explain and defend their position with rational, philosophic argument, they were not looking at Truth with a philosophical eye; theirs was the heart of faith. Put more plainly, if you try to understand Zen from a rational, argumentative point of view, no argument is ever going to be good enough: alternatively, if you try to understand Zen intuitively, using the heart of faith instead of the argumentative mind, no explanation of what I am about to say will be necessary.

It follows from this, then, that Zen is an intuitive RELIGION and not a philosophy or way of life.

Although in this chapter I shall be dealing largely with philosophical and religious arguments these are not the object of Zen. Metaphysics are just so many dead words; to the Zen trainee the only thing that matters is putting the teachings of the Buddha into practice and training himself in the same way as He did. Therefore, after this one chapter, I shall abandon metaphysics and philosophy and go into the realm of practical application.

How, then, did Hinayana Buddhism, with the simple beliefs explained in the previous chapter and its emphasis on the necessity of the trainee renouncing the world for the seeming purpose of pursuing wholeheartedly the path of the Arhat, that is, someone who has thrown away home, family, comforts and ordinary life so as to be free of the chains of birth and death that bind him to Samsara, this world of patience, and so gained the complete peace of Nirvana, irrespective of whether anyone else, if anybody, could follow him, turn into Mahayana Buddhism, with its seeming emphasis on the trainee not entering into Nirvana before he could take every blade of grass with him? The Hinayana idea of the Arhat was, of course, that the aspirant had done everything possible for others that could be done; he had given them a glowing example which they would be able to follow, if not in this life, at least in another; his was the spirit of the pioneer who leads the way. How, then, did this change take place? This is a very difficult question to answer. Doubtless national temperaments had something to do with it but the viewpoint of the Hinayanist concerning Shakyamuni Buddha and that of the Mahayanist concerning Him give us the main clues. The Hinayanist sees a Man Who utterly cleansed Himself from all attachments and became the pioneer of those who free themselves from the suffering which we undergo in our transitory existence; it was natural for Him to take the reward of Nirvana when He had completed this cleansing process. The Mahayanist, however, does not see so much the pioneer as the Prince who gave up all luxuries for the purpose of making the discovery that might benefit all mankind; this He did out of compassion for Himself and humanity. This is emphasised by the fact that He spent forty-five years teaching His fellow men. To the Mahayanist mind His willingness to share His great discovery with all beings was proof that He had truly understood the oneness of all beings and was no longer caught in the desire for self enjoyment which would have been the case had He decided to think only of Himself and enter into Nirvana without a thought about others. This true love for all beings which, later on, I have called the Heart of Samantabhadra, is the hall-mark of the Bodhisattva, that is one who, having reached Nirvana, views the universe and all beings from the standpoint of fully digested Preceptual Truth. Therefore the Bodhisattva ideal was exemplified in the life of Shakyamuni Buddha Himself and not, as some Hinayanists claim, a later addition to the original doctrine.

The way in which this change of aspiration is explained by the Mahayanist is very interesting and touches upon the very basis and core of the teaching of Zen. In the specifically Mahayana Scriptures, written after Buddha's death for the purpose of explaining more succinctly some of His teaching, (such Scriptures may not be recognised by Hinayanists) there is one which is called *The Lotus of the Perfect Law*. Herein, the Buddha is teaching only as much truth as the disciples could, at that time, individually, understand. As each group of disciples developed spiritually He taught them higher Truths: the teachings of Hinayana were for the beginner and the Mahayana ones were for those who had made the greater progress. This means, of course, that Shakyamuni Buddha was aware of the higher

Truths but could not reveal them to people who could not yet understand them. These Truths were inherent in the early teachings and can be seen in them but, because the disciples were not yet ready for them, they could not be fully explained. *The Lotus Scripture*, mentioned above, takes these early teachings and expands them. It was only, in fact, to Makakashyo who, on seeing the flower Shakyamuni Buddha held, smiled, that He revealed the highest Truth of all, in silence, and this intuitional Transmission, which is from heart to heart was, in fact, outside the Scriptures themselves and caused Makakashyo to become the first Zen Ancestor.

It may be argued that, in revealing Truth only so much at a time, the Buddha was deliberately deceiving His disciples. The parable of the householder who has three sons in a burning house, however, taken from *The Lotus Scripture*, disproves this. In this story the father, knowing that his three sons will not come out of the burning house in spite of the great present that he has to offer them, offers them instead the little things that he knows they want and so is able to entice them out. When they are safely at the gate he gives them only the big present that he had for them originally. The parable poses the question, did he deceive them? The scripture has this to say:–

> Even as that father at first attracted his children by the three carts, and afterwards gave them only a great cart magnificently adorned with precious things and supremely furnished, yet that father is not guilty of falsehood; so also is it with the Tathagata; there is no falsehood in first preaching Three Vehicles to attract all living creatures and afterwards in saving them by the Great Vehicle only. Wherefore? Because the Tathagata possesses infinite wisdom, power, fearlessness and the treasury of the laws,

and is able to give all living creatures the Great Vehicle Law; but not all are able to receive it. Shariputra! For this reason know that Buddhas, by their adaptability, in the One Vehicle define and expound the Three.[1]

This idea of "giving only as much food, and of the right kind, as the baby can take" is carried to extremes in Zen Buddhism in Japan as will be seen from the following chapters. The Bodhisattva ideal has too often been neglected by students of Zen, especially in the West, where the metaphysical and philosophical, as well as mystical, elements have attracted people rather more than the deep understanding that service to mankind might be another name for Zen training, therefore it is important that a few more points are made concerning it. A Bodhisattva is obviously someone who has transcended the opposites of self and other and is no longer concerned about his own salvation; the thing that is difficult to grasp is that he is CONSCIOUSLY concerned about the salvation of others but not hindered in that consciousness by emotionalism—just he does that which has to be done. I hope to make this clearer as I proceed in later chapters for it is a very important point. A Bodhisattva is not just an ordinary "do-gooder" in the usual sense of the word. He remains in the world, just as an ordinary person, devoting himself to leading others gently and compassionately with just so much teaching as they can manage at a time, which may be nothing more than just an example, because it is the natural thing for him to do. It is more than just an example, however, because he has realised his eternal oneness with all men; he suffers as they suffer without being conscious of a difference between himself and them although he has overcome the causes of suffering. It is because of this that he continues to train himself endlessly so as to overcome everything that stands in the way of his deepening his oneness with all men; this oneness gives him increased power in their service, including the service of his enemies.

One question has always puzzled beginners in Buddhism: what is Nirvana? and, with the altered viewpoint of the Bodhisattva rather than the Arhat, this question becomes all the more important. If Nirvana is that state into which one enters after attaining enlightenment, as in the case of the Arhat, what happens to the Bodhisattva who, after all his efforts, deserves it just as much but can never enjoy it because of his compassion for others? Obviously, if the Hinayanist view is retained, there can be no Nirvana for the Buddhas and Bodhisattvas. However, as the Bodhisattva proceeds through the stages to Buddhahood, he gradually realises that Nirvana is a state of mind resulting from right effort towards true spiritual perfection rather than a reward in the hereafter as it has sometimes been described. This state of mind has perhaps best been described by Meister Eckhart in the words, "And a man shall be free, and as pure as the day prior to his entry into his mother's womb, when he has nothing, wants nothing and knows nothing. Such a one has true spiritual poverty." This is when compassionate oneness has so transcended all thought of self that not even the oneness exists. So, just by being a Bodhisattva, one is already in Nirvana, according to the above, Nirvana and Samsara not being two different states of existence. Here we see that nothing is, in fact, outside Nirvana and, later, we shall see that even Nirvana does not exist. By giving up Nirvana for the sake of others, one finds oneself in Nirvana in its true spiritual meaning.

This true spiritual state, then, is the Nirvana with which Zen is concerned and, although I have always said that Zen represents the closest Mahayana School of all the ten Chinese ones to the original Hinayana, the ideas of the Bodhisattva and this altered view-point of the concept of Nirvana are a long way away from the Hinayana view-point. However, as stated at the beginning, the basic doctrines of Hinayana and the Precepts, i.e. that which the Buddha Himself taught, remain the same. Zen represents an amplification thereof in many ways and the *Kyōjukaimon* is distinctly an extension of the original Precepts so, although one can see the way in which Zen is connected to the original Hinayana doctrines, one must realise that these are considerably extended. Certain of the Mahayana philosophers, two of whom were direct descendants of Makakashyo, gave reasoned arguments concerning causality and Nirvana to justify their altered concepts of them in the Mahayanist ideal. Asvaghosa, Nagyaarajyuna, Asanga and Vasubandhu were amongst the most noteworthy of these but remember, as stated earlier, that they were men of the spirit and not just men of letters. If one tries to think of them with the usual mind of Western speculative philosophy, one will make no progress whatsoever. The intuitive heart of faith is the all important thing if one wishes to understand what they are trying to convey in words. The purpose being religious, rather than metaphysical, these words were written for the purpose of freeing energetic intellects from mental blocks which they set up of themselves to bar their path to spiritual understanding. Nagyaarajyuna does this by blowing concepts of reason to pieces; he is willing to do this even with basic Buddhist ideas, if they are only concepts, as in the case of Nirvana. Vasubandhu works on the destruction of physical reality and blows to pieces the concepts of atom and perceptual qualities leaving, as real, only such subjective impressions as can exist in the mind. These metaphysical arguments lead quite naturally to the study of the true nature of mind which, when realised intuitively, is the intellectual aspect of enlightenment.

That ultimate reality is Absolute Mind is made clear in certain passages from the *Surangama Scripture* which poses the following four questions:– 1. Where is mind, as functioning through vision, located? 2. If it has no location, how do we determine its reality and nature? 3. To be able to view that which is changing implies a power to view that which is changeless. 4. The power of vision, though changeless, is not, as such, absolute. What, then, is absolute and why?

These theories and metaphysical arguments show the great Zen Ancestors endeavouring down the centuries to clarify the nature of reality and the intellectual aspect of enlightenment; this latter has always been the most intriguing and attractive part of Zen teaching from the Western point of view but ultimate reality transcends what can be expressed in words. Since universal Mind is alone real, one must abandon seeking for anything. This universal Mind is realised only by ceasing to search and by throwing away all theories, ideas and concepts that one knows and believes in. This is the flash of enlightenment explained in philosophical language; later in this book I will explain how it is done through training. However, even in this moment, one must realise that mind itself, and the means by which it has been explained, are a contradiction in themselves for the real Truth lies beyond any kind of verbal expression. Shakyamuni Buddha knew this but, out of His compassion for all beings, gave them something which would be all that they could, at that time, assimilate, hoping that, later on, they could gain a deeper insight. It was for this reason that He never gave answers to certain questions that were asked of Him and, in the Zen system, a teacher sometimes gives an answer to a question that will discourage the questioner from asking questions. This is to teach the student that his difficulty lies in his <u>necessity</u> to ask questions since this shows that his state of mind is still one that clings to reason. It is this actual reason that he has got to throw away in order to perform the leap to perfect freedom.

This leap requires a trust in the heart, that is, intuition, instead of reason, but it does not separate us from the world of the senses. It is simply that, as Shakyamuni Buddha taught, the clear water of the mind has become ruffled by the winds of thought and reason; when we have quietened them, we perceive that the Buddha Light has never ceased to shine upon the water. Here, again, we are using imagery to express Truth. It is we who threw all the dirt into the water and set up the winds that disturbed it; only we can still the winds and throw out the dirt. As Hui-nêng so aptly puts it:–

> The Bodhi is not like a tree,
> The mind is not a mirror bright;
> Since there is nothing from the first,
> Where can the dust alight?

CHAPTER 4.

THE NECESSITY OF ZAZEN
OR MEDITATION PRACTICE.

That a living creature, which is in possession of true faith in Buddhism, shall be able to bring to fruition the seed of Buddhahood, latent in each and every one of us, three things are necessary. Such a person must realise with his whole being, possess and exhibit in his daily life:–

1. The Heart of Avalokitesvara, which is the bringing to fruition of the seed of Great Compassion to be found within us;

2. The Heart of Samantabhadra, which is the bringing to fruition of the seed of Great Love to be found within us;

3. The Heart of Manjusri, which is the bringing to fruition of the seed of Great Wisdom which is to be found within us;

only then can that being return to the world with the bliss-bestowing hands of Maitreya, the Buddha which is to come. These three, Compassion, Love, Wisdom, are like three great drums which, although silent, nevertheless thunder across the world when our whole being expresses them. These three are the keys to the gateless gate of true freedom and it is only we ourselves that prevent us from unlocking it for it was, in fact, never locked. It is only that we, by clinging to our ideas of right and wrong, good and evil, likes and dislikes, prejudices and concepts, in other words, by making choices, have created clouds to hide the brightness of the moon of our True Self. When we sweep all these likes, dislikes, prejudices and ideas, et cetera, away, we discover that the moon had never ceased shining. That which prevented us from seeing it was our belief that we were right in our attachment to opinions and that everyone else was wrong. Therefore the first scripture to be recited during morning service in a Zen temple is that to Avalokitesvara, for Compassion, like a mother, brings forth the child of Wisdom whose father is Love; a love which is non-possessive in the worldly sense and all embracing in the spiritual one. So the first duty of a layman in studying Zen is to find and bring forth the heart of Compassion. We will consider first the method of meditation by which this is done and, in the next chapter, the sort of view-point that goes to make up the exhibition of the heart of Avalokitesvara. Most people who wish to study Zen want to start with the philosophical side but this is wrong. As I said in the previous chapter, the Bodhisattva mind is the first thing to be cultivated by all who wish to study and, in leaving the metaphysical and philosophical side to the very end I am copying Shakyamuni Buddha, in *The Scripture of the Lotus of the Wonderful Law*, by only giving the trainee that which is good for him at the present time.

Zazen teaches the realisation of our True Mind and, once one has this realisation, the mind never again changes back to its old state. Remember, however, that this is not an attempt at stilling the mind for this is an impossibility. It is true that we quieten down the winds of thought, by allowing no thought to disturb us, but it is not possible to stop thinking, nor is this advisable. We simply notice that thoughts arise and that they disappear. A quiet room, in which you will not be disturbed in your own home, is the best place to select if you cannot go to a Meditation Hall. It should not be too bright or too dark, nor should it be too hot or too cold. Generally speaking, it is best to meditate when the body is slightly cool rather than warm. You will need a large, square cushion, about two to three feet square, on top of which you will need another smaller round one, about eight inches in diameter and eight inches high, like a ball; if this is not available use a square cushion doubled up to make it twice its height. Whatever you do, do not wear anything that is either tight or constricting in any way. Trousers, socks, tight skirts and other similar articles of clothing are all to be very carefully avoided as is also clothing that is too short, such as mini-skirts. The Japanese, both priests and laymen, use what is called a *hakama* if they are not wearing special robes. This is a sort of very wide, pleated skirt, with large slits at the sides under which one can place the hands if one is being attacked by insects. It allows for the crossing of the legs in comfort without any unnecessary constriction of the circulation. If one can sit in the lotus position it is, of course, best, but this is not possible for all people. Some people can manage what is called half lotus in which only one foot is placed on top of the other, and others use what is known as the Burmese position. This last is very much favoured by Western people who find that the lotus position is intolerable after a short time. It is possible to use a chair if all these positions are too painful but remember that your body, if it becomes tired, may not be able to keep its stability if it is not sitting on a wide base, such as is provided for it by the three above positions, and there is also the danger of swollen feet if they are left dangling for an indefinite period. In teaching Western people in Sōjiji I found that, although the initial pain of the lotus position is excruciating it is, in the end, perhaps worth the effort for the facility that it gives later on to sit for long periods. The secret of training oneself to sit in this position is not to do it for too long at any one time. After all, Zazen is not an endurance test, despite the fact that it seems to have become so in certain Japanese Zen temples; Dōgen Zenji, who brought this method of meditation from China to Japan, expressly warns against excesses of asceticism saying that Zazen was to be regarded as the "comfortable way." Five minutes a day done properly will lead, in about three to six months, to being able to do twenty to forty minutes not only in comfort but also with serenity of mind. One should increase the amount of time gradually, not force the body to do that which it is incapable of doing all at once. The result of such forcing is invariably the same; the trainee becomes fearful of Zazen and, eventually, loses interest in doing it for fear of the pain. In the beginning the knees will, of course, rise of themselves from the cushions and you will have to repeatedly push them down again. This is a non-volitional action owing to muscle spasm. I can remember watching my left knee rise from the cushions in Sōjiji despite the fact that I was using every muscular effort to keep it from doing so; most teachers realise that this is an involuntary action but there are some who do not and these tend to punish rather than help the trainee in consequence. In large Zen temples the trainee is taught the necessity of sitting still by being hit with the *kyosaku*, or awakening stick, if he moves. Usually this is in the hands of a capable person who realises the possibility of involuntary movements and so does not punish the offender but, occasionally, it finds its way into the hands of a beginner in the disciplinarian's office with unfortunate results. Be this as it may, the important thing is to sit as still as possible and, if one must move, to give up sitting for a few minutes and then go back to it again. Just as Shakyamuni Buddha had to give up unnecessary asceticism, so must we modern trainees not try to do the impossible. This does not mean that we do not strive to conquer our bodies—we do, but we do it gradually and in such a way as to cause the least strain thereto; a strained body leads to a strained mind. There are other positions for the feet which a good teacher can show you if all the above are impossible. Having settled the legs comfortably, place the left hand, palm upwards, in the right one with the thumbs touching each other lightly so that the two hands together look like a slightly flattened oval. This is the procedure for a right-handed person. The necessity of this is in order to repress the active side of the body with the passive; a left-handed person would therefore place his right hand over his left. Opinions with regard to this differ, but I have found, at least for Westerners, that it is the best practice to follow. Since one wishes to gain the highest degree of tranquility possible, the more active side of the body must be tranquilised by the opposite one.

The most important physical thing to remember is that the spine must, at all times, be erect. This does not mean a stiff erectness, indicating pride, nor a sloppy erectness which indicates dejection. Since the state of the body shows the state of the mind, both pride and dejection are obviously no frames of mind in which to do Zazen. Make sure that the small round cushion is only under the tip of the spine at the back and bend the body forward so as to position the buttocks correctly, then sway from side to side, beginning with large swings and ending with small ones, seven or eight times, rather like a pendulum finding its place of rest, until your body positions itself automatically in its natural erectness. This should have the effect of making the body completely weightless from the waist up. The ears and the shoulders should be in one straight line and the nose in a straight line with the navel. The mouth must be closed with the tip of the tongue lightly touching the top of the mouth behind the teeth. The eyes must be open since, to close them, encourages sleep, dreaminess and, sometimes, hypnosis. Since the last named is completely incompatible with Zen meditation it is to be absolutely discouraged. The eyes should be in a sort of half-closed state, not focussing on anything in particular, but resting on a point on the ground that is natural for the range of vision of the trainee concerned. I have heard it said that this must be at least three feet but, since some of us are long-sighted and others short, it is not possible to lay down a firm rule on exact distance. Just allow the eyes to rest naturally on a spot on the ground that is a short distance from the body, thus causing the eyes to be automatically lowered but not closed; this will prevent both eye-strain and fatigue. Also, be sure that the head is erect at all times and that you breathe quite naturally through your nose. The spine must stay absolutely erect since, if it slumps, the digestive and other functions will be interfered with and this will cause you to have trouble of mind, as well as discomfort of body, not to mention a painful back. You should sit facing a wall or curtain since this will prevent your mind from dwelling on the beauty of the scenery or objects in the room. Do not focus your attention on anything; least of all folds in the curtain and knots or cracks in the wall.

When you are completely comfortable take two or three deep breaths; both inhalation and exhalation should be slow and, of course, taken through the nose: this will tend to quieten your mind and allow your breathing to settle down quite naturally. For the purpose of learning concentration at this early stage the best training is to work on counting incoming and outgoing breaths: this will help keep out thoughts of a reasoning nature and pinpoint the mind in one direction only; you will also begin to calm down the thought waves. Under no circumstances go further than ten in your counting; when you reach this number start from the beginning and go up to ten again. At first count both inhalations and exhalations but, as your power of concentration grows, count only inhalations. Thoughts will, in fact, run through your mind and they will do you no harm whatsoever so long as you do not try to hold on to them or try to push them away: many people still think that Zazen is a means of stopping all conscious thought and, although some schools of Yoga do actually aim at this, it is not the purpose of Zen meditation. You cannot stop hearing things and you cannot stop seeing them if they are within your range of vision; they will form thought patterns in your mind however much you work on counting your breaths: they will not impede you in the least unless you try to analyse them and so set up discrimination which will again set the waves of thought going in your head. You must understand that none of these things are, in themselves, obstructions to Zazen; many people misunderstand this and so set up mental blocks in their own minds which are later very difficult to get rid of; just concentrate on your breath counting and do not worry about stray thoughts, words, sounds and sights. Whilst on the subject of this it is advisable to tell you not to sit too close to the wall or too far away from it; two or three feet is a good distance. Natural sounds such as those of birds, insects, water and mechanical motors will not disturb you in the least but human voices, radios and the like can be very distracting, even to experienced sitters, so choose a place that is far from such noises. When in Malaysia I was unable to find a single temple where I was not constantly disturbed by such noises which were usually very loud; all were unsuitable for meditation, at least for people who had not been sitting for several years; of course it is possible to get to a state when no noises whatsoever disturb one but, of the stage of which I am writing, this is not the case. It goes without saying that the room in which one sits must be clean, tidy and, preferably, containing flowers and incense. Zazen should never be done in bed, unless one is a bedridden invalid, since the psychological approach is then all wrong. The ideas of cleanliness, purity and freshness are all important in

Zazen practice and the above mentioned things tend towards this; I personally find that I do my best Zazen after bathing, for then I am freshest, but this is not absolutely essential. In Sōjiji it was not possible for priests, in their junior years, to have a bath more often than once every five days, according to the rules, but still they must do their Zazen every day. Since I was a woman and, during my junior years, the women's bathroom had not yet been built, I frequently had to do without a bath for as long as two months which has proved to me that, although personal freshness is a definite aid to meditation, it is not absolutely essential. The present-day trainees in Sōjiji are much more fortunate than I was for there are now large modern bathrooms for both men and women and the old rule is no longer so strictly enforced. The thing that is important is that you make yourself as clean and tidy as you possibly can under the circumstances and do not wear dirty or night clothes; since man is body and mind, purity of body goes a long way to making purity of mind. The best times to do Zazen are just before dawn and just before dusk but these times are not available to all people. A dark curtain or a small light, in the case of a dark room, can create something of the same effect as these times of day. If I were asked which time is best I would definitely say early morning for the mind is then freshly awakened from sleep, clear, bright and well-rested, there is also the probability of little disturbance since few people are early risers. Any time before a meal is a good time but never try practicing after one for at least half an hour because of the importance of allowing one's digestive processes to work naturally. If you practice regularly for only five or ten minutes a day, without straining your body, you will soon want to increase the amount of time that you spend in sitting because of the increased feeling of bodily health that you will enjoy as well as the great peace of mind that comes from even such a short time. Once you begin to experience bodily discomfort stop sitting otherwise you will grow tired of doing Zazen and grow to dread the time when you think you should be doing it. I myself have experienced this and know what it can be like when one is forced to sit as a result of some over zealous "teacher:" it was only a supreme effort of will on my part which made me continue—and a change of the so-called teacher! The average layman, not being in an actual monastery, is not, perhaps going to have either the same incentive or the same will-power. Normally, even in a big monastery, one does not sit for longer than forty-five minutes at a time without a short break; this is because the strain of keeping the mind taut in the beginning is very great, thus causing a lessening in the value of the actual time spent in sitting; five to ten minutes, done really well, is worth a whole day done badly. The usual system, after sitting for about forty-five minutes, is to do *kinhin*, which is a form of walking meditation, or to do some work such as gardening or cleaning the house, still keeping one's mind in the same tautness and in silence. The same type of meditative walking was, in fact, done by Shakyamuni Buddha Himself since He spent one entire day after His enlightenment walking around the Bodhi Tree. Here again Zen is trying to copy the ancient training system of Shakyamuni Buddha. If one does follow a system of so much sitting, so much walking and so much work it is possible to do "everlasting Zazen" in such a way that one finds that the Meditation Hall is with one wherever one happens to go. This, in fact, is the aim of the ancient system of Zen training and the reason for the numerous activities which many Western people decry as "not being in the spirit of, or a hindrance to, meditation." Dōgen Zenji himself said the same thing to the cook priest whom he met on the ship, on his way to Tendōzan (Mount T'ien-t'ung) in China, and was roundly scolded by the old Chinese for "not beginning to understand the aim and purpose of Buddhism" (see Book Two, "Tenzo-kyōkun"). The conversation ended with the old man telling Dōgen to come to Tendōzan and learn it. In the next chapter I will explain how this manual work helps to cleanse the mind of its impurities and bring about the change of heart that is essential for spiritual growth.

Whatever you do, do not eat too much; I cannot stress this too strongly. Dōgen Zenji taught that one should eat only two-thirds of one's capacity and that it should be all vegetable since meat left acid in the blood which was not good for the body. From his writings I do not doubt that he would have used most of the vegetables to be found in the West to-day, however, he recommends that oil, which is heating to the blood, be avoided, since the body must be cool; one should also avoid wine which clouds the mind and onions and garlic which tend to act as an aphrodisiac when one is meditating. Since the aim is to still the waves of thought in the mind as much as possible, obviously pains from acid indigestion, discomforts from overheated blood, sexual desire and messed-up brains are to be avoided at all costs and these foods, meat, oil of the variety employed in fried foods, and onions, as well as alcohol, are thus taboo in all the really good training temples in Japan at the present time. One can, of course, take milk and similar products in moderate quantities.

Whilst on the subject of food I should perhaps say that there is a theory that wrong eating can cause hallucinations, et cetera, which sometimes beset people in training. These phenomena are called, in Japanese, *makyo*, or "devils of the objective world," but I am not at all sure if bad eating does cause them. Opinions differ. All the authorities agree, however, that they can be caused by bad sitting and incorrect breathing; Dōgen Zenji himself agreed about this. In his writings on how to practice Zazen he speaks of the way in which the body may feel hot, cold or glass-like, hard, heavy or light if the breathing is not well harmonised with the mind. He also speaks of the way in which one can experience the sensations of sinking, floating, feeling hazy or alert, being able to see through solid objects as if they were transparent or experiencing one's body as if it were a translucent substance. One may also see Buddhas and holy beings, receive penetrating insights, suddenly understand difficult passages of the scriptures and many other things. These latter may simply be a proof, when one is a beginner, of not having properly harmonised one's breathing with one's mind however, at a later date, experiences that are actually valid may appear: this will not be, however, until you have had at least one real and large kenshō experience. In former editions of this book I have not mentioned this, preferring instead to err on the side of safety for the beginner. Since one of my later books deals extensively with this matter, however, it is necessary that what I write here shall be clarified. I sincerely hope, however, that this is not taken as a license by beginners to regard *makyo* as valuable. There is a great difference between the *makyo* of a beginner and the visions that sometimes take place during kenshō. Some "beginners," however, are not beginners in spirituality; therefore it is important for even a beginner, whilst setting no store by visions, et cetera, to at least tell his teacher if such things happen to him, whilst not clinging to them, just in case he is having a real kenshō. What I have written in previous editions is an example of how I have used Shakyamuni Buddha's teaching of the burning house, pp. 17–18, for the safety of the beginner. Too much asceticism can cause visions also, as I know to my own cost. Anything that causes the body to live abnormally is likely to raise a corresponding psychological state. This explains how some Christian saints, after great ascetic practices, have had visions of God and angels. These visions do not mean that they are any nearer to heaven but simply that, having punished their bodies excessively, their minds created a balance so as to make them stop doing so; their minds simply gave them the sort of images they wanted to see. Shakyamuni Buddha tried asceticism in the beginning and called the visions that beset Him obstructing devils. It was only after He abandoned these excesses and just sat that He realised the Truth and He had many valid visions thereafter. The danger comes when we attach importance to what we see and hear without having them checked out by a master so, if *makyo* appear, just check them out or ignore them, correct any faults in your sitting, breathing and mode of life as much as you possibly can, and then continue to do your Zazen as if nothing had happened. If once you think that you are becoming holy as a result of visions all progress will stop completely.

When ending your period of Zazen rest your hands, palms upward, on your knees and sway from side to side in the opposite way to which you did when you first sat down, that is, beginning with small movements and ending with large ones, seven or eight times. Get up slowly and gently and commence to do your kinhin. Kinhin is done by making a fist of the left hand, with the thumb inside, and covering it with the right hand; it should not be held tightly against the chest wall but in an oval position. The arms, being held loosely, form an oval at the level of the chest with the elbows extended. The body must always be erect with the eyes again still in their naturally lowered position, not closed nor looking too far ahead of the feet. Continue to count your breaths as you walk, beginning with the left foot. Walk calmly and slowly, with great dignity; do not walk absent-mindedly; a step of not more than six inches at a time should be taken. Walk first on the heel and then along the side of the foot ending upon the toes so that the foot digs itself into the ground as it were. This is done for five to ten minutes after each period of thirty or forty-five minutes sitting. Remember that this is moving Zazen; it is not done for the purpose of stretching the legs as some people think. This completes the actual explanation of the physical side of Zazen. In the next chapter I will speak of the mental attitude to be cultivated by the beginner.

CHAPTER 5.

THE NECESSITY OF UNDERSTANDING THE HEART OF AVALOKITESVARA.

At the beginning of the last chapter I said that it was necessary for a layman to find and bring forth the heart of compassion and I then went into the physical method of doing meditation for this purpose. Now I want to talk about the mental attitude to be adopted in daily life, as well as in Zazen, for this purpose.

In the *Avalokitesvara Scripture* there is the following passage:– "Aksayamati Bodhisattva said to the Buddha, 'World-honoured One, how does Avalokitesvara visit this world of patience? How does he preach the Dharma to all beings? What is the extent of his skillful means?' The Buddha said to Aksayamati Bodhisattva, 'O good man, if there are beings in any country who are to be saved by Avalokitesvara assuming any form from that of a Buddha down to that of a human, animal or devil, Avalokitesvara will manifest in the form of such a being and preach them the Dharma.' "

Originally, in India, Avalokitesvara was definitely male but, on being brought to China, the concept of Avalokitesvara became female. Instead of being the idea of the seed of compassion within each and every one of us she became the Goddess of Mercy. How did this come about? The answer lies in the fact that the Chinese found Buddhism, in its early form, not suitable for spreading to the masses, presupposing, as it did, the perfection of the individual rather than salvation for all. With the growth of the Mahayana ideal, as I explained earlier, new scriptures were written to expand the old doctrines and the Mahayana ideal itself became embodied in the cosmic Buddha Amitabha and the compassionate Bodhisattvas, especially Avalokitesvara. It is believed that Amitabha, or Amida, gained Buddhahood on condition that all who sincerely call on his name shall go, at death, into his Western Paradise where they can continue to liberate themselves under more encouraging and happier circumstances than they enjoyed on earth. In other words, Shakyamuni Buddha was no longer thought of as a historical figure but as one incarnation of a transcendent cosmic reality, Buddha Nature, which is working at all times and in all worlds for the salvation of all sentient beings. Amitabha became the celestial example of Buddhahood: Avalokitesvara, the all merciful, became the goddess who helped to guide the faithful on their road to the Pure Land of the Western Paradise. From this it will be seen that whereas Pure Land, or Shin Buddhism as it is called in Japan, tends more towards the devotional attitude of faith, the Zen beginner's attitude is one of intuitive knowledge within oneself of the existence of the Buddha Nature. By beginners in Zen, Avalokitesvara is seen as a statue, embodying the characteristics of mercy and compassion which the Zen trainee must find within himself; characteristics which he must fertilise and cultivate to good growth through Zazen. There is room in the world for both view-points, the devotional, pietistic and the intuitive, although I have heard it said by some that Pure Land and Zen are incompatible. I now know that, in the deeply spiritual knowledge of religion, they represent opposite ends of the same tunnel and, according to the beginner's temperament and character, so he or she enters at the entrance of his or her own choice. Although externally these entrances seem to be very different, it is impossible to say which end of the tunnel is the right one to enter for they are not separate and the way in which one starts training can only be decided by the individual concerned. Zen temples do not usually recite the *Amitabha Scripture* but they do recite the Avalokitesvara one for the purpose of raising the seed of compassion in the beginner trainee.

The statues of Avalokitesvara in Japan appear female until, on looking at them closely, one realises that they are neither male nor female but something which is beyond both. This is because, if someone truly realises the heart of Avalokitesvara, he becomes a new creature, beyond the opposites of male and female, right and wrong. Therefore, in every large Zen temple, there are two Meditation Halls, one for laymen and one for *unsui*, a word which translates as Zen trainee. The statue in the Layman's Meditation Hall is that of Avalokitesvara because laymen have not, as yet, learned to transcend duality and, until reaching the heart of Avalokitesvara, are still in the "world of patience" where the opposites of male and female, right and wrong exist. The statue in the Unsui Meditation Hall is that of Manjusri, Great Wisdom, and those who enter there should be no longer conscious of male and female, right and wrong, like and dislike. They should be unsui, free as the clouds and strong and gentle as water, with the determination of both to wander across the universe in search of truth and wisdom, swirling all obstacles from their path as they go, for they have undergone true rebirth.

When a layman arrives to study he is taken to the Layman's Meditation Hall and shown the statue. He is told that he must become as Avalokitesvara Bodhisattva which it represents; all-compassionate, all-seeing, all-helping. Just as the statue has a thousand arms to help in all places at once and a thousand eyes to see where the help is needed, so the

The statue of Avalokitesvara, the compassionate aspect of the Buddha, at Shasta Abbey. The Hall is also used as a Tombstone Hall. This particular hall is commonly used for housing memorials of the dead in eastern temples.

lay student must search within himself for a means to benefit mankind throughout the world. He must find within himself the strength of a thousand arms and the sight of a thousand eyes. He must so cleanse his heart that no attachment to anything of his old selfish self remains within him and this is done by the power and training of the meditation I described in the previous chapter. But he must not train for the sake of helping others only, nor for the sake of helping himself. He must just train for training's sake and nothing more. In some ways this type of meditation could be called brainwashing for it is a constant criticism of oneself in the minutest details, but it is brainwashing with the difference that it is done by one's own wishes and not by those of another.

The motive for coming to a Zen temple is all important. It was Shakyamuni Buddha's love for the people of the world that made Him go in search of the cause of suffering, old age, decay and death; and at a later date He just trained for training's sake, albeit in the service of mankind. Those who wish to study Zen should consider this point carefully. The purpose of Zazen is NOT to think about gaining anything; this will become clearer as I progress. Shakyamuni Buddha already longed for and exhibited the characteristics of Avalokitesvara prior to His setting out on His journey: He was, in fact, already half-enlightened. Too many people nowadays want to study Zen solely for the benefit of themselves and, without the Bodhisattva mind, which is the heart of Avalokitesvara and Samantabhadra, they will never achieve it. All the pictures of the East warn that this is so if one has the eyes to see them clearly. Always Avalokitesvara appears as a mother pouring out the waters of mercy upon the sea of the world and, behind her, walks her little son, Maitreya, the Buddha which is to come. Those who seek only wisdom, and are unwilling to seek for the heart of Avalokitesvara, will never find either for their basic motive is selfish. Nor is training to attain the heart of Avalokitesvara by itself enough. One trains neither for self nor others in true training; one trains for training's sake.

It is for this reason then that a Zen student should first find his true heart, the heart of Avalokitesvara, before he can be allowed to enter the great Meditation Hall of the unsui. He will be expected to meditate from three in the morning until nine at night, he will be watched minutely and his slightest action regulated: since he must be of impeccable moral character the smallest infringement of the Precepts will bring down strict censure. But all meditation is not just sitting. If one puts one's slippers correctly, and this is the first thing to be taught to a new-comer to a temple, it becomes a form of meditation. Slippers must be placed neatly together, with their backs to the door, so that they do not offend the eyes of others nor get

Ringing the great bell at Shasta Abbey at 11 A.M. and 3 P.M. to announce that the temple is open to visitors. This bell was a gift from Rev. Gikō Yokoyama of Keizō Temple, Rev. Keizan Watanabe of Gishō Temple, Rev. Gi Hirokō of Jishō Temple, Rev. Tatsuhara Yokoyama of Saikō Temple and Mrs. Haruyo Ōnichi, laywoman, all of Japan.

in their way when entering and leaving rooms. This is the first attitude of mind to be cultivated—the thought of order, tidiness and other people's comfort. The small ceremony, performed by oneself prior to bathing, has the same purpose. The words of the prayer are, "I must cleanse my body and my heart." When the bath is over the prayer becomes, "I have cleansed my body; I pray that I may cleanse my heart." In the Bathroom itself strict rules govern the placing and folding of the clothes on the necessary rails and shelves, the way in which they are to be folded must be so as to cause no offence of sight to others and also so as not to occupy too much room in case there is no room for others. In the bath no soap must be used, since it is communal, and no towel or face cloth allowed to be placed in the water. All washing must be done at a separate washing place outside the bath, in a special position, and the water disposed of in such a way that it does not soil the feet of others. Only then may the actual bath be entered. When in the bath one sits in the Zazen position with the washing cloth upon one's head so that it shall not be in others' way. All bathing is, like everything else, done in silence since one must consider that others are working hard on cleansing their own hearts and do not wish to be disturbed by idle chatter. There is a special small ceremony prior to the use of the lavatory, and also one for after it; a special position of the body must be used, not the conventional one, so as to remind one that all habits of mind and body must be changed completely if one is to understand the Truth of Zen. One must make no noise in walking, stand and sit in attitudes that are neither disrespectful nor arrogant to others and one must sleep on one's right side, with one's head on a meditation cushion instead of a pillow, and the coverlet tied by two strings around one's body lest, during the night, someone in the Meditation Hall may awaken and be disgusted by the sight of a partially uncovered body. Since all sleep in the Meditation Hall together this is a wise precaution. The *Tenkien*, or senior on night duty, who walks around the Meditation Hall with a lantern to make certain that all is well, carries a kyosaku and is empowered to thrash any sleeper who is uncovered, or partially uncovered, during the night. This is one of the strictest rules of the temple.

The prayer before meals also reveals the Zen idea of others rather than self (see "Fushuku-hampō," Book Two). When the eating is over, and it must, of course, be done in silence for the purpose of considering the necessity of eating as explained in the prayer, the washing-up water is passed around. Each trainee must wash up in his own bowl and later make an offering of the washing-up water by drinking it during the recitation of the following prayer, "We offer this water to the hungry ghosts so that they too may be filled." So nothing is left, the bowls are polished clean reminding the trainee that, just as the bowl is immaculate with nothing left, so must he himself become. The bowl from which one eats, which is also the begging bowl, is called "the round head of the priest" in Zen terminology and it must always be pure and immaculate, empty of all defilement; meal taking is a very important thing in Zen—within it can be found all the teaching of Zen Truth. The house-work must be done in the same spirit. One does not think only about cleaning one's own living space but helps all others to clean theirs for the mind is such that he who just cleans up himself is selfish—one takes the Bodhisattva vow for all beings as well as oneself. The garden is cleaned and tended in the same way and periods of meditation in the Meditation Hall are interspersed with manual labour in the garden, kitchen and house: these periods must not be regarded as chores but as a means of doing moving meditation. The Cook and his assistants must live and think in such a way that they can see the Buddha Body in a stalk of cabbage and cherish it just as much when handling it in their cooking. He who regards anything as clean or unclean, holy or unholy, is still in the realm of the opposites and thus very far from the Zen way of life. Herein lies a grave difficulty for the beginner who can understand that one must work hard to reach immaculacy of mind and then is shocked out of it by the teacher who does some wicked act so as to teach him not to cling even to immaculacy. In fact, in order to teach his pupils, friends and acquaintances this a teacher will often resort to very strange and fantastic methods of teaching, appearing sometimes unreasonable, angry, grumbling, cajoling, dishonest or even mad. Whenever the teacher behaves strangely one must remember that he is holding a mirror in front of the person being taught; that person should study himself carefully and not criticise the teacher, however bewildering and worldly his behaviour may seem; if he is licensed to teach he knows what he is doing. Dōgen Zenji does not tell us so much in words but, from the many references in his writings and the actual "Tenzo-kyōkun," or "Manual for the Monastery Cook," which he wrote, I strongly suspect that he got far more understanding from his wanderings near, or work in, the kitchen than from a good many other places. In fact some Zenists go so far as to say that the monastery's understanding of Zen can always be tested by a careful study of the Chief Cook whose character must be so kaleidoscopic as to be able to embrace all Buddhism in a grain of rice. Doing one's washing is another important thing for a Zen trainee. Here it is very obvious that the idea of cleaning up one's own dirt is synonymous with throwing out the stupid ideas and notions that one has in one's head. Mending clothes, the idea of tidying oneself up, and shaving heads each have their own appropriate spiritual meanings within the same scheme of thought. Thus every aspect of life is made into a meditation on how to think of others and purify oneself. Each one of us also has something that he must do something about—a secret vice, a rasping voice, heavy footfalls, unsightly dress—anything that can offend others must be carefully attended to. Never for a moment must one consider oneself only.

In the beginning one concentrates one's mind on counting the breaths when meditating but later, as problems present themselves such as painful legs and other portions of the body, sights that may be disturbing and sounds that distract, one must learn to deal with them by neither trying to hold on to them nor trying to thrust them away. Just one observes that they arise and disappear.

Gradually the trainee will realise that his powers of concentration are growing; the peace within him will deepen. He will begin to ask questions as to what Avalokitesvara is and how she actually appears and he will realise that all Avalokitesvaras do not appear as ladies in white dresses but sometimes as judges who punish in order to make one better, doctors who employ a knife which is painful in order to cure, teachers who are cruel to be kind to their pupils. The true meaning of compassion is often misunderstood.

Many people also misunderstand the role of the Inō priest, or Disciplinarian, whose thankless job it is to see that the temple rules are kept and mete out punishment to all offenders, however slight their offences may be. He also has the job of beating all trainees twice a month with his kyosaku to encourage them to greater efforts and to teach them that praise and blame are but two sides of the same coin. He is the embodiment of the saying that the "kindest Avalokitesvara is to be found in hell." Do not misunderstand the use of the words heaven and hell; both places are here and now and of our own creation. Gradually, as the trainee's meditation deepens, he will discover that it is a joy to be alive and that all people, irrespective of colour, race, sex or religion, always have been, and always will be, one. When this moment comes right and wrong, male and female, like and dislike cease to exist and the trainee finds himself or herself bathed in a joy that seems to fill the universe. From this point there is neither self nor other and one trains for training's sake.

Without realising it, the trainee will have become the living incarnation of Avalokitesvara and proved the Truth of the scripture that Avalokitesvara can be seen in any form from that of a Buddha to that of a human, animal or devil. He or she will have been reborn in heaven upon earth and that heaven will always be with him or her for it is, in fact, his or her own discovery and his or her own creation.

CHAPTER 6.

ACTIVITY IN THE HEART
OF SAMANTABHADRA.

Up to now it has been possible to write of things that are easily comprehensible to the ordinary mind, for the reaching of the compassionate state, described in the last chapter as the heart of Avalokitesvara, can be understood without difficulty as a signpost on the road to True Spirituality and, indeed, to some people, spirituality needs to go no further. If it does go any further it is not, to the minds of some, spirituality. This is because the world does not clearly understand the true meanings of the words activity and stillness. Spirituality might be described as activity in stillness or stillness in activity. Let me make this clearer. Just to be passively peaceful and serene may be very nice for the person concerned but it is not particularly useful to anyone except, perhaps, as an example of what can be achieved with self-discipline; quietism is not a substitute for true Zen practice; from the Zen point of view something more must take place, which I call passive activity, and this is extraordinarily difficult to describe.

If we are to truly fulfill the Bodhisattva vow, we must do something more practical than be passive about everything; we must exhibit dynamic activity in the way in which we teach others, and this dynamic activity is often very painful to the pupil. This is because the Zen mind, if it has truly understood the heart of Avalokitesvara, Compassion, and heart of

46

Samantabhadra, Love, is going to think quite differently from the way in which the world thinks, and it is also going to behave quite differently. This 'strange' behaviour has often acquired Zen teachers bad characters, bad reputations and many difficulties but, if the teacher is a true one, he will accept all of this simply because he knows that what he did was done from the stand-point of non-self for the purpose of teaching others.

It follows logically from this that the pupil must have absolute faith in the Buddha Nature of the teacher, otherwise he will always be criticising his actions in his own mind and not be able to breed the necessary trust which is absolutely essential between master and pupil before Transmission can occur. It also means that we must study very carefully what is the true meaning of the words "love" and "compassion." Compassion means to be merciful but true mercy does not necessarily wear a white dress and look like a beautiful lady as I said in my last chapter; nor does its active side, love, necessarily express itself in gentle action. Every doctor knows that when patients are suffering from hysteria it is better to slap them than to make a fuss of them—this is not cruelty, it is kindness. The Zen teacher is in the same position as the doctor in this respect. He must first diagnose the spiritual "illness" from the trainee's questions, and then administer the cure thereof, and he will not be gentle in the way in which he does it. Obviously then, without faith in the teacher, the pupil will get no-where; the teacher, for his part, must put up with the bad reputation, et cetera, including ill-treatment, which he acquires, since this is the logical karmic consequence of his own actions, despite the fact that he was doing what he did for the benefit of others. It is this fact alone that makes what may seem a right action into a wrong one and a wrong one into a right one. For the teacher understands the doctrines of anicca, change, and anatta, no separative self, and from the former he knows that what may be right now will be wrong later on, and again, at a later date, right again; this swing of the pendulum is often misunderstood by the worldly mind; I have known students completely bewildered and even driven away from the study of Zen because they could not understand the two-facedness, as it seemed to them, of the teacher who one minute said one thing and the next the exact opposite and who sometimes imputed things to the student which he never said or did and literally turned black into white and then back into black again. (These techniques are not used at Shasta Abbey, J.K.) It is easier for an Oriental to get away with this kind of teaching than it is for a Western teacher. Whereas the average Western student will accept two-facedness from an Oriental, whitewashing the contradiction with the thought that it is inexplicable as part of the mysterious East, when faced with the same situation presented by a Western teacher he has no way of rationalising it and so either ends up hating and distrusting the teacher or walking completely out of Zen. If he took the trouble to look a little harder, he would realise that the problem for an Oriental student with an Oriental teacher is exactly the same as his own one with this difference—the Oriental student does not try to rationalise the behaviour of his teacher, he simply accepts it, however irrational it may seem to us. The Western student, with his sharpened critical faculties, has great difficulty in trusting a teacher to this same extent and so is hardly ever capable of surmounting the problem. But if the student from the West is seeking true religion and not Eastern mysticism and culture, he will trust his teacher completely for the teacher is seeing beyond the opposites to the true heart of the matter; that others cannot see this heart as clearly as he can is a source of grief to him and he wishes deeply that they may share with him the joy of knowledge and true freedom. The lot of Zen teachers is an extremely lonely one and they are often forced to grieve very deeply, not for themselves, but because of the misunderstanding of others. The average Westerner is too critical, and too unwilling to give up his negativity and distrust, to make an ideal disciple in the Eastern sense of the word and it is impossible to teach Zen orientally without complete trust between master and disciple as I have already stated. In the *Transmission of the Light* (see Book Three), which is simply the explanation of how the Truth was Transmitted from Ancestor to Ancestor in the Buddhist apostolic line, each individual Ancestor had a besetting fault or sin, as a Christian would call it, and, as the book is read through, one gradually discovers that the Ancestors were no better and no worse than present day men; but all trusted their teachers implicitly once they found them.

Each Ancestor represents a type of person to be found in the world at the present time. In one respect almost all Westerners come under the same category as the second Ancestor, Ananda, in that they love argument and are proud of their erudition. As a warning to my fellow Westerners I would like to point out that it took Ananda almost five times as long as it took anybody else to realise the Truth of Zen simply because of his love of clinging to books and knowledge. Keizan Zenji, who wrote the *Transmission of the Light* early in the fourteenth century, writes the following therein:–

> I know well that the very Truth is not in the clever and the erudite, nor is it in those who gain worldly rank. This is the proof: Ananda followed Makakashyo as a servant for twenty years before his enlightenment. He was born on the same night that the Lord [Shakyamuni Buddha] was enlightened. He liked erudition and, because of this, he was not enlightened. Shakyamuni Buddha, however, concentrated His mind in Zazen and so was enlightened.

I know well that erudition disturbs enlightenment and, in the above, lies the proof. Therefore the following saying is in the *Kegon Scripture*, "A poor man who counts others' treasure cannot have his own. Erudition is as this." If you wish to understand the Truth really, you should not like erudition; just concentrate on Zazen.

Ananda was always thinking that there must be something other than the *kesa* that was given at the Transmission—there HAD to be something mysterious—just giving a kesa was too ordinary. Keizan continues:–

The Truth cannot be gained by erudition. Although a person is like Ananda, is clever and has sharp ears and can understand every character in the Scriptures and doctrines, if he cannot understand their real meaning with his whole being, he is counting another's treasure. This is not because there is no meaning in the Scriptures and doctrines. Therefore, in Japan and other countries, they are understanding the meaning of the Scriptures in words and so they cannot understand fully. Of course the Truth should be thought about very sincerely yet Ananda, who could understand the Scriptures and doctrines of the Lord better than any other and who was His actual disciple, was unable to realise the Truth. Who of us is able to understand by words if he could not? Yet, after spending many years as the servant of Makakashyo, he realised the Truth. If you want to become one with Truth as one fire combines with another, throw away selfish opinions, old emotions, arrogance and obstinacy concerning your own learning and realise the True Mind of the Lord with the naïve, simple mind of a child. You yourself are the manifestation of Truth. If you can realise Truth you disappear at once. As this is so, we should not look for it outside of ourselves in erudition.

Because of this solemn warning, I have eschewed erudition as much as possible in this book. All those of my readers who love book learning are heartily advised to take the comments of Keizan to heart for they are far truer than they will ever realise this side of Zen understanding.

To make all the foregoing clear it would be appropriate for me to do what all the other writers on Zen do and quote stories of the Zen teachers of old to prove my various points, but any intelligent reader can get the appropriate books of stories and work this side of Zen out for himself. Concerning the people who criticise the actions of teachers I have this to say. Just as the ocean is undisturbed in its depths by the storms that sweep its surface and create gigantic waves, so is the heart of the licensed and trained Zen teacher. Students who suffer from the idea that such a teacher is exhibiting emotionalism had best plumb the depths of their own emotions before criticising the mirror that the teacher is holding up before them for, just as the mirror is undisturbed by the reflection upon its surface, so is the Zen teacher undisturbed by the reflection in his actions of what the students are exhibiting in front of him.

Now it is extremely difficult, even after reaching the stage of understanding compassion, for a trainee to reach the point where he can exhibit the correct behavioural traits of a teacher. This is because, in reaching the stage of compassion, he was, as it were, climbing up a side-branch of a tree rather than the main trunk. He had reached compassionate passivity which all could comprehend, thereafter he must swing to the opposite branch, compassionate activity, i.e. love. The way in which a trainee is forced to make the change is again somewhat cruel to the ordinary thinking mind. When one is given the kyosaku to carry, not just for routine purposes of *jikidō*, or monitor, in the Meditation Hall, but as a junior teacher, one knows that it has been decided that it is time to learn to become active. Many people find it almost impossible to use the kyosaku for some time after being handed it for it is now one's duty to be cruel to others for the purpose of being kind. (It is now only used on those who ask in Shasta, J.K.) In some Zen temples there is a picture of a trainee being thrashed with the title, "Deeds of the Utmost Kindness." In the religious sense this is true but, looked at with the discriminating mind, it appears cruel. To be put in charge of a bunch of raw trainees is another way of teaching activity to the third stage trainee who can then no longer sit as he wishes in the physical Meditation Hall; he has to learn to find that Meditation Hall within himself. So always both the trainees and the teacher are being taught; this is one of the meanings of the words "endless training" or training for training's sake.

At this stage and, indeed, in most of the others, the teacher's job is an extremely thankless task. Since a true Zen teacher is, in any case, beyond the necessity of thanks, it does not much matter but those who wish to study Zen should consider this point well for they are likely to acquire a bad reputation from those who misunderstand what they are trying to do when giving genuine teaching. If their trainees do not have complete faith in them, they may well find themselves with a bad reputation. I cannot emphasise this enough. If they are true teachers, this will not worry them in the least—since Shakyamuni Buddha was content with only a tree under which to live and nothing more He could teach as He wished—once one requires the financial support of others, limitations are placed upon one's teaching of Truth. The "Shushōgi," the most popular of all the Zen scriptures in Japan, has this to say:– "When you meet with a teacher who preaches the Right Law, you should not think of his caste, nor attend to his outward features, consider his shortcomings or criticise his methods of teaching; simply venerating his wisdom, you should bow before him three times a day and never worry him."

It is said that there is plenty of room at the top of the tree of fame and there is certainly plenty of room in the rarefied air of fourth and fifth stage meditation. Few indeed are they who have the courage to complete their training and fearlessly throw away both friends and enemies for the sake of giving True teaching. There is also the fact that to shock a person out of the passivity of the third stage of compassion can be very difficult. This stage, which is the stage of many priests and some laymen, is so comfortable and enjoyable that it does not seem possible that there could be anything better. There is, however, a greater experience and a joy and freedom beyond the powers of imagination. The true teacher can tell when the trainee has truly acquired the characteristics of Samantabhadra by watching his actions and reactions to the situations that he is bound to create as a result of his teaching methods, and the proof of whether he truly loves mankind with the heart of Samantabhadra is given when, in face of all opposition, distrust and misunderstanding, he is willing to carry on in the path that he has chosen, truly caring nothing for material things, fame, fortune, reputation, honour, life or death. The person who thinks that a teacher can tell, by just looking at a trainee, whether or not he has had a realisation of the Truth, is completely mistaken—the only way any teacher can tell if a change has taken place in a person whom he is training is by meditating deeply with that person over a period of time. Teachers are not sorcerers—they are human beings, and those who go around imputing almost magical powers to "Zen Masters" deserve a sound box of the ears for doing a grave disservice to a great, deep and wonderful religion.

CHAPTER 7.

THE HEART OF MANJUSRI.

When Shakyamuni saw, sees and will see the morning star and was, is and will be enlightened, He said, says and will say, "I was, am and will be enlightened instantaneously with the universe." This saying has not received enough attention from those who would study Zen, and it is all important for, within it, lies one of the greatest of all clues to understanding Buddhism.

When I first asked my former master how to go about my studies he told me, quite simply, "Expect nothing, seek nothing, just live." This, to someone who had travelled around the world in order to study, did not seem, at the time, an adequate answer; yet he spoke nothing more than the literal truth. The analytical and critical mind of Western man desires something more than the above and it is this analytical and critical mind that Zen seeks to transcend. In order to do this, one has to come to an understanding of what is real "mind" and what is misconception.

In the last two chapters I talked about the ways in which Zen teachers train their pupils to go beyond duality; then seemingly back into duality through activity in stillness. Now I want to talk about the way in which both stillness and activity, compassion and love, dissolve into wisdom, which is the immaculacy of nothingness, leading to being able to just live, expecting nothing, seeking nothing and knowing nothing— the acme of perfection of spiritual poverty which possesses the universe. To do this we must consider the philosophic and spiritual way of thinking that produces the activity of both compassion and love as well as the true meanings of the words "mind" and "enlightenment."

In the *Surangama Scripture*, as stated earlier, four main questions are posed:– a. Where is mind, as functioning through the senses, located? b. If it has no location in such senses, how do we determine its reality and nature? c. To be able to view the changing implies that we are also able to view the changeless, and d. Although the power of the senses is changeless, they are not, as such, absolute. What, then, is absolute and why?

Without going into a long and detailed explanation of these questions, I will summarise them quickly. If mind is located within the senses, obviously a blind or deaf man would not be in possession of a mind as far as these senses were concerned, yet the blind and deaf both have cognisance of darkness and silence. As this is so, it cannot be located in the senses. However, that which sees and that which hears perceives things undergoing changes; it notices that the hand becomes wrinkled with age; that leaves wither and fall; yet that which has cognisance of these things does not, of itself, change. The fourth question is the all important one. The power of the senses, though changeless, is not, as such, absolute. What, then, is absolute and why? The illustration given by Buddha in the Scripture is an excellent one so I will quote it in full:–

Although we exercise the power of sight through the medium of this very sight-power, seeing still does not depend on this sight-power; even whilst "seeing," we may be still at a distance from "true sight;" nor by the exercise of sight do we necessarily exercise the power of "true sight." Consider a man whose eye is afflicted with a cataract. At night, when the light of the lamp shines before him, he thinks he sees a round shadow encircling the flame, composed of the five colours interlacing one another. Are these beautiful colours in the lamp or in the eye? If they are in the lamp, then why does not a man with healthy sight see them? It is in the sight of the person concerned then, as it is the result of an act of vision; so what name shall we give to the power that produces these colours? We must conclude that the object looked at, the flame, is dependent on the lamp, but that the circle is the result of imperfect vision. Now all such vision is connected with disease and to see the cause of the disease (that is, the cataract) is curative of the disease. Therefore, what you and other creatures now see is the result of an original fault, as of sight, of the cataract, on the true and ever-glorious power of sight which I possess. If the ordinary power of sight be a cataract on the eye of my true sight, it follows, as a matter of course, that the pure and bright mind of my true knowledge[2] in seeing all these unreal associations is not afflicted with this imperfection; THAT WHICH UNDERSTANDS ERROR IS NOT ITSELF IN ERROR; therefore, having laid hold of this true idea of sight, there will be no further meaning in such expressions as "hearing with the ears" and "knowing by the sight." This faculty which we, and all the twelve species of creatures, possess, and which we call sight—this is the same as the cataract on the eye—it is the imperfection of true sight; but that true and original power of vision which has become thus perverted and is, in its (True) nature, without imperfection—that cannot properly be called by the same name.[3]

The obvious deduction from all this is that Mind[2] only is absolute Buddha, shining brilliantly and perfectly in everything, manifesting itself in all things and at all times, and this universal Mind,[2] which is Buddha, can only be realised by leaving behind all reason, analysis, belief and knowledge which it knows and trusts. This awakening to reality can only be achieved by Zazen and the intuitive understanding which the teacher is always exhibiting to the pupil. But here again we have a difficulty for the very fact that mind has been explained in such a way as above, which is the teaching of the Ōbaku Church of Zen is, in itself, contradictory, the real Truth lying beyond any kind of verbal explanation or expression.

Ōbaku teaches that the mind is a mirror bright. Sōtō teaches that the mind is not a bright mirror since there never was anything from the beginning. However, it is necessary to know this Ōbaku belief for it leads naturally to the Rinzai one and, eventually, to the highest of all, that which lies beyond this last pair of opposites, Sōtō. There is only one way to understand what I have written here and that is to do Zazen and get your own realisation; I can tell you that fire burns but you will not know what I mean by "burns" unless you put your hand in the flame for yourself; I cannot give you my understanding; you must find your own. The scriptures say very clearly, "Remember thou must go alone—the Buddhas do but point the way." Although Shakyamuni Buddha was aware of these facts, He still gave the beginnings of these teachings out of sheer compassion for others, hoping that, as people progressed in knowledge and understanding, they could come to greater realisation.

It was for the above reasons that Makakashyo, the first Ancestor after Shakyamuni Buddha, was Transmitted silently in the famous story of the flower and the smile; no words were capable of expressing that which they both knew. The

great Chinese teacher, Hsi-yün (Ōbaku Kiun) puts it rather
well:–

> If students of the Way desire to become Buddhas they
> need not study anything whatsoever of the Dharma. They
> should only study how to avoid seeking for, or clinging
> to, anything. If nothing is sought, the mind will remain
> in its "unborn" state and, if nothing is clung to or known,
> the mind will not go through the process of destruction.
> That which is neither born nor destroyed is the Buddha.
> The eighty-four thousand methods for counteracting the
> eighty-four thousand forms of delusion are merely fig-
> ures of speech for attracting people towards conversion.
> In fact, none exist. Relinquishment of everything is the
> Dharma and he who understands this is a Buddha, but the
> renunciation of ALL delusions leaves no Dharma on which
> to lay hold. If the student of the Way wishes to under-
> stand the real mystery, he need only put out of his mind
> attachment to anything whatsoever, especially his own
> opinions and criticisms. To say that the real Dharmakaya
> of the Buddha is like the void means that it actually is void
> and that the void is the Dharmakaya (conception of Cos-
> mic Buddhahood). The void and the Dharmakaya do not
> differ from each other, neither do sentient beings and
> Buddha, the phenomenal world and Nirvana, or delusion
> and Bodhi. When all such forms are left behind, that is
> Buddha. Ordinary people look outwards whilst follow-
> ers of the Way look into their own minds, but the real
> Dharma is to forget both the external and the internal. The
> former is easy enough, the latter very difficult. Men are
> afraid to forget their own minds, fearing to fall through
> the void with nothing to which they can cling. They do
> not know that the void is not really void but the real realm
> of the Dharma. This spiritually enlightened nature is

without beginning or end, as old as space, neither subject to birth nor destruction, neither existing nor not existing, neither defiled nor pure. . . . It cannot be looked for or sought, comprehended by wisdom or knowledge, explained in words, contacted materially or reached by meritorious achievement. If a man, when he is about to die, can only regard the five aggregates of his consciousness as void, . . . if he can only awake to this in a flash and remain free from the remaining entanglements of the Triple World, (past, present and future) he will indeed be one who leaves the world without the faintest tendency towards rebirth. If he should behold the lovely sight of all the Buddhas coming to welcome him and yet feel no desire to go towards them, if he should behold the devils and evil forms surrounding him and yet have no fear, remaining oblivious to self and at one with the Absolute, he will indeed achieve the formless state. (This is not only true of the time of death but also during Zazen.) When analytic thinking concerning the past, present and future does not take place, it is called complete relinquishment of the Triple World. Since the time when the Buddha entrusted Makakashyo with the Dharma until the present day, the Transmission has been from mind to mind, yet these minds are identical with each other. In fact, however, mind is not really mind and the reception of the Transmission is not really reception. WHEN THE BUDDHA WAS ALIVE HE WISHED TO PREACH THE TRUE VEHICLE BUT PEOPLE WOULD NOT HAVE BELIEVED HIM, SCOFFING AT HIM INSTEAD. Hence a Transmission of mind cannot be made through words, and any transmission in concrete terms cannot be that of the Dharma. So the Transmission is made from mind to mind and these minds are identical with each other. On the other hand, if the Buddha had said nothing, that would have been selfish. So he adopted the expedient of preaching the Three Vehicles (that is, only revealing as much as people could understand at any one time). None of these vehicles represents the real Dharma, so it is said that there is only a One-Vehicle Way for, wherever there is division into this or that, there is no Truth. However, there is no way whatsoever of expressing universal mind. Therefore the Buddha called Makakashyo to the Seat of the Law on which he sat and commanded him to practice this branch of the Dharma separately, saying that, when a silent understanding of it is obtained, the state of Buddhahood is reached.[4]

I have paraphrased this considerably owing to its great length and in order to make it clearer in places for Western minds. But the question that all those who read this will be asking is, "How and when does one reach this state of understanding and what is the standard by which the teacher judges the pupil's ability?" This is one question, not two, and is easily answered. When the pupil is just living, without thought of self or other, doing that which has to be done without fear or elation, taking notice of neither praise nor blame as a result of his actions and when the Wheel turns in the teacher when he meets, sees or talks to the pupil, the teacher will know that the pupil has, in fact, refound his Original True Self. He will be living as a top spins; whilst seemingly busy outside, his centre will be still and unmoving. When this stage has been reached and the master and disciple behold each other face to face, they will know that their minds (Buddha Nature) always have been and always will be one, just as they are one with the mind of Shakyamuni Buddha and all the Buddhas of the past, present and future. (Please note the similarity of the teaching here with that for Zazen, i.e. do not try to think and do not try not to think, just sit; here he who exhibits

Questions are asked by all trainees on the first and fifteenth of every month in Sōtō temples. Unlike Rinzai however, all such questions are asked in public, not in private, and all Zen masters in residence in the temple take turns in being questioned. Here the author asks a question of the Director. The ceremony is called Shōsan and the actual question and answer are called mondo in Sōtō. Mondo is the Sōtō equivalent of the Rinzai kōan, however the asking of the latter always takes place in private. Once a term the Abbot rises upon the altar, as the living Buddha, to be questioned by all trainees in a ceremony similar to the above called Jōdō.

true Buddhahood neither clings to anything nor pushes it away, he just lives; Zazen is the key to the whole of Buddhahood.) But this past, present and future, too, are again non-existent for time, also, has been transcended and, as this is so, for those who have the instantaneous perception of true understanding, this very time that you are reading this NOW is none other than the time when Shakyamuni Buddha smiled at Makakashyo in India, and YOU are Makakashyo; it is the time when Hui-nêng was Transmitted at midnight, in secret, and YOU are Hui-nêng in ancient China; it is the time when

Dōgen looked upon Koun Ejō in Japan in the thirteenth century and YOU are Koun Ejō. If you want the Truth as much
as a hanged man wishes to loosen the rope around his neck,
you will understand these words instantly and know that YOU
yourself ARE Buddha, always have been and always will be;
you are enlightened in all ages simultaneously with the whole
universe. To those who realise the heart of Manjusri, not only
is duality transcended into unity but the very unity itself is
also transcended and the truth of Meister Eckhart's words
proved for all time:– "And a man shall be free, and as pure as
the day prior to his conception in his mother's womb, when
he has nothing, wants nothing and knows nothing. Such a one
has true spiritual poverty." Bodhidharma put it this way:–
"The nature of the mind (Buddha Nature), when understood,
no human words can compass or disclose. Enlightenment is
naught to be obtained, and he that gains it does not say he
knows."[5]

This is true spirituality and true enlightenment, but do
not stay with unity any more than you stay with duality for if
you do you will be the embodiment of the saying, "(and he
who thinks that he is Buddha), there he sits upon his throne,
unseen by any save himself."

Every philosopher knows that to reach perfection is to
reach an ending from which one must again start from the very
beginning. One is only Buddha when one is always becoming
Buddha by keeping the Precepts in their Absolute State. He
who reaches Buddhahood is the one who is himself and nothing more. He is not pretending to be holy or unholy, nor is it
his problem if others dislike or worship him for being the way
he is. He just does that which has to be done and nothing more,
without ever saying that he is Buddha or that he is not. He is
always becoming Buddha and leaving Buddhahood behind
every moment of the day; he cannot hold on to Buddhahood

any more than you who read this can hold on to the moment at which you read the words that I have just written.

They who know the turning of the Wheel never say they do or do not know to those who do not—they just live, doing that which has to be done. Despite the thanklessness of the job that he does, the Zen teacher has his compensations, but he is not attached to them. He goes on, making himself as perfect as possible as he goes, doing that which has to be done.

The last stage of training is to return to the world with the bliss-bestowing hands of Maitreya, the Buddha who is to come. In D.T. Suzuki's book, *The Manual of Zen Buddhism* there is the following verse:–

> Returning to the city with bliss-bestowing hands, his thatched cottage gate is closed, and even the wisest know him not. No glimpses of his inner life are to be caught for he goes on his own way without following the steps of the ancient sages. Carrying a gourd he goes out into the market, leaning against a staff he comes home. He is found in company with wine-bibbers and butchers, he and they are all converted into Buddhas.
>
> > Bare-chested and bare-footed, he comes out into the market-place;
> > Daubed with mud and ashes, how broadly he smiles!
> > There is no need for the miraculous power of the gods,
> > For he touches, and lo! the dead trees are in full bloom.[6]

It is the duty of every trainee to share with the world the glory of his own understanding and this is done in many ways, not being confined to any one method. Remember that

Avalokitesvara reveals herself in the world in all walks of life and spheres of activity. The trainee may take up the work of a priest, a doctor or a nurse, a teacher, hotel keeper or a servant but his nature, if he continues to keep up his training and does not become either ambitious, power hungry or superior in his own mind with regard to others and especially his former teachers, will be so different from that of ordinary men that all the world will notice and want to copy him. Just by being an Arhat one is, in fact, a Bodhisattva. By the above gentle method of teaching, which is always devoid of proselytising, he will gradually lead others away from the idea of personal gain to higher things; thus Avalokitesvara manifests herself at all times in the world of patience.

Unfortunately I must end this chapter on not quite so lofty a note as I would like to; previously this chapter ended here but, as a result of at least two people misunderstanding it from the selfish viewpoint, I am forced to add this paragraph. There is a great difference between the way in which sainthood is looked at in Christianity and the way in which it is looked at in Buddhism. Because Christianity believes that there is a separate soul in each individual the outlook with regard to saints is that they themselves are holy and fit to be in heaven; in Buddhism, since there is no separate soul, the persons concerned cleanse themselves of all past karma to such an extent that that which belongs to the Eternal may be seen in them and it is not theirs; thus Avalokitesvara appears in them in this world in all walks of life but they are not individual saints. Such a person is not exhibiting holiness that is his personal property; he is exhibiting that which comes from the Eternal—in the case of Avalokitesvara, the Compassionate Nature of the Eternal which is synonymous with Avalokitesvara. The above could be regarded as the difference between a saint and a Bodhisattva but such an explanation may <u>still</u> lack for something. One thinks of Christian saints as special people with special souls; one thinks of Bodhisattvas as non-special people who are exhibiting the Eternal. In Christianity one aspires to be a saint; one is ambitious to become a saint. In Buddhism there is no aspiration to sainthood and no ambition; having cleansed one's karma one merely exhibits the Eternal without being conscious of exhibiting the Eternal and without caring whether one exhibits it or not since it is the natural and right thing to do. The poet of the oxherding picture quoted above lived in a Buddhist country where what I have just said was naturally understood—at least at that time; when we in the West can understand it, as naturally-born Buddhists understand it, what I have written in this last paragraph will not be necessary. Until that time, however, the difference must be clearly understood and the Westerner who suffers from the ambition to wander across the world doing good must know that he is courting spiritual disaster.

CHAPTER 8.

WHAT ARE KŌANS?

It is essential to do Zazen if one would understand the world we live in with anything deeper than the usual superficial understanding of the average person, and it is not a matter of doing anything out of the ordinary since all religions have practiced contemplation and meditation in various forms throughout the centuries. Even dogs and cats love to sit quietly for long periods of time, however, most Western people, being intellectually oriented as I said earlier, are plagued by either fear or boredom during such periods if they have nothing specific to think about and this is the main reason why the Rinzai system of kōans appeals to the average Westerner; it simply gives him something to think about until he comes to the realisation that there are no <u>real</u> questions that can be answered by the processes of thought. Such a practice is concentration, <u>not</u> Zazen.

It was Daie Sōkō, born 1089, who advocated the use of kōans during Zazen as preferable to the old method of quiet sitting, known as *shikan taza* in Japanese, which had prevailed up to then and on which he himself had been trained, as had, indeed, all the great masters up until that time, including Rinzai himself. Since Daie Sōkō was known to be brilliantly intellectual, I strongly suspect that he found the older method of meditation too difficult to practice; only the intellectual types seem to have difficulty in practicing the old method of meditation (see the chapters on Ananda and other intellectuals in Book Three). Since the whole purpose of Zazen is to quieten the thought waves so that one may realise one's True Nature, the present day use of kōans for many Westerners, that of seeing how many they can solve like puzzles, is utterly wrong. In Japan I have so often seen, with disgust and sadness, a snobbish pride taken by these people in telling their fellow trainees how many kōans they have already solved and what "heights of understanding" they have reached. Many have a mistaken idea of what Zen "freedom," about which so much has erroneously been said, is.

Sōtō Zen does not make it a rule of training that trainees must "solve" a matter of three hundred or so kōans before being given their master's seals and this for the very simple reason that training is not for the purpose of gaining seals or anything else but solely to teach the trainee the True Way of Buddhism. Because the connection between kōan technique and the teachings of Buddha is obscure, many people have, with some reason, believed in the past that Zen is not a branch of Buddhism at all and I, for one, do not blame them for, as yet, I have never seen any book which explained the connection between the two. It would be wrong, however, to believe such nonsense for Zen is the very essence of Buddhism itself. Without Zazen, Buddha could never have reached enlightenment; the very first "kōan" was Shakyamuni Buddha's own. After seeing the four sights (see Chapter 1) and realising the need for finding the cause of suffering and removing it, He sat under the Bodhi Tree doing Zazen until the "kōan" was solved with the discovery of the Four Noble Truths. Thereafter He taught the Four Noble Truths; His whole life of forty-five years of service to mankind was an extended explanation, and applied use, of the answer to His own "kōan."

To just use kōans as puzzles or, worse still, to believe that all must be solved and then graduation is automatic, is a waste of time. Sōtō Zen does occasionally use kōans as, and when, applicable to a situation but never more than necessary.

In the *Most Excellent Mirror—Samadhi* it says, "When a trainee asks a question, a matching answer always comes from the Zen master—who uses all means, so varied, even so to say that black is white (when teaching) because delusions in the trainee's mind are all topsy-turvy." In other words, because the trainee has no idea of what Buddhism REALLY is, i.e. the TRUE use and keeping of the Precepts, his early attempts at answering questions are rejected by the teacher although the trainee may have, and frequently has, given the right intellectual answer to the kōan set. The teacher refuses the answer because the trainee's spiritual growth is not, as yet, great enough for it to receive the seal of the teacher. Each time the pupil comes to the teacher with his answer it is rejected and each time the pupil comes back to the same answer, frequently in different wording, with greater spiritual conviction than he had in the beginning when answering it, until he eventually explodes the answer and comes to the teacher no longer caring whether the latter agrees with him or not because he KNOWS with his whole being that his answer is right. This is the right use of kōans.

The important point to remember here is that the teacher always gives matching answers to the trainee's questions; in other words, it is the pupil that makes the running and not the master, the latter acting only as a mirror reflecting the reactions and actions of the pupil: this is the master's reason for sometimes making black white, although he knows that this is only muddling the pupil more. If a student is already in a muddle, and is deliberately made to see that his thinking and behaviour are muddled by a skillful teacher, he can do something to help himself, always presuming that he <u>knows</u> that the muddles shown to him by the teacher are reflections of himself.

Now this system is excellent as a means of character training for Precept keeping and helping to strengthen faith in the Eternal. When a trainee first comes to a temple he knows the beliefs and basic tenets of Buddhism, the Ten Precepts and other necessary doctrines, but he only knows them in his brain and not deeply as the conviction of his blood and bones. By the time he has undergone the strict moral training of the temple for several years, his character is, if, after reflecting him, the teacher gave him an excellent example, beyond reproach and he keeps the Precepts because it is his inclination to do so and not because it is a moral code which it is incumbent upon him to keep as a result of an outside deity. Here again the connection of Zen training with the old Buddhist Precepts is exemplified. The moral codes of most religions are enforced by a deity from outside but the Buddhist takes the moral discipline of Buddhism upon himself. Because an external deity is lacking, conviction of the Truth of the Precepts must be generated from within the trainee; this is the use of the conviction-stimulating reflection and example, i.e. correctly understood kōan technique. When the teacher sees that the pupil has made the moral code his natural way of life, he knows that the latter has finally taken the Buddha, Dharma and Sangha for refuge in the True meaning of the words. One has to live Buddhism, be Buddhism and, to do this, the Precepts must flow through one's veins as does one's very life-blood. Just as we do not notice the coursing of our blood but permit it to flow unhindered, so the Buddhist lives the moral code of the Precepts, unhindered by them and unhindering them. The certainty of understanding that comes at various times, the *kenshō*, as a result of meditation, deepens the spirituality and character of the person and enables him or her to enter into the Precepts more deeply. Once it is second nature to be constantly exemplifying the Precepts, one is not conscious of doing so and so is not conscious of being either bound or Buddha. Therefore Buddha recognises Buddha when the trainee beholds the master, and the master beholds Buddha in the pupil when both keep the Precepts with no smell of holiness and no taint of evil for Buddha then walks, sleeps, sits, eats and works in both of them without any knowledge of Buddha and no attachment thereto. This is spiritual autonomy. Many can reach this state successfully without kōans of the orthodox type at all. Rinzai forces the kōan book on everybody; Sōtō studies the individual and artistically suits the teaching to his or her needs.

In order to bring the student to the above level of acceptance of the Precepts it is imperative to raise his conviction of faith to its highest peak, and the first thing, which every pupil must be certain of, is the possession of, i.e. faith in, his own Buddha Nature.

It is important to find the Buddha within animals and inanimate things. Once the certainty of one's own Buddha Nature has been established beyond doubt, the stream of Buddhism has been entered and the trainee is then free to progress, deepening his understanding as he goes.

If kōans are ever used, it must be clearly understood that the solving of each one is not a separate gaining of enlightenment but a deepening of original enlightenment. Enlightenment is not obtained piece-meal; it is one and undivided. A shallowy glimpse is no less enlightenment than is a deep one; and the fact that we all possess the Buddha Nature from the beginning of time proves that we are already enlightened anyway but must train ourselves in order to realise it. It is useless, after reading the above, to consider that merely to know one possesses the Buddha Nature is the equivalent of being enlightened, as some critics of Sōtō Zen have, at times, claimed as its most glaring fault, for to have something with no awareness of its possession is, practically, the same as not to possess it; awareness, the knowledge of possession, must be awakened. One has to know of this possession, and still train, in order to realise it to the full. To this end kōans are used when appropriate in Sōtō Zen.

How is it, then, the reader may ask, that a teacher, when using kōans, may, on occasion, do evil acts, if the whole purpose of the kōan system is to teach the pupil the correct understanding of the Precepts? The answer is that it is impossible to harmonise right and wrong unless one knows fully what right and wrong are and represent. One cannot know heaven without also knowing hell; one cannot fully understand them without transcending both. Most people are bound by the moral code of their religions, but Buddhism teaches its followers how to be freed by their moral code. This does not mean that immorality is countenanced and encouraged as some drug addicts and advocates of free love seem to think. Unless one knows, with one's whole being, that an act is evil, one does not understand evil; unless one knows, with one's whole being, that an act is good, one does not understand good; unless one knows, with one's whole being, that a good act and a bad act partake of both a Buddha and a devil action, being the reverse and obverse of the same 'coin' so to speak, one does not understand that the kindest Avalokitesvara is to be found in hell and the worst devil occupies the highest heaven. The teacher must accept the karmic consequences of any evil act he may do in order to teach the transcendence of good and evil to his pupils. Only after this paradox has been transcended can the pupil fully understand the Goi Theory and the Precepts for only then will he know how to keep these Precepts without being bound by them or being attached to them. It is as bad to keep the Precepts out of <u>attachment</u> to morality as it is not to keep them at all; a teacher sometimes breaks the Precepts in order to teach the immorality of morality to those still suffering from attachment to morality (and the teacher who does this will still carry the karmic "can" for doing so). The grave danger of <u>attachment</u> to the keeping of the Precepts is the creation of spiritual pride. Eventually the Precepts are so transcended that there is neither morality nor immorality to such an extent that even the Precepts themselves do not exist and the pupil is, instead, the very living embodiment of them. Such a person could never be either a drug addict or an advocate of free love, and he would not be able to explain to anyone the reason why since it would be his nature to live a moral life. This is the true keeping of the Precepts.

CHAPTER 9.

APOSTOLIC SUCCESSION.

So far as I can discover, no one has ever yet talked about the priestly ranks to be found in Sōtō Zen nor have the various terms and titles used been explained. Since these things are a source of much controversy in Western countries, I have decided to devote a whole chapter to them. First and foremost the term *tokudō* must be explained.

This is the most misunderstood word in Zen terminology. Strictly speaking, it means ordination, but the Japanese have stretched it to include the meanings, and equivalent status, of Christian baptism and confirmation without employing a qualifying word to differentiate between the three meanings. Since this is so, many Western people return to their own countries from Japan suffering from the idea that they are priests when, in fact, they are only confirmed laymen. The blame for this must be laid squarely at the door of the Japanese—after all, if you insist on having only one word, meaning three different things, you cannot blame the unfortunate foreigner who looks it up in his dictionary, reads that it means ordination, understands this in the same way that he would understand it if he were a Christian, since this is its meaning in his own culture, and goes away thinking that he is a full priest. It is important to counteract such misunderstandings, and prevent recurrences in the future, but doing so is a bit like locking the stable door after the horse has bolted. I have known of at least three people who were going around dressed as priests, and doing various ceremonies, when they were actually only confirmed laymen. A fair way of judging whether or not the ceremony you have undergone is that of a layman or a trainee priest is to ask if you are expected to shave your head, wear robes and enter a training temple. If the answer is no then you can safely take it that you are a confirmed layman and not a priest, even if the priest who does the ceremony looks up the word in his dictionary and tells you otherwise. To become a confirmed layman you agree to keep the Precepts and are given a small, token rakhusu, or kesa, to wear; it is this last which misleads people more, perhaps, than the actual terminology since the kesa has always been the badge of the priest in Buddhism. If you are planning on going to Japan, it would be best to make exhaustive enquiries of any priest to whose temple you may go, should you receive tokudō, since, to say you are a priest when you are not one, upsets the Japanese very considerably and no one wants to be branded a religious fraud; especially when he is innocent.

Next let us look at the words *monk* and *nun*. In Zen temples the Japanese again have only one word for both of these— *unsui*. This word is made up of two Chinese characters, the first of which means "cloud" and the second "water." In combination, their meaning is as follows:– an unsui is a person, male or female, who wanders across the world, as free as a cloud, in his search for Truth but yet has the strength of an ocean to wash away the mountains that stand in his or her way. Obviously this is a very different meaning from that usually given to the words *monk* and *nun* in countries which have a Christian culture or background. A monk or nun lives a dedicated life in the service of God under vows of poverty, chastity and obedience, but the unsui takes no such vows; his only vow is that of the Bodhisattva which is:– However innumerable beings may be, I vow to save them; however difficult the teachings are, I vow to master them; I vow to cleanse my own heart (of karma). This is very different from the Christian vows quoted above: there is another difference also. Both male and female unsui in Sōtō Zen are expected to become members of the priesthood, i.e. priest or priestess, they are not supposed to be content with just being unsui. This brings into focus the difference between Christian and Buddhist monasticism; the former does not permit nuns to become full priests, but the female unsui in Zen is expected to become the priestess of a temple. The ideal in the Buddhist scriptures is that male and female are alike in the Buddha Mind and so men and women can go up the ranks of the priesthood equally. Unfortunately, Japanese custom (or prejudice, whichever word you prefer) gets in the way of the female far more often than it should with the result that there are not nearly as many full priests among the women as there should be and those who have made it have much poorer temples than the men. Prejudice apart, the ideal in Japanese Sōtō Zen (see "Shushōgi," p. 99, first para.) is complete equality of the sexes and a woman, if she is energetic and resourceful, can go all the way up the seven ranks of the priesthood although this is not so in many other Buddhist Churches; quite a number of my friends have gone up these ranks. Before the war, the obstacles placed in a woman's way were so great as to be almost insurmountable. However, with the influx of new ideas from outside Japan, life has become a lot easier for the female members of the priesthood and a really energetic woman, if she is willing to put up with slights from the male priests can, as stated above, become a full priestess. It is easier for Western women than it is, perhaps, for Japanese ones since the former possess more tenacity concerning this than do their Japanese sisters.

Because of the great difference in meaning between the English words *monk* and *nun* and the Japanese *unsui*, the former are never used in describing Zen trainees in this book. Scholars argue between the words *trainee* and *seminarian* as translations of *unsui*, but I feel sure that the former is by far the closer to its true meaning since the word *seminarian* does not adequately describe the actual activities of the temple unsui. Perhaps the very best solution would be to keep the Japanese word *unsui* and carry it over into the English language since no one English word can really convey its true meaning.

With regard to the words *priest* and *priestess*, the Japanese characters present no such difficulties as those of *unsui*. *Oshō* literally means *"honorable" priest* and *ni-oshō* means *female "honorable" priest*, i.e. priestess. These terms are applied to unsui after reaching the fifth grade of the priesthood and cause no complication once they are truly understood according to the above meaning. It is, of course, the duty of every member of the priesthood to serve his fellow men to the best of his ability and this may involve him in performing duties that are not particularly of a priestly nature, such as working in commerce or industry. Since every priest or priestess was at one time an unsui, this fact is another one of the reasons why the word *unsui* cannot be translated as *monk* or *nun*.

Let us now look at the various ranks of the priesthood. These are seven in number.

1. Jūkai Tokudō (equivalent of laymen's confirmation in the Christian church and so not, strictly speaking, a rank of the priesthood but, whilst it is not incumbent on every Buddhist layman to undergo this ordination ceremony, it is imperative for all aspirant priests to do so).

2. Tokudō (ordination to the priesthood as a trainee).
3. Shusōshō, or Chief Junior, (the ceremony of Hossen is undergone after the trainee has reached a certain level of understanding, can recite all the scriptures, lead all the other trainees in the temple in debate and perform various ceremonies).
4. Transmission (once this ceremony has been performed upon an unsui, it is impossible for him to leave the priesthood since he has then been joined to the apostolic line of his own master. They who would understand the apostolic line and the Transmission should study the *Denkōroku* of Book Three in detail).
5. Zuisse (this is a special, congratulatory ceremony, only held in the head temples of Sōjiji and Eiheiji, at which trainees receive their certificates of priesthood. When I was in Japan, the ceremony itself used not to be obligatory, and many young trainees saved themselves the expense of travelling to the head temples by paying a sum of money to the head office of the Church after taking the examination to prove their ability to perform certain ceremonies, notably those of funeral, wedding and Segaki. The ceremony was instituted by imperial command and, as a ceremony, is therefore of little use to Western trainees who naturally are not subject to the emperor of Japan; for them it is sufficient to take the test and pay the fee).
6. Shinzan and Kyoshi (the Kyoshi is the divinity and teaching degree bestowed by the temple in which the new priest underwent his training and, after receiving it, he may do the ceremony of Shinzan, or "ascending the mountain;" it is the induction ceremony of a new priest of a temple).
7. Kessei or Angō (the four ceremonies of Kessei or Angō are performed when a priest or priestess has a

disciple whom he or she has trained from Tokudō to Shusōshō. Strictly speaking, the terms *Kessei* and *Angō* refer to the two periods of a hundred days, during the rainy seasons of spring and autumn, during which the priesthood undergoes its strict training. Nowadays it is used somewhat loosely to mean the four principle ceremonies, mentioned above, which are then not spread out over a hundred days but compressed into the space of less than a week. The differences between the words "Kessei" and "Angō" are solely sexually prejudicial, Kessei being used for men, since it is very polite, and Angō being used for women since it is not particularly polite; the two words, however, stand for identically the same thing).

Often children were registered as future priests at a very young age when I was in Japan—perhaps at birth, however, I gather that this no longer takes place. Here again the word tokudō was a misnomer in that it implied simply a paper registration in an office of something that might never become actual fact. Should a young person be so registered, he could take Jūkai Tokudō, if he did not want to be a full priest when he grew up, or he could merely keep Jūkai. To this day, it is possible to sidestep the second and do the two simultaneously; the second is renewable each year and many people come, year after year, for this purpose. Both involve the person concerned in living in the temple for about a week, under exactly the same discipline as that of the priesthood, and attending ceremonies. Those who only come to Jūkai, and do not undergo Jūkai Tokudō, do not usually attend the actual confirmation ceremony nor do they receive the token rakhusu. It is usual for people to take the priesthood tokudō, or unsui ordination, after Jūkai Tokudō, if they so wish, but sometimes the priesthood ordination is done first. This is not a good practice since it puts the cart before the horse, but priestly fathers, who wish to ordain their own sons without having to go to the great expense of holding Jūkai Tokudō in their own temples, often resort to it. The unfortunate young unsui, whose ceremonies are done in this order, is made to do all the menial tasks in a training temple until the next Jūkai ceremony which always takes place in the spring. After this ceremonial error has been corrected, he can continue his training normally.

Like Shakyamuni Buddha before him, the trainee has two masters from whom he learns prior to finding his *honshi*, or true master, with whom he will undergo the Transmission ceremony. The first master is regarded as the trainee's "father" in Buddhism since he gives him birth in the family of the Buddhas at ordination, a new name in religion and the opportunity to be set free from the world of samsara. It is the first master's duty to teach his new disciple the scriptures, to watch and correct his morals in accordance with the Precepts and to feed, clothe and otherwise watch over his welfare, as a parent watches over a child, providing him with financial aid at all times. It is because of this last fact that it is so extraordinarily difficult for Western people to get themselves ordained by Japanese teachers. A little thought will make the reason for this very clear. To be financially responsible for a young boy or girl, in their 'teens or early twenties, and who is, moreover, a member of your own nation, is one thing, but to become financially responsible for an adult foreigner, of whom you know little or nothing, is a very different matter and some priests have been very badly treated by unscrupulous foreigners in the past. There is also the fact that it is extremely difficult for a priest to make an adult foreigner, of whose language he is not certain and whose Japanese is probably bad, to behave as a Japanese disciple, doing all the chores of scrubbing, cleaning, cooking and waiting on the priest's wife and children, as if he or she were a servant in the priest's house, whilst being scolded and sometimes beaten. Such behaviour is required of disciples in Japan by all teachers: to behave thus is reasonably easy when you are young, although even twenty-year-old Westerners have difficulty with this sort of thing, and the Japanese teachers are incapable, it seems, of understanding that an adult cannot be treated in the same way as an adolescent; as far as they are concerned, the disciple is a <u>baby</u> Buddha who, having just been born, must be taught accordingly. In the religious sense this is a good practice, but it becomes ludicrous when it is carried over into everyday life to such a degree that the person is being treated in the same way, physically, as a small child. I know that there are some types of Western mentality to which this appeals, at least for a short time, but never for very long! As a result of all that I have written above, it is extremely difficult to get one's head shaved, and enter the priesthood in Japan, if one wants it done by a Japanese, and those teachers who do do it, the number of which is extremely small, are not all exactly out of the top drawer, their aim being frequently more to show off the number of foreign disciples they have than to give those disciples a genuine insight into Buddhism. One of the favourite occupations of Japanese priests is to force foreign disciples to appear on television or in newspapers for the teacher's, or temple's, own glorification. The effect of this type of publicity on the pupil is terrible since the very last thing that a sincere student wants is anything of the sort whilst undertaking his search for Truth; such banal, personal questions as these publicity hounds ask are frequently rude in the extreme and tend to turn the unfortunate trainee into an insincere public show rather than to give a true picture of him or her. I say the above with considerable feeling for I myself was subjected gravely to this sort of thing until Kohō Zenji, lately Chief Abbot of Sōjiji, found out about it and stopped any further interviews. Those who wish to go to Japan to study should consider this information carefully. I was lucky enough to find a true friend in my Master but many are not.

At the end of a year from ordination, or a little earlier, the trainee can become a Shusōshō, i.e. Chief Junior. If he is being taught by his own father a much longer time may elapse. The Shusōshō's duties are as described earlier in this chapter: the period of time during which he is in charge of the various ceremonies and debates is one hundred days. For this special training period he takes his second master—or should do: in practice, in Japan, it is frequently the first master who does not only the duties of the second but also the third as well.

The next grade, as stated earlier, is that of Transmission. There is no way of gauging when this will take place since it takes as long as it takes for a person to become truly converted and decide to dedicate himself to his true, spiritual potentiality, the Truth of Zen; under no circumstances can the ceremony be done until this stage has been reached. It does not, however, ALWAYS take a long time and age and sex have no effect upon it: the majority of Transmissions take place between the ages of twenty-five and forty-five and, although there are exceptions, you will find, if you go through the *Denkōroku* (Book Three), that this was true in ancient times as well as now: Shakyamuni Buddha was approximately thirty-five, Christ around the same age whilst Dōgen was twenty-eight. The only people who really take a long time to arrive at realisation are the ones who love book-learning and argument. Unfortunately a good ninety-five per cent of all foreigners, studying Zen, fall into the book-learning class; I cannot emphasise too strongly the danger of book-learning as a hindrance to Zen understanding: like Keizan, I too say that erudition is a grave hindrance.

There is an interesting, historical link between the original Shakyamuni and the present day Transmission ceremony in the placing of the mats belonging to the master and disciple. In the history of Shakyamuni Buddha, (see Chapter 1) is the story of His being brought, as a child, to the ascetic Asita and placing His feet on the latter's head, thus indicating that He would be the greater. In the Transmission ceremony, the mats of the master and disciple are placed first so that the top edge of the master's one overlaps the disciple's very slightly as they bow to each other and, later on, the side edge of the disciple's mat is placed over the master's as they bow side by side to the altar. In the text it says, "Although the disciple stands beneath the master's feet, he must also stand on the master's head." This means that, if Buddhism is to remain a living religion, the disciple must aim at Buddhahood. In Japanese, Shakyamuni Buddha is called the "dai honshi," or Great, True Teacher, and the title given to the Transmission master is that of "honshi," or true teacher. Although Shakyamuni Buddha had only two masters and then decided to "go it alone," the Zen trainee, as stated earlier, usually has three, the last one standing in place of Shakyamuni Buddha as His representative and descendant in the apostolic line. There is a grave danger in this knowledge in that people think that they cannot reach the Truth of Zen without a master but nothing could be further from the meaning of Zen. After all, Shakyamuni Buddha did not have a honshi—He made His own way to realisation, and He was a man, not a god, from the beginning of His life until His death: He was not gifted with any power that we do not, ourselves, possess. So long as we believe that we possess the Buddha Nature, and follow the system of meditation taught by Shakyamuni Buddha, we can rediscover that same Buddha Nature within ourselves without any outside help—all that is really necessary is that we have sufficient belief in its existence: once again I quote, "Remember thou MUST go alone, the Buddhas do but point the way." However, in this day and age, it is essential that a person present himself to a master for certification in order to protect the public from fraud if he wishes to act as a priest after realising the Truth by himself. Many honshis act as catalysts for their disciples; they do it by means of acute observation and spiritual intuition, not by any magical power, although it may seem they possess extraordinary powers to the ordinary man or woman.

This last sentence may seem somewhat sweeping to some so I will try to make it clearer. The honshi is the person who ratifies the final realisation of Zen Truth, but we should remember that many stories tell of people arriving at their realisations as a result of inanimate objects: in these cases the objects were the catalysts. Such a realisation is afterwards confirmed by the trainee's honshi as a realisation and the honshi adds his spiritual certainty at confirmation. Spiritual certainty, the Turning of the Wheel, and observation over a long period of time—it is debatable which of the two is the more valuable since a person may Turn the Wheel and still have a long way to go in order to perfect himself—will tell the teacher when the disciple is truly ready for Transmission. The Turning of the Wheel tells both master and disciple of the meeting of Buddha Nature with Buddha Nature; of heart with heart; the flowing of the two into one and the one merging into the immaculacy of nothingness. This spiritual intuition and certainty apart, a person may still not be ready for Transmission for some time after his realisation since his character training may not be finished but, in this sense, no disciple is ever fully ready for Transmission since a perfect character is impossible: a real kenshō, however, will make the character training a thousand times easier for both the master and the disciple.

Because of the importance of character training, and herein the master's observation comes into play, the honshi must at all times set an example of being as perfect as possible within the Precepts, and it is the duty of the disciple to copy his good points and not his mistakes. All masters make mistakes, being human, and some make them deliberately so as to make sure that the disciple does not stay with immaculacy but learns that there is nothing holy or unholy anywhere; at the same time, knowing that both master and disciple are imperfect, they must still continue their own training whilst remaining perfectly themselves, sometimes even performing a seemingly evil act (for which they will bear the karmic consequences) in order to teach the disciple the TRUE meaning of right and wrong. A honshi, after observing the trainee over a long period of time, affirms or denies the latter's understanding by either giving or withholding the sealed, silken certificates of Transmission and doing the actual ceremony.

The tragedy of most Western people in Japan is that they are hunting for a "god the father" figure who will teach them everything. This is wrong. They MUST do Zazen and realise that no one can help them except themselves. They must clearly understand that all things are teaching at all times if they are truly looking for teaching. Anything, or anyone, that is the catalyst for the realisation of Zen Truth for a person is Buddha. If the reader is searching for a special person as a "master" he will get nowhere for he is very definitely in the world of the opposites; he is saying that one thing is Buddha and another is not. Do not be misled by the popular trend in the West of going master hunting. Transmission from a honshi is necessary for the purpose of apostolic succession in the priesthood and is a certification of spiritual understanding; since this is so, it is never permitted to laymen. This is not because laymen cannot reach the Truth of Zen—they can and often do—however, they neither get, nor need, a certificate to prove it that is the same as a priest's.

Do not think that the Ancestors in the apostolic line in the *Denkōroku* were different from yourself. First there was Makakashyo who, being a deeply spiritual type, could understand things easily by intuition; then came Ananda who was so busy running around in erudite circles in his own head that it took him years and years just to accept a very simple fact—one that was so simple that his erudite brain could not believe it was true. Shōnawashyu carried around a personal, psychological problem concerning clothes and so was the prototype of the present-day psychological problem cases that come all the time to Japanese temples. Mishaka liked playing with supernatural arts until he found something better to do in religion; Bashumitsu was probably one of the worst dipsomaniacs the world has ever known until he accidentally met a true priest—up to that time he thought intoxicating liquor was the finest thing there was—simply because he knew of nothing better. Such things as the above do not prevent a person from reaching sainthood so long as they are not clung to with a closed mind. All these people had to admit to themselves that perhaps they were wrong—they had to do *sange suru*, admission of being at, and acceptance of, fault before they could make any progress spiritually; if the reader wants to study Zen seriously he must take a good look at himself, decide that he does not think very much of what he appears to be, and do sange suru too. After all, most people cling to things because they know of nothing better—it is the willingness to believe that there may be something better that makes spiritual growth possible; it is the willingness to recognise that one was, up to the time of seeing that better thing, mistaken that results in sange suru. So Transmission is recognition of Buddhahood, spiritual autonomy and confirmation thereof. The ceremony cannot be performed before reaching the age of majority and, in actual fact, is almost never done before the age of twenty-five.

Zuisse is of little use to Western people since it is part of Japanese custom, rather than original Buddhism, and so no deeper explanation is made of it here. Kessei is useful in foreign countries both as a ceremonial form, since it contains the ceremonies needed for the testing of a teacher and a Shusōshō, and as a certification of their ability. The West needs to keep the teaching of Zen in its original purity and, for this, gorgeous ceremonies, such as Zuisse, are quite unnecessary. The degree certificates issued by various training temples are valuable in some ways but there is no reason why, after the establishment of Western training temples, similar certificates cannot be issued in English with examinations in the same language. Such certification would be far more valuable than in Japanese since the language difficulty is insurmountable for many Westerners.

The title of "Rōshi" is much misunderstood in the West. Since the word means "Reverend," it is often applied as an honorific by people when greeting a priest. Most priests are not too happy with the term since it has the connotation of old and useless as well as noble; they prefer, instead, the last half of the word, or its second Chinese character, which is *shi*, or *sensei*, meaning "teacher" or "master" in Japanese. There are many titles in Zen with somewhat similar uses and meanings as rōshi, one being *Zenji* which means, literally, "Zen Master," but there is a difference in the use of the term *rōshi* in the Rinzai and Sōtō Churches. After receiving the title from his master, a Rinzai priest is always called by it whilst a Sōtō priest is not necessarily so called. Although the Sōtō priest's master may have thought him worthy of the title, as a result of his spirituality, other persons may not necessarily have the same opinion. This does not mean that the priest concerned is a bad one or unworthy of the title—there are priests who are good for some trainees and not for others. The title should only be conferred by a master on a really worthy disciple in both Rinzai and Sōtō: a Sōtō priest may be a rōshi to his master and not to anyone else. The Sōtō practice has the advantage of keeping rōshis from temptations which, being only human, they may succumb to—remember that, although a priest may have understood true spirituality and become a rōshi, he is still as much subject to making mistakes and creating bad karma as is the next man; for this reason Dōgen wrote, in the "Shushōgi," that it was wrong to consider a priest's shortcomings and criticise his actions if he was teaching true religion—one's duty was to be grateful for such teaching and not criticise, remembering that perfection is impossible.

The above has been written to clarify many points about which there seems to be much misunderstanding in the West. Whilst I realise that this short explanation is inadequate, I do not wish to bore the reader with details that are not of importance to his studies. Anyone who has been to Japan, and received an "ordination" there, had best consider what that ordination really means, unless he has spent many years going up all the ranks described in the foregoing list. Only if they have gone through them ALL, and continue to pay taxes for them, are they really priests of the Sōtō Zen Church IN JAPAN; in Western countries it may be sufficient to have only gone up as far as Transmission since we are not trying to follow in the steps of the Japanese but in those of Shakyamuni Buddha.

BOOK TWO.

THE TEACHINGS OF DŌGEN ZENJI.

INTRODUCTION
TO THE TRANSLATIONS.

Dōgen Zenji, 1200–1253, was born in Japan and entered the priesthood at the age of twelve. He studied Tendai Buddhism on Mount Hiei but, finding the teaching there unsatisfying from the religious point of view, went to Kyoto where he studied Rinzai Zen under Myozen, a pupil of Eisai, founder of Rinzai Zen in Japan. He left for China, with Myozen, in 1223, again because he could find no real depth in the Rinzai teachings. He studied much in various temples in China, eventually receiving the Transmission from the Abbot of Tendōzan, Tendō Nyojō Zenji, and returning to Japan in 1227. He stayed for a time at Kenninji, in Kyoto, but left there, since he felt that he was not yet competent to teach, in order to retire to a small temple; here he commenced his now famous writings. He became the first Abbot of Koshōji, in 1236, and was offered the opportunity to become the founder of Daibutsuji, later Eiheiji, by Hatano Yoshihige: he died in Kyoto. He is known in Japan either as Eihei Dōgen Zenji or by his posthumous title of Kōsō Jōyō Daishi.

Dōgen Zenji brought with him from China both the Transmission and the teachings of the Sōtō Zen Church of Buddhism. This Church, which is the oldest of all the Zen Churches (both the Ōbaku and Rinzai Churches are derivatives), is perhaps the only Church of Mahayana Buddhism to retain some of the original Indian elements of Hinayana Buddhism. There is no doubt that Dōgen's way was, and still is, hard to follow, for he was a somewhat puritanical mystic, but there is equally no doubt that he inspired Japanese Buddhism with a new spirit. His major works are *Shōbōgenzō, Eihei-kōroku, Eihei-shingi, Gakudō-yōjinshū* and *Kyōjukaimon.*[7] The *Kyōjukaimon* is essential if one would understand the moral training and the scope of Sōtō Zen teaching.

The translation in this book is not literal for the very good reason that, were it so, the book would lose much of its true feeling and flavour; instead, I have tried to give the religious fervour, with which Dōgen obviously wrote, its full value. The main teaching of the Sōtō Church that he brought with him was that no words or scriptural text could adequately express the Spirit of Buddhism and therefore those who were bound by such words and scriptures could understand nothing of the Truth which had been Transmitted by the Buddha Himself to His first disciple, Makakashyo, who had, in his turn, handed it on, from disciple to disciple, down the line of Ancestors to the present day.

The following translated writings must be understood as exhortations to his followers to be earnest and strenuous in their training and his own sentiments on this subject are clearly expressed. Serenity, simplicity and purity were his ideal and his whole life was a living expression thereof. They who would follow in his footsteps must live immaculately pure lives, within the Precepts of the Buddha, without in any way being bound thereby, thus morality becomes the norm without being hindered by either morality or rules and regulations. Purity of life and thought, harmony within the community and the destruction of all rules and regulations that did not lead to the complete freeing of the mind to commune with the One Mind of the Buddha were absolute essentials for all his followers and, at the heart of the teaching, as the lode-stone to which all returned, was silent meditation during which one just sat as had the Buddha, in utter serenity of contemplation, Buddha Nature communing with the Buddha Mind: theology, as far as he was concerned, was of no importance whatsoever. His was an intuitive method of spiritual training which resulted in a lofty transcendence over worldly care and desire; it led to the elimination of suffering, and the attachment thereto, of which the Buddha speaks in the Four Noble Truths.

When words appear in brackets in the text of Dōgen, it should be understood that the words contained therein have been inserted by me for the purpose of clarifying the text.

SHUSHŌGI.

WHAT IS TRULY MEANT BY
TRAINING AND ENLIGHTENMENT.

Introduction (The Reason for Training).

The most important question for all Buddhists is how to understand birth and death completely for then, should you be able to find the Buddha within birth and death, they both vanish. All you have to do is realise that birth and death, as such, should not be avoided and they will cease to exist for then, if you can understand that birth and death are Nirvana itself, there is not only no necessity to avoid them but also nothing to search for that is called Nirvana. The understanding of the above breaks the chains that bind one to birth and death therefore this problem, which is the greatest in all Buddhism, must be completely understood.

It is very difficult to be born as a human being and equally difficult to find Buddhism however, because of the good karma that we have accumulated, we have received the exceptional gift of a human body and are able to hear the Truths of Buddhism: we therefore have the greatest possibility of a full life within the limits of birth and death. It would be criminal to waste such an opportunity by leaving this weak life of ours exposed to impermanence through lack of faith and commitment.

Impermanence offers no permanent succour. On what weeds by the road-side will the dew of our life fall? At this very minute this body is not my own. Life, which is controlled by time, never ceases even for an instant; youth vanishes for ever once it is gone: it is impossible to bring back the past when one suddenly comes face to face with <u>impermanence</u> and it is impossible to look for assistance from kings, statesmen, relatives, servants, wife or children, let alone wealth and treasure. The kingdom of death must be entered by oneself alone with nothing for company but our own good and bad karma.

Avoid the company of those who are deluded and ignorant with regard to the Truth of karmic consequence, the three states of existence and good and evil. It is obvious that the law of cause and effect is not answerable to my personal will for, without fail, evil is vanquished and good prevails; if it were not so, Buddhism would never have appeared and Bodhidharma would never have come from the west.

There are three periods into which the karmic consequences of good and evil fall; one is the consequence experienced in this present world, the second is consequence experienced in the next world and the third consequence experienced in a world after the next one; one must understand this very clearly before undertaking any training in the way of the Buddhas and Ancestors, otherwise mistakes will be made by many and they will fall into heresy; in addition to this, their lives will become evil and their suffering will be prolonged.

None of us have more than one body during this lifetime, therefore it is indeed tragic to lead a life of evil as a result of heresy for it is impossible to escape from karmic consequence if we do evil on the assumption that, by not recognising an act as evil, no bad karma can accrue to us.

Freedom is Gained by the Recognition of Our Past Evil Acts and Contrition Therefor.

Because of their limitless compassion the Buddhas and Ancestors have flung wide the gates of compassion to both gods and men and, although karmic consequence for evil acts is inevitable at some time during the three periods, contrition makes it easier to bear by bringing freedom and immaculacy: as this is so, let us be utterly contrite before the Buddhas.

Contrition before the Buddhas brings purification and salvation, true conviction and earnest endeavour: once aroused, true conviction changes all beings, in addition to ourselves, with benefits extending to everything including that which is animate and inanimate.

Here is the way in which to make an act of perfect contrition. "May all the Buddhas and Ancestors, who have become enlightened, have compassion upon us, free us from the obstacle of suffering which we have inherited from our past existence and lead us in such a way that we may share the merit that fills the universe for they, in the past, were as we are now, and we will be as they in the future. All the evil committed by me is caused by beginningless greed, hate and delusion: all the evil is committed by my body, in my speech and in my thoughts: I now confess everything wholeheartedly." By this act of recognition of our past behaviour, and our contrition therefor, we open the way for the Buddhas and Ancestors to help us naturally. Bearing this in mind, we should sit up straight in the presence of the Buddha and repeat the above act of contrition, thereby cutting the roots of our evildoing.

Receiving the Precepts.

After recognising our evil acts and being contrite therefor, we should make an act of deep respect to the Three Treasures of Buddha, Dharma and Sangha for they deserve our offerings and respect in whatever life we may be wandering. The Buddhas and Ancestors Transmitted respect for the Buddha, Dharma and Sangha from India to China.

If they who are unfortunate and lacking in virtue are unable to hear of these Three Treasures, how is it possible for them to take refuge therein? One must not go for refuge to mountain spirits and ghosts, nor must one worship in places of heresy, for such things are contrary to the Truth: one must, instead, take refuge quickly in the Buddha, Dharma and Sangha for therein is to be found utter enlightenment as well as freedom from suffering.

A pure heart is necessary if one would take refuge in the Three Treasures. At any time, whether during the Buddha's lifetime or after His demise, we should repeat the following with bowed heads, making gasshō:– "I take refuge in the Buddha, I take refuge in the Dharma, I take refuge in the Sangha." We take refuge in the Buddha since He is our True Teacher; we take refuge in the Dharma since it is the medicine for all suffering; we take refuge in the Sangha since its members are wise and compassionate. If we would follow the Buddhist teachings, we must honour the Three Treasures; this foundation is absolutely essential before receiving the Precepts.

The merit of the Three Treasures bears fruit whenever a trainee and the Buddha are one: whoever experiences this communion will invariably take refuge in the Three Treasures, irrespective of whether he is a god, a demon or an animal. As one goes from one stage of existence to another, the above-mentioned merit increases, leading eventually to the most perfect enlightenment: the Buddha Himself gave certification to the great merit of the Three Treasures because of their extreme value and unbelievable profundity—it is essential that all living things shall take refuge therein.

The Three Pure, Collective Precepts must be accepted after the Three Treasures; these are:– Cease from evil, Do only good, Do good for others. The following ten Precepts should be accepted next:– 1. Do not kill, 2. Do not steal, 3. Do not covet, 4. Do not say that which is untrue, 5. Do not sell the wine of delusion, 6. Do not speak against others, 7. Do not be proud of yourself and devalue others, 8. Do not be mean in giving either Dharma or wealth, 9. Do not be angry, 10. Do not debase the Three Treasures.

All the Buddhas have received, and carefully preserved, the above Three Treasures, the Three Pure Collective Precepts and the ten Precepts.

If you accept these Precepts wholeheartedly the highest enlightenment will be yours and this is the undestroyable Buddhahood which was understood, is understood and will be understood in the past, present and future. Is it possible that any truly wise person would refuse the opportunity to attain to such heights? The Buddha has clearly pointed out to all living beings that, whenever these Precepts are Truly accepted, Buddhahood is reached, every person who accepts them becoming the True Child of Buddha.

Within these Precepts dwell the Buddhas, enfolding all things within their unparallelled wisdom: there is no distinction between subject and object for any who dwell herein. All things, earth, trees, wooden posts, bricks, stones, become Buddhas once this refuge is taken. From these Precepts come forth such a wind and fire that all are driven into enlightenment when the flames are fanned by the Buddha's influence:

this is the merit of non-action and non-seeking; the awakening to True Wisdom.

Awakening to the Mind of the Bodhisattva.

When one awakens to True Wisdom it means that one is willing to save all living things before one has actually saved oneself: whether a being is a layman, priest, god or man, enjoying pleasure or suffering pain, he should awaken this desire as quickly as possible. However humble a person may appear to be, if this desire has been awakened, he is already the teacher of all mankind: a little girl of seven even may be the teacher of the four classes of Buddhists and the mother of True Compassion to all living things. One of the greatest teachings of Buddhism is its insistence upon the complete equality of the sexes.

However much one may drift in the six worlds and the four existences even they become a means for realising the desire for Buddhahood once it has been awakened: however much time we may have wasted up to now, there is still time to awaken this desire. Although our own merit for Buddhahood may be full ripe, it is our bounden duty to use all this merit for the purpose of enlightening every living thing: at all times, there have been those who put their own Buddhahood second to the necessity of working for the good of all other living things.

The Four Wisdoms, charity, tenderness, benevolence and sympathy, are the means we have of helping others and represent the Bodhisattva's aspirations. Charity is the opposite of covetousness; we make offerings although we ourselves get nothing whatsoever. There is no need to be concerned about how small the gift may be so long as it brings True results for, even if it is only a single phrase or verse of teaching, it may be a seed to bring forth good fruit both now and hereafter.

Similarly, the offering of only one coin or a blade of grass can cause the arising of good, for the teaching itself is the True Treasure and the True Treasure is the very teaching: we must never desire any reward and we must always share everything we have with others. It is an act of charity to build a ferry or a bridge and all forms of industry are charity if they benefit others.

To behold all beings with the eye of compassion, and to speak kindly to them, is the meaning of tenderness. If one would understand tenderness, one must speak to others whilst thinking that one loves all living things as if they were one's own children. By praising those who exhibit virtue, and feeling sorry for those who do not, our enemies become our friends and they who are our friends have their friendship strengthened: this is all through the power of tenderness. Whenever one speaks kindly to another his face brightens and his heart is warmed; if a kind word be spoken in his absence the impression will be a deep one: tenderness can have a revolutionary impact upon the mind of man.

If one creates wise ways of helping beings, whether they be in high places or lowly stations, one exhibits benevolence: no reward was sought by those who rescued the helpless tortoise and the sick sparrow, these acts being utterly benevolent. The stupid believe that they will lose something if they give help to others, but this is completely untrue for benevolence helps everyone, including oneself, being a law of the universe.

If one can identify oneself with that which is not oneself, one can understand the true meaning of sympathy: take, for example, the fact that the Buddha appeared in the human world in the form of a human being; sympathy does not distinguish between oneself and others. There are times when the self is infinite and times when this is true of others: sympathy is as the sea in that it never refuses water from whatsoever source it may come; all waters may gather and form only one sea.

Oh you seekers of enlightenment, meditate deeply upon these teachings and do not make light of them: give respect and reverence to their merit which brings blessing to all living things; help all beings to cross over to the other shore.

Putting the Teachings into Practice and Showing Gratitude.

The Buddha Nature should be thus simply awakened in all living things within this world for their desire to be born herein has been fulfilled: as this is so, why should they not be grateful to Shakyamuni Buddha?

If the Truth had not spread throughout the entire world it would have been impossible for us to have found it, even should we have been willing to give our very lives for it: we should think deeply upon this: how fortunate have we been to be born now when it is possible to see the Truth. Remember the Buddha's words, "When you meet a Zen Master who teaches the Truth do not consider his caste, his appearance, shortcomings or behaviour. Bow before him out of respect for his great wisdom and do nothing whatsoever to worry him."

Because of consideration for others on the part of the Buddhas and Ancestors, we are enabled to see the Buddha even now and hear His teachings: had the Buddhas and Ancestors not truly Transmitted the Truth it could never have been heard at this particular time: even only so much as a short phrase or

Before breakfast all the trainees carefully clean the monastery grounds. Here the author sweeps leaves in the grounds of Dai Hon Zan Sōjiji. The gate for the Imperial envoy may be seen in the background.

section of the teaching should be deeply appreciated. What alternative have we but to be utterly grateful for the great compassion exhibited in this highest of all teachings which is the very eye and treasury of the Truth? The sick sparrow never forgot the kindness shown to it, rewarding it with the ring belonging to the three great ministers, and the unfortunate tortoise remembered too, showing its gratitude with the seal of

Yōfu: if animals can show gratitude surely man can do the same?

You need no further teachings than the above in order to show gratitude, and you must show it truly, in the only real way, in your daily life; our daily life should be spent constantly in selfless activity with no waste of time whatsoever.

Time flies quicker than an arrow and life passes with greater transience than dew. However skillful you may be, how can you ever recall a single day of the past? Should you live for a hundred years just wasting your time, every day and month will be filled with sorrow; should you drift as the slave of your senses for a hundred years and yet live truly for only so much as a single day, you will, in that one day, not only live a hundred years of life but also save a hundred years of your future life. The life of this one day, to-day, is absolutely vital life; your body is deeply significant. Both your life and your body deserve love and respect for it is by their agency that Truth is practiced and the Buddha's power exhibited: the seed of all Buddhist activity, and of all Buddhahood, is the true practice of Preceptual Truth.

All the Buddhas are within the one Buddha Shakyamuni and all the Buddhas of past, present and future become Shakyamuni Buddha when they reach Buddhahood. This Buddha Nature is itself the Buddha and, should you awaken to a complete understanding thereof, your gratitude to the Buddhas will know no bounds.

EIHEI-SHINGI
DŌGEN'S MONASTIC RULES.

TAITAIKOHŌ.
HOW JUNIOR PRIESTS MUST BEHAVE
IN THE PRESENCE OF SENIOR PRIESTS.

A Taiko is a senior member of the priesthood (male or female) who has been in training for a period of five years or more longer than the priest in his presence. Since they have spent much time in training, they are very excellent in their understanding of Buddhism and all junior members of the priesthood must show their respect for these senior ones in their daily behaviour. This code of behaviour of sixty-two rules is excellent for juniors of the present day to follow.

1. The kesa must be worn and the mat carried at all times when a senior is present.

2. The kesa must not be worn merely as if a covering for the shoulders in the presence of a senior. One of the scriptures says, "If all we do is cover our shoulders with the kesa in the presence of the Buddha, priests and seniors we shall fall into the worst of hells."

3. Clasp your hands respectfully when you see a senior; do not allow them to hang down.

4. Sit upright without leaning back when in the presence of a senior and never stare at him.

5. Do not laugh loudly, suddenly or with disrespect in the presence of a senior.

6. All seniors must be served with the same respect as that which you would accord your own master.

7. Be grateful for all teaching given by a senior; be attentive and do not require its repetition.

8. Always show humility when with seniors.

9. When with a senior never scratch or hunt vermin.

10. Do not spit or blow your nose when with a senior.

11. Do not clean your teeth or rinse your mouth when with a senior.

12. Always wait for a senior's permission before sitting down in his presence.

13. Do not sit on any raised surface whereon the senior may sit or sleep.

14. Never touch a senior when near him.

15. A senior of five years has the rank of Acarya; one of ten years has the rank of Upadhyaya; this is the law of Buddha and you must remember it well.

16. Never sit down before the senior permits you and then clasp your hands, sit down respectfully and upright, showing no sign of laziness or disrespect.

17. Never lean to right or left when with a senior; this is gross impoliteness.

18. Show humility when giving information to a senior and never say all you wish to.

19. When with a senior never give a large yawn; if you must yawn cover your mouth.

20. Never touch your face, head or limbs when with a senior.

21. Do not sigh heavily; behave yourself with respect when with a senior.

22. Stand as if at attention when with a senior if you must stand.

23. If another senior enters the room in which you are sitting with another senior stand and bow respectfully.

24. If there is a senior's room next to yours never read scriptures loudly.

25. Never give information on religion to others without the direction of a senior no matter how many times you may be asked.

26. Always give truthful answers to seniors' questions.

27. Be careful to neither disappoint nor anger a senior and look at him straightly when addressing him.

28. Never bow to another junior when you are with a senior.

29. Never receive reverence from another in the presence of a senior.

30. Work faster than the seniors at laborious work and slower than they at that which is agreeable if you are living with them.

31. Never be slow in giving respect to a senior whenever you meet one.

32. Always ask the meaning of scriptures or the Vinaya if you are fortunate enough to become acquainted with a senior; you must never be contemptuous of him or idle in his presence.

33. Should a senior become ill it is your duty to nurse him.

34. Never jest in the presence of a senior either about himself or his room and do not indulge in idle chatter.

35. Never criticise or praise a senior in the presence of another senior.

36. Do not show contempt for a senior by asking frivolous questions.

37. Shaving the head, cutting the nails or changing the lower garments must never be done in the presence of a senior.

38. No junior may go to bed before all the seniors in the house have retired.

39. No junior may take food prior to seniors.

40. No junior may bathe prior to seniors.

41. No junior may sit down before a senior does.

42. If you meet a senior you must bow and follow him; you may only return home when he directs you to do so.

43. If a senior becomes absent-minded be respectful when refreshing his memory.

44. If a senior makes a mistake do not sneer at him either publicly or in private.

45. When entering a senior's room snap your fingers three times to announce your entrance.

46. When entering a senior's room never do so by the centre of the doorway for this indicates pride; always do so from either the left or right side of the door.

47. If you go regularly to a senior's room always enter and leave by the left side of the door; never go boldly through the centre of the entrance.

48. Do not take meals before a senior has taken his.

49. You may not stand up before a senior does so.

50. If a benefactor or donor comes to see a senior you must sit down, erect, and listen politely to the sermon that the senior may give; you may not leave the room abruptly.

51. Do not scold others in the presence of a senior; not even if they deserve it.

52. If a senior is present do not call to others from a distance.

53. If you take off your kesa do not leave it in a senior's room.

54. No junior may criticise a senior's sermon or lecture.

55. Do not clasp your hands around your knees if a senior is present.

56. Do not bow to a senior if he happens to occupy a less important seat than you at some function or meal.

57. Always leave your room before bowing to a senior.

58. You must never bow to a senior if you are sitting on a chair and he is sitting on the floor.

59. If the senior has teachers be mindful thereof.

60. If a senior has disciples be as respectful to them as you are to him; never waver in your respect to a senior.
61. When one senior is with another senior the seniority of either is of no account to the other.
62. For you seniors will always exist; there will always be someone senior to you both when you are a first grade unsui and when you become a Buddha.

The foregoing code of behaviour represents the True Body and Mind of the Buddhas and Ancestors; if you do not realise this to the full the Pure Law will disappear and the Way of the Buddhas and Ancestors will be laid waste. Only those who have done good works in former existences will be able to comprehend the value of this behavioural code; it is the very perfection of Mahayana.

SHURYŌ-SHINGI.
TRAINEES' HALL RULES.

The behaviour in the Trainees' Hall must be in accordance with the Precepts of the Buddhas and Ancestors as well as with the teachings of the scriptures of the Hinayana and Mahayana, paying special attention to the rules of Hyakujō. Hyakujō states in his rules that our every action, whether great or small, must be in accordance with the Precepts of the Buddhas and Ancestors, therefore we must read the Vinaya and other scriptures in the Trainees' Hall.

The scriptures of the Mahayana and the words of the Ancestors must be read when in the hall; one must meditate deeply on the teachings of the old Zen Masters and try to follow those teachings.

Nyojō Zenji, my former master, once said to his trainees, "Have you ever read the scripture delivered by the Buddha on His deathbed? Within this hall we must love each other and be deeply grateful for the opportunity of possessing a compassionate mind which enables us to be parents, relatives, teachers and wise priests; because of this compassionate mind our countenances will for ever show tenderness and our lives will for ever be blissful. We must never speak ill of another even if his language is coarse. We should speak tenderly to such a one, gently pointing out his fault, rather than defame him when he is not present. When we hear something of value we should put it into practice; by so doing we gain great merit. How fortunate it is that we are together. How fortunate it is that we, in this hall, have been able to make the acquaintance of those who, in former lives, performed good works and have thus become the treasures of the priesthood. What joy! Amongst the laity there is a great difference between related and unrelated persons, yet the Buddhist brotherhood possesses greater intimacy than most persons have with themselves. Zen Master Enan, of Ōryuzan, once said, 'the fact that we are in this boat is due entirely to our good deeds in past lives; that we are blessed with the opportunity of spending the training period together in the same monastery is equally due to the same cause. Although we are now in the position of master and trainees, one day we will all be Buddhas and Ancestors.'"

We must not disturb others by reading scriptures or poetry in a loud voice when in the hall, nor may we hold a rosary when in others' presence. Herein all that we do must be gentle.

Visitors must never be permitted to enter the hall, nor may they be conversed with there, whatever their occupation. Those who must speak to shop-keepers must do so elsewhere.

Never talk idly or joke when in the hall. However great is the desire to laugh it must not be indulged in; we must always remember the four views of Buddhism:– there is impurity of body, pain in sensation, mind is transient and things have no ego; we must always remember to be devoted to Buddha, Dharma and Sangha. How can there be pleasure in a world wherein life is as transient as that of fish in a tiny pond? We must not chatter with fellow trainees; if we live an energetic life we can train our minds to become as mountains despite many others around us.

Never leave one's place to look at books which others may be reading: such behaviour is an obstacle both to one's own progress and to that of others in the study of Buddhism; than this, there is no greater misfortune.

If the rules of the Trainees' Hall are broken, and the offence is of a trifling nature, the guilty one must be duly warned by the seniors; if the offence is serious, the Disciplinarian must deal with the offender suitably after hearing the facts. Beginners, and those who have entered the priesthood late in life, must be warned compassionately and respectfully: as to whether or not they will obey this warning will depend upon the depth of sincerity in the mind of the individual trainee. The Temple Rules state that speech, deeds, and actions must be in accordance with the Trainees' Hall rules. Seniors must show an example to juniors, leading them as parents would lead their own children: this behaviour is in accordance with the mind of the Buddhas and Ancestors.

Worldly affairs, fame, gain, war, peace, the quality of offerings, et cetera, may never be discussed in the hall: such talk is neither significant nor useful, pure nor conscientious, and is strictly forbidden. It is to be understood that, since the Buddha has been dead for so long a time, our ability to gain enlightenment is too low to speak of. Time flies as an arrow and life is transient if we are slow in training. Wherever trainees may be from, they must make titanic efforts to train themselves just as they would, if their hair were to catch fire, make titanic efforts to extinguish the flames: time is precious and must never be wasted with idle chatter.

One must not pass in front of the holy statue in the hall, neither from the right nor left thereof, nor may one take notice of, or speak about, others' presence or absence; it is forbidden to look at others' seats.

One may not lie down, stretch the legs, lean against the woodwork or expose one's private parts when on one's seat for such behaviour is disturbing to others. The old Buddhas and Ancestors sat beneath trees, or in open places, and we should remember their very excellent behaviour.

Gold, silver, other money and clothes may not be hoarded in the hall: the old Buddhas made this clear in the Precepts. Makakashyo, the first Ancestor, when a layman, was a thousand times richer than King Bimbasara; in fact, his wealth was greater than that of all the sixteen countries of the time put together; however, once he left home and entered the priesthood, he wore ragged robes and had long hair, going begging until his death on Mount Kukkutapada: always the *funzoe* of the trainee comprised his clothes. One should understand very clearly that, since Makakashyo always appeared thus, we trainees of a later generation must be careful of our manners (if we are in the presence of those who are unkempt).

When speaking to another in the hall it must be in a quiet and polite voice. No noise must be made with slippers and noses may not be blown loudly; others must not be disturbed by spitting, coughing loudly, or yawning; one must learn the teaching of the Buddhas and Ancestors and not waste time with poetry. One may not read the Buddha's teachings loudly in the hall for this is rude to others.

If someone is impolite, he must be warned by the Disciplinarian; however important a senior is, he may not behave rudely or impolitely to others.

If one loses something, such as robes, bowls or anything else, the following notice must be exhibited on the board specially provided therefore:–"Trainee. . . . .lost. . . . .on. . . . . at. . . . .I beg that whoever may find it shall exhibit a notice, similar to this, saying that it has been found." A great priest once said that, although one may be guilty in the sight of the law of the world and be punished, in the law of Buddhism one is beyond such punishment, therefore we must not make judgements or guesses of our own that may be detrimental to others' characters: the matter of dealing with lost articles must be in accordance with the rules of the temple. If a lost article is found by anyone, the fact must immediately be made public by a notice to the effect that it has been found.

Worldly, astrological or geographical books, heretical scriptures, philosophy, poetry or scrolls may not be left in the hall.

Bows and arrows, military equipment, swords, armour and other weapons are not permitted in the hall: if any person shall be in possession of a sword, he must be immediately expelled from the temple. No instruments for immoral purposes are permitted within the temple.

Musical instruments may not be played, nor dancing performed, in or near the hall.

Wine, meat, garlic, onions, scallions and horse-radish may not be brought into the hall.

When there are many in the hall, juniors must be quick to do laborious work; it is not, however, necessary for seniors to be so; this is traditional. Juniors must be slower than seniors in doing enjoyable work for this is the true law of the Buddhas.

All sewing must be done behind the hall: during this time, no idle chatter is allowed, for thoughts must for ever be upon the Buddhas and Ancestors.

Since the hall is for training only, no ill-mannered person is permitted to either enter or lodge there; those who are weak-minded, even if good-mannered, may not sleep therein or wander about for fear of disturbing others.

Worldly affairs and commerce may not be dealt with in the hall.

These rules are the Precepts of the Buddhas; in Eihei Temple they must be observed for all time.

FUSHUKU-HAMPŌ.
MEAL-TIME REGULATIONS.

"When one is identified with the food one eats one is identified with the whole universe; when we are one with the whole universe we are one with the food we eat,"—this comes from the *Vimalakirti Scripture*. The whole universe and a meal are identical in quality.

If the whole universe is the Dharma then food is also the Dharma: if the universe is Truth then food is Truth: if one is illusion then the other is illusion: if the whole universe is Buddha then food is Buddha also: all are equal in all their aspects. "Both concept and reality are equal as they are in the eye of the Buddhas, there being no difference between them whatsoever,"—this comes from the *Lankavatara Scripture*.

"If the universe is seen to be the realm of the spirit, there is nothing outside the realm of the spirit; if it is seen to be Truth then there is nothing other than Truth; if it is seen to be the equal essence then there is only essence; if it is seen as 'different appearance' then there is only 'different appearance,'"—these are the words of Basō.

Here "equal" is not relative but absolute, meaning the Buddha's Wisdom: there is no difference between the whole universe and the Truth when they are seen with this Wisdom eye for the very manifestation of Truth is the above mentioned equalness. We are, therefore, the personification of the universe when we eat—this is a fact that only the Buddhas fully understand—and the universe is the personification of Truth. When we eat, the universe is the whole Truth in its appearance, nature, substance, force, activity, cause, effect, relatedness, consequence and individuality. The Truth manifests itself when we eat and, when eating, we can realise the manifestation of Truth. The correct mind, when eating, has been Transmitted from one Buddha to another and creates ecstasy of both body and mind.

When the bell rings for the end of morning Zazen, breakfast is taken in the Meditation Hall, each trainee remaining in the same place that he occupied for meditation. The drum is struck thrice and the bell eighteen times to announce to all the trainees that it is time for breakfast. In city temples the bell is rung first; in country ones the drum is beaten first. At the sound of the drum or the bell, those facing the wall turn around to face each other across the *tan* and those who work outside the Meditation Hall cease to do so, washing their hands and returning to the Meditation Hall with dignity. After hearing the three slow strokes on the wooden *han*, they enter the hall in silence and without looking about them. No speaking is permitted in the hall.

Whenever a trainee enters the hall, he must make gasshō; this means that the tips of the fingers must be just below the tip of the nose. If the head is dropped, tilted or kept upright the finger tips must always be in alignment therewith and, when making gasshō, the arms must be kept away from the chest wall and the elbows away from the sides. When entering the hall through the front door, all except the Abbot must enter by the left side, irrespective of where his seat may be, using the left foot as he passes the left pillar of the door lintel. The Abbot enters the hall by the right side of the door or straight through the middle of the doorway. In either case he enters with the right foot first, which is the traditional manner, bows to the statue of Manjusri, turns right and sits in his chair. The Chief Junior trainee goes through the gaitan and enters to the left of the front entrance. If trainees enter by the rear door of the hall those in the right half thereof enter by the right side of the rear door, using their right foot first, and those in the left half enter at the left side using their left foot first. They bow to the east behind the statue of Manjusri and go to their seats.

Seats in the Meditation Hall are allotted according to the date of ordination, admittance to the temple or the work done by the trainee however, during the training period of ninety days, the first of these three considerations is the one always taken into account.

When wishing to sit on the tan, a trainee must first bow to his own seat, which means that he bows to his neighbours' seats, turn round clockwise and bow to the trainee on the opposite side of the tan, push the left sleeve of his *koromo* under his left arm with his right hand, the right sleeve under the right arm with the left hand, lift the kesa in front with both hands, hold it with the left hand, put the feet together, sit down on the edge of the tan and remove the slippers. He next presses on the tan with his right hand, lifts first the left leg and then the right one, pushes the body backwards on the seat from the edge so that he is not sitting on the part used as a table, sits upright and places his left leg on his right one. The kesa is then spread over the knees so as to hide the inner robes from others' eyes. Robes must never be allowed to fall over the edge of the tan and enough space must be left between the seated trainee and the edge for the food bowls to be spread out, this space being regarded as pure. The three reasons for this are called the "Three Purities:–" a. the kesa is laid there, b. bowls are spread there, c. heads point there during sleep.

The Director, Disciplinarian, Cook, General Maintenance, and Abbot's Assistant priests sit on the right side of the gaitan and the Guest Master, Bathhouse, Sickroom, Librarian, Outdoor and Teacher priests sit on the left side of it at this time.

After the wooden fish has been struck three times all must be in their seats and no one may enter the hall thereafter. The *umpan*, which is hung outside the kitchen, is then struck several times to tell the trainees to rise, collect their bowls from above their seats and carry them to the pure place in front of their seats; all do this at the same time. All stand up quietly, turn to the right, bow reverently to the name over their seats, make gasshō, hold up the bowl with both hands, taking care that it is neither too high nor too low, turn to the left with the bowl near the chest, sit down and put the bowl to the left behind them. All trainees must be careful not to disturb their neighbouring trainees by bumping against them with any part of the body or turning so fast that the holy kesa flies out and scrapes their faces or shaven heads.

After this the senior who is in charge of the statue of Manjusri offers boiled rice thereto, making gasshō, accompanied by a serving monk who carries the rice box. He then bows to the statue, goes behind it, removes the crêpe cover from the mallet found on the wooden block behind the altar, returns to the front of the statue with his hands in gasshō, bows again, turns to the right, leaves the hall and goes to his own seat, passing the tan of the officers in charge of the eastern half of the temple.

After three strokes on the drum, the bell is struck seven times in front of the Meditation Hall: the Abbot then enters and the trainees immediately leave their seats. The Abbot bows to Manjusri and the trainees and sits down in his chair: the trainees then take their seats again. When they are settled, the attendant priest who has followed the Abbot to the hall and is waiting outside it, bows immediately, enters, places a table in front of the Abbot's chair, bows and leaves the hall. The Abbot's bowl is placed upon this table: the trainees, sitting upright and in a straight line, place their bowls in front of them. The Disciplinarian enters, bows to Manjusri, offers incense, bows again and walks to the mallet making gasshō. After the wooden block has been struck once with the mallet, the trainees unfold their bowl covers.

In order to set out the bowls, one must first make gasshō, untie the knot on the bowl cover and fold the dishcloth to an unobtrusive size, twice crosswise and thrice lengthwise, placing it, together with the chop-stick bag, just in front of the knees. Spread the pure napkin over the knees and put the dishcloth, with the chop-stick bag on top of it, under the napkin. The cover is then unfolded and the farther end is allowed to fall over the edge of the tan, the other three corners being turned under to make a pad for the bowls to be placed upon. The lacquered-paper table-top is taken in both hands, the under fold being held in the right hand and the top one in the left, and is unfolded as if to cover the bowls. Whilst holding it in the right hand, take the bowls with the left and place them in the centre of the left end of this table-top, thereafter taking them out of the large one separately, in order, beginning with the smallest. Only the ball of the thumb of each hand is used for removing them so as to prevent any clattering: when the meal is a small one, only three bowls are used. The chop-sticks are then taken out of the bag followed by the spoon; when the meal is over they are put in again, in reverse order; the bowl-washing stick remains in the bag. The chop-sticks and the spoon are placed with their handles to the right on the table-top in front of the bowls. The bowl-washing stick is then re-moved from the bag and placed between the soup bowl and the pickle one, with its handle pointing to the edge of the tan. After this all trainees wait for the offering of rice to be made to the hungry ghosts. The empty chop-stick bag is folded in three and replaced under the napkin, on top of the lacquered divider, the latter being on top of the dishcloth.

When the meal has been offered by a donor, the Sick-room priest enters the hall carrying the incense-burner fol-lowed by the donor. After offering incense to Manjusri, he leads the donor all round the hall: at this time the donor holds his hands in gasshō and keeps his head bowed. The trainees make gasshō, without speaking, laughing, looking from side to side or moving their bodies, just sitting calmly and quietly.

The Disciplinarian then strikes the wooden block once and recites the following:–

> We take refuge in the Buddha,
> The completely Perfect Scriptures,
> The Saints and Bodhisattvas
> Whose merit is beyond all understanding.
> To-day a donor has offered food; I pray you all to
>   understand well his reasons for doing so which I
>   am about to read to you.

> (The statement of the donor is read.)

> I have read the donor's reasons for his offering and I
> call upon the Buddhas and Bodhisattvas to witness its

sincerity for they are endowed with holy eyes which can see beyond both self and other. Now let us chant the names of the Ten Buddhas in chorus.

The Disciplinarian and the trainees make gasshō, chanting as follows:–

> The completely pure Buddha, Vairocana Buddha, Dharma Itself;
> The complete Buddha Who has been rewarded for His previous training;
> Shakyamuni Buddha, one of the many Buddhas Who has appeared in the many worlds;
> Maitreya Buddha Who will appear in the future;
> All the Buddhas in all directions and in the Three Worlds;
> The great and excellent *Dharma Lotus Scripture*;
> Holy Manjusri Bodhisattva;
> The great and wise Samantabhadra Bodhisattva;
> The great and kind Avalokitesvara;
> All the Bodhisattvas and Ancestors;
> The *Scripture of Great Wisdom*.

The Disciplinarian continues:–

> In the beginning the mallet will strike the Buddha on the foot; later it will strike Him on the head.

If the meal is an ordinary breakfast or lunch, the Disciplinarian will again strike the wooden block, saying:–

> Having taken refuge in the Three Treasures,
> All will be able to grasp them perfectly.

When the names of the Ten Buddhas have been chanted,
the Disciplinarian strikes the wooden block once. In order to
show that a true trainee will be willing to offer food to all
other creatures, the Chief Junior makes gasshō and chants the
following verse loudly:—

(For breakfast)

The ten benefits bless the breakfast gruel
And all trainees profit greatly thereby;
Since the results thereof are limitless and wonderful,
Pleasure is ours for eternity.

(For dinner)

Since I will give Three Merits and six tastes
To all the Buddhas and the members of the priesthood,
All sentient beings within the universe
Will enjoy this offering.

When the Chief Junior is not present, the priest next in
rank chants the above verses. A trainee then enters and says
in a loud voice, "Breakfast is served." This trainee must enter the hall to the left of the door, bow to Manjusri, bow to
the Abbot, bow to the Chief Junior, stand near the left side of
the front door, bow to Manjusri again and make gasshō. The
words must be spoken clearly and no errors made in their an-
nouncement since, if these words are pronounced incorrectly,
the meal cannot be taken: should this happen, the announce-
ment must be made again. The Chief Junior bows to the food
in front of him, meditates and then he and all trainees start to
eat. If a donor has offered money or food, the Disciplinarian
comes from behind the statue of Manjusri, bows to the Chief

Junior and asks him to give thanks for the gift. The Disciplinarian strikes the wooden block once and the Chief Junior recites the thanksgiving verse loudly:–

> The two kinds of alms, material and spiritual,
> Have the endowment of boundless merit:
> Now that they have been fulfilled in this act of charity
> Both self and others gain pleasure therefrom.

The rice must be served carefully and never in a hurry for, if the serving is hurried, they who receive the food will be flustered; it must not be served slowly, however, for then the recipients will become tired. The rice must be served by those whose duty it is to act as waiters; no one who is sitting on the tan may serve himself. The first person to be served is always the Chief Junior, the Abbot being served last. During the serving, the hands of others and the brims of bowls must never be soiled with either soup or gruel. In order to indicate how much they wish to receive, those sitting on the tan must hold a spoon in their right hand, with the bowl towards the chest and the handle towards the serving trainee. The handle must be moved up and down gently two or three times, when enough has been placed in the bowl, and the body bowed slightly: the amount of gruel received depends entirely upon this. The spare hand must never hang down when a soup bowl, or other bowl, is being put down; it must be kept in a one-handed gasshō. Trainees may not sneeze or cough whilst receiving food: if, however, either is unavoidable, the trainee must turn his back to the others present before sneezing or coughing. The Precepts of Buddha must always be followed whenever one carries the rice box.

One must be respectful, when receiving gruel or rice, for the Buddha Himself said that we must receive food with respect; this fact must be carefully remembered. When receiving food, the bowl must be held up horizontally with both hands underneath it; only the correct amount of gruel or rice may be placed therein—there must never be so much that some is left uneaten and those who are doing the waiting must be notified when enough has been received by the lifting of two fingers of the right hand. When the food has been received, it must not be consumed greedily by seizing a spoon or chop-sticks from the trainee doing the waiting, nor may a trainee receive food from a waiting trainee to whom he has lent his own spoon or chop-sticks for the purpose of dishing it out. It was said by one of the Ancestors that one must have the correct mind when receiving food, holding the bowl horizontally. Both the rice and the soup bowls must be filled and the rice, soup and other food taken in regular sequence. Food may not be eaten with the knees drawn up. Should a waiting trainee be in so great a hurry that even a grain of rice, or a drop of soup, is spattered in another's bowl, the serving must be done again. The bowls may not be held up, nor may the trainees take food, until the Inō (Disciplinarian) has struck the wooden block to announce that the food has been served.

When the block is struck, the trainees make gasshō, bow to their food and recite the verse of the Five Thoughts:–

> We will first share the merits of this food with the Three
>   Treasures of the Dharma;
> Second, we will share it with the Four Benefactors,—the
>   Buddha, the President, our parents and all people;
> Third, we will share it with the Six Lokas;
> With all of these we share it and to all we make offer-
>   ing thereof.
> The first bite is to discard all evil;
> The second bite is so that we may train in perfection;

The third bite is to help all beings;
We pray that all may be enlightened.
We must think deeply of the ways and means by which
    this food has come:
We must consider our merit when accepting it.
We must protect ourselves from error by excluding
    greed from our minds.
We will eat lest we become lean and die.
We accept this food so that we may become enlightened.

Rice offerings for the hungry ghosts may not be made before this verse is finished. To make this offering, seven grains of rice are placed on the handle of the bowl-washing stick or the edge of the lacquered table: the offering is always made with the thumb and middle fingers of the right hand. If the food served is rice cakes, vermicelli or buckwheat, a ball, the size of a dime, should be taken from the bowl and placed as above; if the meal consists only of gruel, no offering is made, although there was a time when this was actually done; no spoon or chop-sticks were used for the purpose. After the offering, all trainees make gasshō and keep silent.

The following is the correct way to eat breakfast. The gruel is received in the largest of the set of bowls which is then replaced upon its holder. After a few seconds wait, the second bowl is taken with the right hand, placed on the left palm and held there by the top of the thumb which is turned slightly inwards. The spoon is taken in the right hand and seven or eight spoonfuls of gruel are transferred from the first bowl to the second one, the latter being put on the left side of the former. The brim of the second bowl is put to the lips and gruel may be taken with the spoon: all the gruel is thus to be eaten up by repetitions of this sequence. Should gruel be left in the first bowl, the second bowl must be replaced upon the table, the first bowl taken and the gruel consumed with the spoon. The bowl is then cleaned with the bowl-washing stick and replaced upon its holder. The second bowl is picked up and any gruel left therein consumed; the trainee must wait for the water to be brought for washing-up after cleaning the bowl with the bowl-washing stick.

The following is the correct way to eat lunch. The first bowl is raised as high as the mouth and rice is put therein: this bowl may not be left on the table nor may it be put to the lips: the Buddha said that food must be eaten with respect and never with arrogance for, should we have an arrogant appearance, we are only equal to children or harlots: the upper part of the bowl is regarded as pure and the lower part as defiled. The first bowl is held with the fingers underneath and the thumbs in the brim, the second and third fingers only being on the outside and the fourth and fifth being kept away from the bowl entirely—this is the correct way to hold the bowls.

In far-off India, Shakyamuni Buddha and His disciples used neither chop-sticks nor spoons, simply making the rice into balls with their right hands—we present-day Buddhists must remember this fact; many heavenly deities, Cakravarti Raja and emperors did the same thing—we must understand that this was the ancient way. Only sick monks used spoons; all others ate their food with their hands. In India they have neither heard of, nor seen, chop-sticks: they may only be seen in use in China and certain other countries and it is only due to local customs that they are used in Zen monasteries. The Buddhist Precepts must be followed at all times; the custom of taking food with the hands has long died out. Since there are no teachers left whom we can question about the old traditional way, we use a spoon, chop-sticks and bowls.

When picking up, or replacing, bowls, spoons and chop-sticks, no noise may be made, nor may rice be stirred in the

All meals in large temples are taken formally in the Meditation Hall. Here the author eats formal breakfast in Dai Hon Zan Sōjiji.

middle with the spoon. Only sick trainees may ask for extra food. The extra bowls may not be filled with rice, nor may a trainee look into a neighbour's bowl or disturb him. Lunch must be eaten carefully, large lumps of rice may not be crammed into the mouth nor may balls be made and thrown into the mouth. Not even a grain of rice that has fallen on the table may be eaten; the lips may not be smacked whilst chewing rice and it may not be chewed whilst drinking soup. The Buddha said that tongues must not be long nor lips be allowed to be licked whilst taking food: this must be studied well. The hands may not be waved whilst eating; the knees may not be held with the elbows nor the food stirred. The Buddha said that food may never be stirred as if by a cook, thus leaving the hands soiled, nor may it be consumed noisily: He also said that food may not be piled up, like the mound on a grave, or the bowl heaped full; soup may also not be poured upon food, as if to wash it within the bowl, other food may not be mixed with that in the bowl and other food may not be mixed with rice, and held in the mouth, after the manner of monkeys.

Meals may not be taken either too quickly or too slowly in the Meditation Hall: it is very impolite to eat everything up so fast that one sits and watches others eat with one's arms folded. Noise may not be made with bowls, or spittle swallowed, before the waiting trainee announces "Second helpings" in a loud voice. No rice may be left uneaten or anything else asked for. It is not permitted to scratch the head during a meal; dandruff may not be allowed to drop into the bowls and the hands must not be soiled. The body may not be shaken; the knees may not be raised or held; yawning is not permitted nor may the nose be blown loudly; if a fit of sneezing comes on, the nose must be carefully covered with the hand. If any food becomes jammed between the teeth, it must be removed with one hand covering the mouth from the sight of others. Fruit seeds and other similar waste must be put in a place where it will give no offence to others—a good place being on the lacquered table top in front of the bowl, slightly hidden by the bowl's rim—others must never be allowed to become disgusted by such a sight. If another tries to give food or cake that is left over in his bowls to another it may not be received. No waiting trainee may use a fan in the Meditation Hall during the heat of summer, especially if a neighbouring trainee feels a chill; if a trainee feels that he has a chill coming on he should tell the Disciplinarian and take his meal elsewhere. If a trainee wishes to ask for something he must do so quietly. If, at the end of the meal, any food remains in the bowl, it must be wrapped in the dishcloth. The mouth may not be opened wide nor may rice be eaten in large spoonfuls; rice may not be spilled into the first bowl nor the spoon soiled. The Buddha said that one may not wait with one's mouth open for food nor speak with one's mouth full: He also said that trainees must not try to get extra food by covering the food in their bowls with rice or by covering the rice with other food: careful notice must be taken of this advice. The Buddha also said that tongues must not be smacked at meal times, lips may not be licked or food blown upon to warm or cool it; this must also be carefully remembered. After breakfast, all bowls must be cleaned with the bowl-washing stick. If each mouthful is ladled carefully three times before eating it will become of a suitable size. The Buddha said that, when eating, rice-balls must be made neither too large nor too small.

The whole of the bowl of the spoon must be put completely into the mouth when eating lest food be spilled; no food or rice may be spilled upon the napkin—if any food is found upon the napkin it must be given to the waiting trainee. If any unhusked rice is found in the rice in the bowl it must be husked and eaten; it may not be thrown away nor swallowed without being husked.

In the *Scripture of the Three Thousand Manners* it says that, if something unpleasant is found in the food, it may not be eaten and its presence may not be made known to any neighbouring trainee; also the food may not be spat out. If any rice should be left in the bowl it must not be kept in the presence of a Senior but given to a waiting trainee. When the meal is over, trainees must be satisfied with it and require nothing more. From both the rational and practical outlook, one should try never to waste a single grain of rice at mealtimes; the whole universe is completely identified with the meal. The bowls may not be struck with the chop-sticks or spoon, thus causing noise, nor may the lustre of the bowls be impaired. If the bowls lose their lustre they will become unuseable as a result of dirt and grease. When water is drunk from the bowls no sound may be made with the mouth in doing so and it may not be disgorged into the bowl or other utensils. The face and hands may not be wiped with the napkin.

In order to wash the bowls, the sleeves of the robe must be carefully arranged so that they do not touch anything; after this hot or cold water must be received in the first bowl. After receiving the water, the bowl must be carefully washed with the washing-up stick, the bowl being turned carefully from left to right. The used water is poured into the second bowl and the first bowl is washed carefully again, both inside and out, with the washing-up stick; the bowl is turned with the left hand whilst the washing-up stick is held in the right hand. The bowl is then held in the left hand whilst the dish-cloth is unfolded with the right one and spread out as if to cover it. After this the bowl is taken in both hands and wiped with the unfolded dishcloth; it is turned from left to right in the wiping. The dishcloth is put into the bowl so that it may not be seen from the outside and the bowl is replaced on its stand. The spoon and chop-sticks are washed next in the second bowl and wiped with the dishcloth. During this time, the dishcloth must remain in the first bowl to hide it from view, only a corner of it being used to wipe the spoon and chop-sticks. When the spoon and chop-sticks have been wiped, they must be put into the chop-stick bag and placed in front of the second bowl. The second bowl is then washed in the third bowl; it and the washing-up stick are held lightly with the left hand and the third bowl is taken in the right hand and put in

the place that the second one occupied. The water is transferred from the second bowl to the third one, and the second
bowl is washed in the third one in the same way as the first
bowl was. The same sequence for washing is used for the third
and fourth bowls. No spoon, chop-sticks or bowls may be
washed in the first bowl. The sequence is:– the first bowl is
washed and wiped, then the spoon, then the chop-sticks, and
the second, third and fourth bowls. All the bowls are then
put separately into the first one as each is washed; the bowl-
washing stick is wiped and put into the chop-stick bag last.
The napkin may not be folded before the dirty water has been
discarded; this water may not be thrown upon the floor—also
the Buddha said that left-over food may not be put into the
water; this point must be studied carefully. When the dirty-
water bowl is brought, trainees must make gasshō and empty
their dirty water into it taking care to see that it does not soil
the sleeves of the robe. Fingers may not be washed in the water
and the water may not be thrown away in an unclean place.
The second, third and fourth bowls are put into the first one,
with the thumbs only, in the reverse order from when they
were removed.

The first bowl, containing the other bowls, is then held
up with the left hand and placed in the middle of the bowl
cover, the lacquered table-top being taken out from underneath
it with the right hand. This table-top is folded with both hands
above the first bowl and placed on top of it. The bowls are
covered with the cover, the nearer end of it being put over the
bowls first and the far end then folded over them towards
the trainee. The napkin is folded and placed on the cover
and the chop-stick bag is placed on top of the napkin. Originally the washing-up stick was put on top of the napkin but
now it is put into the bag. The dishcloth is put on top of the
chop-stick bag and the two other corners of the cover are tied

together over the bowls. Both ends of this tie should be on the right in order to tell the right way round of the bowls and to make their untying simple. When the bowls have been wrapped, the trainees make gasshō and sit quietly. The wooden block is struck once by the Manjusri statue attendant to signify that the trainees may leave the Meditation Hall.

The trainee sitting to the left of the Abbot's attendant on the gaitan rises, bows to the Manjusri statue, goes to the west side of the wooden block on the south side of the incense bowl, bows to the block, makes gasshō and waits for the Abbot and the trainees to wrap their bowls completely. When they have all finished, he hits the wooden block once, covers the mallet with the mallet cover, makes gasshō and again bows to the block. The Disciplinarian then recites the following:–

> The universe is as the boundless sky,
> As lotus blossoms above unclean water;
> Pure and beyond the world is the mind of the
>   trainee;
> O Holy Buddha, we take refuge in Thee.

Abbot Eisai Transmitted this traditional way of ending meals and so we continue to do it thus.

The Abbot leaves the hall: when he leaves his chair the Manjusri statue attendant must immediately leave the place where he has been standing beside the wooden block and hide behind the curtain of the Manjusri statue lest he should be seen by the Abbot.

The trainees rise and replace their bowls above their seats; the bowls must be held with both hands as the trainees stand up, turn to the right and place them above their seats with their right hands, hanging them, by the tied covers, on their hooks whilst supporting them with their left hands. The trainees then make gasshō, come back to the edge of the tan and descend slowly; they put on their slippers and bow to each other. When tea is taken in the Meditation Hall the trainee's behaviour is the same as the above and the method of sitting down on the tan and descending from it is always the same at all times.

The cushions are placed under the tan and the trainees leave the hall. When the Abbot has left the hall, the end of morning Zazen is announced by three strokes of the bell: if Zazen is to be continued no bell is sounded. If, however, a donor asks the trainees to go to the Meditation Hall, they must do so even if the bell has already been rung and, thereafter, the bell must be rung again to announce the end of morning Zazen. When tea is over in the afternoon and the Abbot has bowed to Manjusri and left the hall, the bell is struck three times to tell the trainees to leave the hall and they then descend from the tan: they leave the hall in the same way that they entered it as described earlier. All walking in the Meditation Hall must be in the manner of kinhin—half a step to each breath—as in the manner of the kinhin periods during Zazen.

BENDŌHŌ.
HOW TO TRAIN IN BUDDHISM.

Only because of the way in which it shows itself in the Dharma have the Buddhas and Ancestors ever been able to grasp the Way of Buddhist training. When sitting down, or when lying down to rest, all trainees must behave in exactly the same way; most of their actions must be done in an identical manner. As long as they live, trainees must live a life of purity in their monastery; one must realise clearly that wilful acts against other trainees are valueless, being contrary to the behaviour of true Zen trainees: the correct ordering of daily life is, therefore, the heart of Buddhism. When, by the correct ordering of our daily life, we exhibit the heart of Buddhism, we are free from delusive body and mind; as this is so, the disciplined life of the trainee is the embodiment of both enlightenment and practice, pure and immaculate since before time began. This disciplined life is the first appearance of the kōan; for those who follow it, there is never any need to try to grasp enlightenment.

Evening Zazen commences with the sound of the evening bell; the trainees put on their kesas and go to their places in the Meditation Hall. The Abbot does his evening Zazen in his chair facing the Manjusri statue, the Chief Junior sits quietly facing the edge of the tan and the other trainees do their Zazen facing the wall. The Abbot's attendant, or other serving trainee, sits on the stool behind a screen which is placed behind the Abbot's chair so that he may attend the Abbot.

The Abbot enters, with the right foot, on the right-hand side of the front entrance of the Meditation Hall, goes to bow three times to Manjusri, offers incense, bows again, goes around the Meditation Hall, in the fashion of kentan, making gasshō, returns to Manjusri and again bows three times. He then goes to his seat, bows thereto, turns around clockwise to face Manjusri, bows again, sits down and pulls up the sleeves of his robe tidily after having taken off his slippers and covered his feet with his robe; he sits in *paryanka*. The attendant, or serving trainee, does not do kentan with the Abbot but waits inside, and to the left of, the front door. After the Abbot has sat down, this attendant goes to his seat, from whence he bows to Manjusri, before sitting down behind the Abbot. The attendant always carries the Abbot's incense box and, should the Abbot wish to sleep in the Meditation Hall, his bed must be made ready to the left of the Chief Junior; when he awakens, he at once leaves his bed to continue his Zazen in his chair. It is customary for the trainees to wear no kesa during morning Zazen and that of the Abbot is hung on his chair.

The drum and bell are struck at the end of evening Zazen in order to tell the time at which the Abbot wishes to do his morning meditation; both hour and minutes are struck and then the han is struck thrice.

At the sound of the han, the trainees make gasshō, remove and fold their kesas, put them in their cases and place them upon the top of their cupboards; the Abbot does not remove his kesa. The Abbot leaves his chair, bows to Manjusri and leaves the hall, left foot first, by the right-hand side of the front entrance; his attendant and serving trainee wait for him in front of the Meditation Hall door; this is also the place where they stand when he enters the Meditation Hall. Should the Abbot sleep in the Meditation Hall one or two of his serving trainees must stay on the stool, or form, behind his chair, whilst some of his five attendants sleep on the left of the Manjusri statue attendant on the gaitan; this is where the new trainees have their sitting place. All trainees must continue to do Zazen until the Abbot leaves the Meditation Hall: when he has gone, they quietly make their beds, set their pillows and lie down together. No one is allowed to remain sitting in Zazen by himself nor is he allowed to observe those who are sleeping; no one may deliberately leave his seat to go to the lavatory. This is correct behaviour in the Meditation Hall for the *Scripture of the Three Thousand Manners* says that there are five rules when sleeping:– 1. heads must always be pointing in the direction of the Buddha statue, 2. no one may observe the Buddha from a lying position, 3. legs may not be stretched out, 4. trainees may not face the wall or lie on their faces, 5. the knees may not be raised.

The right side, never the left, must always be on the floor of the tan when lying down or sleeping; heads must be towards the edge of the tan in order to be in the direction of the Manjusri

Manjusri seated in meditation upon the beast of self which never sleeps. This particular statue is in the Meditation Hall of Dai Hon Zan Sōjiji where the author spent seven years in training.

statue. It is forbidden to lie on the face or back with the knees up or the legs crossed. The legs may not be stretched out, the night clothes may not be pulled down and the body may not be stripped as is the fashion amongst the unbelievers. At all times, when lying down, our minds must be filled with light as brilliant as that of the heavenly beings.

The han in front of the Chief Junior's room is usually struck at three in the morning—as stated above, however, the exact hour depends upon the Abbot's wishes—and the trainees rise, in silence, without making any fuss. No one is permitted to remain in bed, alone, on the tan; this is impolite to others. Each trainee puts his own pillow in front of his own cupboard in silence for fear of disturbing his neighbouring trainees, all then remain in their own places, wearing part of their bedding as a covering, and sitting on their Zazen cushions: no one is permitted to close his eyes for, should anyone do so, he will feel sleepy—trainees must strive to open their eyes over and over again—it is the morning breeze that eventually opens them completely. All are far from understanding the Way of the Buddhas and time flies as does an arrow; should a trainee feel sleepy he must not shake himself, straighten up, yawn, sigh or disturb others; respect for others must always be the first consideration when with fellow trainees; no one may despise another. The head may not be covered with any part of the bedding; if sleep becomes overwhelming, the bed cover must be removed and Zazen continued in light clothes. The correct time for washing the face and hands behind the Meditation Hall is when there are not too many other trainees doing so: a long towel, folded double, must be carried over the left arm with both ends hanging inside. The trainees rise and leave the tan, leaving the Meditation Hall by the rear door as quietly as possible after rolling up the bamboo screen outside it. Those who sit to the right of Manjusri leave the hall on the right-hand side of the door, using their right foot to step through it: those who sit on the left side use their left foot and leave by the left side. Slippers may not be dragged when walking nor may trainees walk noisily: they may not speak to anyone they meet on the way to the washroom or chant any scripture even if no one else is present. The hands may not hang down whilst walking; they must be kept folded. In the washhouse, trainees may not dig others in the ribs with their elbows when waiting their turn to wash; they must wait quietly. Having secured a place in which to wash, the trainees do so.

The correct way of washing the face is to hang the towel round the neck with both ends hanging on the chest. These ends are taken under the arms, crossed at the back, brought back to the chest and tied securely. This causes the sleeves to be tucked in as if beneath a sash and, by so doing, the collar and sleeves are tied above the arms under the armpits, thus protecting them.

All trainees then take their tooth-brushes and make gasshō, reciting the following:–

> I take this tooth-brush so that all living things may
> profit;
> May they understand the Truth quickly and become
> naturally pure.

The teeth are then cleaned and the next verse recited:–

> Our teeth are cleaned this morning so that all living
> things may profit;
> Let us not only clean the fang of delusion, but crush de-
> lusion as this tooth-brush is crushed in the mouth.

The Buddha said that we should not crush the tooth-brush over more than one-third of its thicker end; in both cleaning the teeth and cleansing the tongue, the Buddha's teachings must be carefully followed. The tongue should not be scraped with the tooth-brush more than three times and, if the tongue bleeds, trainees must cease scraping at once. The old regulations for trainees say that the crushing of the tooth-brush, the rinsing of the mouth and the scraping of the tongue are the proper way to cleanse the mouth. When others are present at this time the mouth must be covered so that the sight of its cleaning may not disgust them: blowing the nose and spitting must also be done discreetly. In great Sung most temples had no washhouse behind the Meditation Hall but here it is found there.

The wash-basin is placed by the water-heater, hot water ladled into it and carried to the place for washing. Water is then taken in the hands and the face carefully washed; the eyes, nostrils, ears and mouth must be washed so that they become the embodiment of the purest immaculacy in accordance with the Buddha's Precepts. Trainees must be careful in the use of hot water so that they are not wasteful of it; water, with which the mouth has been rinsed, must not be disposed of in the wash-basin but spat out elsewhere. The body must be bent, or the head lowered, whilst the face is washed; trainees may not stand upright, thereby splashing others or their basins; all dirt, grease and sweat must be washed from the face, the water being scooped up by the hands. The right hand unties the knot in the towel and the face is then wiped; however, if there is a public towel, this should be used instead. Others must not be annoyed as a result of noise made with the basin and the ladle, nor may the throat be gargled. According to the old regulations, face washing at four in the morning is part of Buddhist training; the regulations also say that it is not permitted for trainees to spit deliberately or disturb others with noise as a result of mishandling the basin.

Trainees return to the Meditation Hall in the same way that they left it. After returning to their seats, they continue to do Zazen correctly, using part of the bedding as a covering, if they so wish, but no kesa is worn at this time. Trainees may not leave their seats when changing their night clothes for day ones: to do so they must put their day robes over their heads, unfasten their night ones carefully, take their arms from the sleeves and slip them off of their shoulders so that they drop to the knees like beds. The day robes are then fastened and the night ones taken by the sleeves and folded; after this they are put inside the trainees' own cupboards; the procedure is the same when changing from day to night clothes. Nakedness is strictly forbidden on the tan; trainees may not fold clothes standing up; they may not scratch their heads or recite their rosaries, thus being contemptuous of other trainees; they may not talk to their neighbouring trainees, sit, or lie, in a crooked line. Trainees may not creep about on the tan when getting on, or leaving, it; when so doing, they must be careful not to make a rustling noise with their robes as a result of sweeping the tan with either their sleeves or skirts. The han in front of the Chief Junior's room is struck at four in the morning: no trainee may enter by the front entrance after the Abbot and the Chief Junior have sat down. Beds may not be put away in cupboards until after the umpan has sounded in the kitchen and the hans in front of the various buildings been struck to announce the end of Zazen. At the sound of these, beds and pillows are put away, the curtain is raised, the kesa is put on and all turn round to face each other. The serving trainee belonging to the Sickroom Attendant priest rolls up the bamboo screens at the front and back doors of the Meditation Hall, offers incense and lights the candle in front of Manjusri.

The correct way to fold the top cover of the bed is to take two corners and put them together, double the cover lengthwise and then fold it in four; it is then folded in four again crosswise, making sixteen folds altogether, and put into the trainee's cupboard, with the pillow inside it, the creases of the bedding facing the cupboard door. The trainees make gasshō, take their kesa cases and put them on top of the bedding, open them, make gasshō, turn two sides of the case downwards so as to cover the bedding to the right and left but not to the front or back.

The trainees make gasshō again, place the kesa on their heads, again make gasshō and recite the following verse:–

> How great and wondrous are the clothes of
>   enlightenment,
> Formless and embracing every treasure;
> I wish to unfold the Buddha's teaching
> That I may help all living things.

The kesa is then unfolded and put on and the trainees turn round to sit facing each other, folding any bedding carefully in case it should touch the seat of a neighbouring trainee. All trainees must behave prudently, never being either rough or noisy, the Law being ever with them. Trainees must respect other trainees in their every act, never at any time doing anything against them. When the bell for the end of Zazen has been rung, it is not permitted for any trainee to remake a bed and lie thereon. When breakfast is over, all trainees return to the Trainees' Hall, have tea or hot water, or sit quietly in their places.

The notices saying "Zazen" are hung outside the Meditation Hall, the Trainees' Hall and the Chief Junior's room, as well as the Abbot's room, by the Sickroom Attendant's serving trainee. The Chief Junior and all the other trainees put on their kesas, enter the Meditation Hall, go to their places and all, except the Chief Junior, meditate facing the wall; the trainees who live in the western half of the monastery are included in this; the Abbot sits in his chair facing Manjusri. No trainee may turn his head in order to observe others entering or leaving the hall or for any other purpose.

If a trainee wishes to leave the hall in order to go to the lavatory he must remove his kesa before leaving his seat, put it on top of the folded bedding, make gasshō, and leave the tan. Such a trainee must turn round, facing the edge of the tan, put his feet over the edge and put on his slippers. The eyes must be lowered when entering or leaving the Meditation Hall since no trainee may observe the backs of other trainees. When walking, the feet and body must move in such a way that their movements are naturally combined, the eyes being fixed upon the floor on a spot approximately eight feet in front of the feet. The correct length of a step, when walking, is the length of the trainee's own foot; the walking must be done slowly and silently so as to give the semblance of standing still; the feet may not be dragged, causing the slippers to make noise, and trainees may not make a pit-pat noise with them for fear of being impolite and disturbing the minds of other trainees. All walking must be done with the hands folded, the sleeves never being allowed to hang down to the legs.

The kesa may not be folded whilst standing on the tan, nor may the ends thereof be held in the mouth; it may not be shaken, trodden on or held under the chin; it may not be touched with wet fingers, hung beside Manjusri or on the edge of the tan. When a trainee sits down whilst wearing his kesa he must be careful to see that he does not sit upon it, he must also make sure that no part of it is under his feet; it may only be put on after making gasshō. Trainees must also make gasshō when they place their kesas in their cases for this is the traditional manner and must be carefully followed.

It is strictly forbidden to leave one's seat and go out of the hall whilst wearing the kesa. When the umpan is struck in the kitchen, all trainees make gasshō at the same time, this being the signal for the end of morning Zazen. If it is early morning Zazen, the trainees put on their kesas after hearing the umpan and leave the hall, leaving their cushions on their seats since these may not be put away until lunch time. The Sickroom Attendant priest tells the serving trainee to put away the notice announcing Zazen after hearing the closing bell of the later morning Zazen; this is the only period of Zazen at which this notice is hung up. Should there be no evening Zazen, the notice which says that there will be no Zazen that evening is hung up until the evening bell is sounded. The correct way to announce Zazen is to strike the han in the morning and the bell in the evening. When hearing these, each trainee puts on his kesa, enters the Meditation Hall and, after sitting down, does his Zazen facing the wall. For early morning Zazen, and for evening also, the kesa is not worn when entering the Meditation Hall; in the evening all trainees enter the hall carrying their folded kesas over their left arms, go to their seats, take out their cushions and do Zazen, beds not yet having been made, although originally the traditional way was to make half of each trainee's bed. The folded kesa is taken from the left arm, folded in four, and put on top of the bedding, after which Zazen is done. During early morning Zazen the kesa is put on the top of the cupboard; the kesa may not be moved about as trainees wish.

Cushions must always be used during Zazen. The correct way of sitting is completely cross-legged with the right foot resting on the left thigh and the left foot resting on the right thigh. It is also permitted to sit half cross-legged which means that the right leg is placed over the left one and nothing more.

The back of the right hand is then rested on the left leg and the back of the left hand is placed on the right palm, both hands having the thumbs touching each other lightly. All must then sit upright, their heads in a straight line with their spines, leaning neither to right nor left, bending neither backwards nor forwards. The ears should be in line with the shoulders and the nose with the navel. The tongue must be rested lightly behind the top teeth, with the lips and teeth firmly closed. The eyes must be kept naturally open, the pupils not being covered with the eye-lids; the back of the neck must be in a straight line with the back. Breathe quietly through the nose without being hard or noisy; the breaths must not be too long or too short, too fast or too slow. Sitting in this steady position of both body and mind, trainees should breathe deeply once or twice and sway from right to left seven or eight times. Thoughts must not be discriminated about as in "this is good or this is bad;" understanding is only possible when one is beyond discriminative thought: this point is vital to Zazen.

When wishing to leave the tan, trainees must do so quietly and slowly after standing up. They must not walk quickly and their hands must be in a folded position; they are not permitted to dangle. When walking, trainees are not permitted to look about them; they must look modestly at their feet taking gentle steps. All trainees must perform all their actions together regularly and in a timely manner; this is the correct way to practice Buddhism.

If there is to be no evening Zazen this fact is announced after afternoon Zazen. The trainees put away their cushions after dinner and leave the Meditation Hall in order to go to the Trainees' Hall to rest in their places. After about two hours, which is roughly around three in the afternoon, they return to the Meditation Hall, take out their cushions and do Zazen; after this they leave their cushions until the time for dinner on the following day. The Chief Junior enters the Meditation Hall from the gaitan, using the left-hand side of the front door, before it is announced that there will be no evening Zazen. Prior to doing this, he sometimes strikes the han in front of his room three times. After entering, he offers incense to Manjusri, goes round the Meditation Hall, following the edge of the tan as in kentan, and sits down in his place. The Sickroom Attendant priest's trainee server then goes to all the rooms in

The trainee is arriving for meditation in the Meditation Hall of Dai Hon Zan Sōjiji; the author is already seated. Each trainee has only one tan, or sitting space, upon which he sits in meditation, sleeps and eats his meals, the wide wooden edge being his table. The two cupboards at the end of each tan hold his bedding and personal belongings; this is all he may own. In the top right corner may be seen the back of the Manjusri statue as well as the wooden mallet and block, covered by a cloth, used in reciting the meal-time scriptures; the lanterns carried all night long around the Meditation Hall by the nightwatch, to insure decency, may also be seen. The name plate of each trainee may be seen over his cupboard; the round cushion in the foreground is called a zafu. The light coloured cushion on the dark square one, just below the trainee who is entering, indicates the seat of a temple officer.

the temple to tell the other trainees that the Chief Junior is now in the Meditation Hall. If there is no evening Zazen, the han in front of the Trainees' Hall is struck three times. On hearing this, the trainees return to the Meditation Hall, put on their kesas and sit down facing each other on the tan; those who usually look at the wall put on their kesas and then turn round and face each other. The Sickroom Attendant's serving trainee hangs up the notice which says there will be no evening Zazen, this having been permitted by the Abbot. He then rolls up the bamboo screen, re-enters the hall, bows to Manjusri and goes to bow to the Chief Junior, making gasshō. After bowing, he says softly that the Abbot has released all trainees from evening Zazen. The Chief Junior acknowledges this with a silent gasshō and the serving trainee goes to Manjusri, bows, rises, makes gasshō and says in a loud voice, "Rest," which means that there will be no evening Zazen; he leaves the hall and strikes the bell three times to announce this to everyone. The trainees bow to each other, making gasshō in the same way as at meals: if the Abbot is present he rises, bows to his chair, bows to Manjusri and leaves the hall. The trainees leave the tan, bow to each other and get on to the tan again to make their beds: one lowers the bamboo screen and they all go to the Trainees' Hall. After arriving there they bow to each other and sit on their seats facing each other: if they wish they may take supper.

An offering of hot water is respectfully made to Manjusri, after the Chief Junior has sat down, and the priest in charge of the hall thereafter offers incense; during this incense offering, all trainees must make gasshō. Whilst making this offering, the priest in charge may have a kesa hanging over his left arm if the Abbot has so directed or if it is the custom of the temple.

The priest in charge then bows to Manjusri, offers incense with his right hand, makes gasshō, turns right, for the incense offering was made at the censer, returns to Manjusri, bows, makes gasshō, goes to the centre of the right half of the hall, bows, makes gasshō, turns right, goes to the centre of the left half of the hall, passing in front of Manjusri, bows, makes gasshō again, turns right, returns to Manjusri, bows, makes gasshō, makes the hot water or tea offering, offers incense again and bows as previously.

TENZO-KYŌKUN.
INSTRUCTIONS TO THE CHIEF COOK.

From its inception, Zen Buddhism has had six chief offices, called the *Chiji* in Japanese, and the priests who hold them, as the Buddha's sons, are jointly in charge of all the affairs of the temple; among these the office of *Tenzo* is that of Chief Cook and this post is always held by a senior priest.

None but the finest priests, fully awakened to, and eager for, Buddhahood, have, up to now, ever been trusted with the office of Tenzo for, unless there is an earnest desire for Buddhahood, however great an effort the priest holding this office may make, he will not be successful therein. The *Zen Temple Regulations* state that the desire for Buddhahood must for ever be kept active within the mind of the Tenzo priest and he must, at various times, devise such dishes as will create great pleasure for the monks who partake thereof.

Excellent priests, such as Tōzan, once held this office; it is important to understand that the Tenzo priest is utterly different from a royal cook or waiter.

I often asked questions of the senior priests, when I was undergoing my training in China, and all of them were very kind in telling me what they knew of the duties of the Cook, saying that they who were entrusted with this office were the very cream of Buddhism as it has been handed down to us from the enlightened Buddhas and Ancestors. If we would understand the duties of a Cook we must study the *Zen Temple*

Regulations thoroughly, listening, in the minutest detail, to the explanations thereof given by seniors.

Every twenty-four hours, after lunch, the Cook has a consultation with the Treasurer and Assistant Director concerning the food to be used for the following breakfast and lunch; how much rice and the quantity, and type, of vegetables. Once the food has been prepared it must be cared for in the same way as we care for our own eyesight: it was said by one Zen teacher that the common property of the temple must be accorded the same care as that accorded to our own eyes. This food must be dealt with as if it were for the royal table; exactly the same care must be given to all food, whether raw or cooked.

After the above mentioned consultation another is held in the temple kitchen for the purpose of deciding which vegetables shall be eaten, which tastes relished and what gruel made. The *Zen Temple Regulations* state clearly that, when food is prepared, the Cook must consult with all the officers—the Treasurer, Assistant Director, Guest Master, Disciplinarian and General Maintenance personnel—as to what tastes shall be relished at breakfast and lunch and the number of vegetables to be used. When the above matters have been decided, the menu for the day is written upon the boards which are hung in front of the Abbot's room and the Trainees' Hall: thereafter the following morning's breakfast gruel is cooked.

When rice and vegetables are being examined and washed it is imperative that the Cook be both single-minded yet practical, ensuring that the work is done to the very best of his ability and without allowing contempt for any foodstuff to arise in his mind: he must be diligent in all his work without discriminating against one thing as opposed to another. Although he dwells within the ocean of merit, he must never waste so much as one drop of that ocean's water,—not even if he may have his hut upon the very summit of the mountain of good works: however minute may be the merit of anything he does, he must never forget to accumulate that merit, even if it seems to him to be infinitesimally small and therefore not worth bothering about.

The *Zen Temple Regulations* say that, unless the Cook has carefully arranged the six kinds of tastes to be relished and cooked with a gentle, pure heart, bearing in mind utter respect for the food, he has not fulfilled his duty as Cook to his brother trainees. He must, therefore, be very careful in all things—for example, the removal of sand from rice—and, by so doing, he will naturally cook with a gentle and pure heart as well as properly arrange the six kinds of tastes.

Seppō, when holding the office of Cook under Tōzan, was once washing rice when Tōzan came into the kitchen. "Is there rice or sand left when you have finished the washing?" asked Tōzan. "I wash away both at the same time," replied Seppō. "If you do that, what will the trainees eat?" asked Tōzan. At this question, Seppō turned over the rice-bin. "One day you will be enlightened," said Tōzan, "but it will be under someone other than me." By such methods as this, the old and excellent teachers trained their disciples when in the office of the Cook, and we of the present day must never be lazy should we ever be appointed thereto. When cooking, the Cook must seek for Buddhahood with as much zeal as men of the present time apply to their work when stripped to the waist. It is imperative that we ourselves look carefully at both rice and sand and make certain that we never mix them; the *Zen Temple Regulations* say that the Cook must personally examine all food carefully and ensure its cleanliness. The water with which the rice is washed must not be idly thrown away; in the old days a straining bag was used for the purpose of ensuring that no rice was ever left in the water: rice must also be protected against rats and the curious after being put into the pot.

The following day's breakfast vegetables are prepared first and thereafter the rice and soup for lunch. The dining table, rice-box, and all necessary tableware must be washed and kept carefully clean in a convenient place ready for use; whether chop-sticks, ladles or other articles, they must all be made ready in the same single-minded way as the food and handled just as gently.

The following day's lunch rice is prepared after all rice-weevils, green-peas, bran, dust, sand and grit have been removed therefrom: the *Scripture for the God of Fire* is always recited if rice and vegetables are mixed, the recitation being done by a junior trainee.

Hereafter all vegetables, liquids and other raw food are made ready; that which has been provided for the temple officers must be cooked with the same care as that shown to ordinary food, irrespective of quantity or quality. The Chief Cook must never be concerned about the unappetising appearance of food, nor must he complain about it: he must be so single-minded in his own training that no resting place can ever be found between him and the actual food, the two being identical with each other.

The following day's breakfast must be completely prepared before midnight and cooked after that hour has struck; the following morning, when breakfast is over, the pot is cleaned and the lunch rice steamed together with the soup. Every grain of rice must be washed carefully in the scullery by the Chief Cook personally; he must never leave until the washing is over and he must, on no account, cast away even a single grain: when the washing has been completed, as well as the soaking, the rice is put into the pot and steamed over the fire. It was said by one old priest that the pot in which the rice is cooked must be thought of as our own heads; the water in which the rice is washed must be regarded as our own life. In summer, all rice must be put in a rice-chest before being put upon the dining table.

The vegetables and soup must be cooked as soon as the Chief Cook commences the cooking of the rice and, here again, the Chief Cook himself must handle the work: he occasionally gives orders for the necessary utensils to be prepared by a serving trainee, servant or stoker however, in olden times, only the Chief Cook was allowed to handle the cooking. Recently there are some serving trainees with the titles of Rice Cook, or Meal Supervisor, (being specifically in charge of rice and gruel) and Accountant; all are allowed to assist in the actual cooking in the larger temples.

The Chief Cook must not eye the food superficially or with a discriminatory mind; his soul must be so free that the Buddha Land appears within a blade of grass, whenever he and others behold it, and he must be capable of giving a great sermon even on the very heart of a particle of dust. He must not be contemptuous when making poor quality soup, nor should he be overjoyed when he makes it with milk: if he is unattached to the last, he will not hate the first. There must be no laziness in him, however unappetising the food may be; should the food he beholds be of good quality his training must become all the deeper so that he may avoid attachment thereto. His speech in the presence of all men must be the same, unchanging in mode for, should he change it, he is not a true seeker after Buddhahood. He must be polite in all he does and strenuous in perfecting his efforts at cooking for these actions will lead him in the path of purity and care once trodden by the excellent priests of old: I myself long to be thus. How is it possible to be so single-minded at all times? It is true that, once, a very fine, old, Chief Cook made a poor soup for only three small coins, but a true Chief Cook must be able to make a fine soup for exactly the same price; most modern Chief Cooks would find this very difficult for there is as big a difference between ancient and modern as there is between heaven and earth: it is extremely difficult for a modern Chief Cook to be as those of olden times but, if he strives with all his might, and is gentle when cooking, he will go even farther than they did. People of the present day seem to be completely unaware of this fact, primarily because they give free reign to their own pettiness, discrimination and feeling to such an extent that they are as wild horses prancing or wild monkeys swinging about from one tree to another. Should one meditate deeply upon oneself, discarding the pettiness, discrimination and feeling, the oneness of self and others will be realised. Therefore, if one is moved by things and people, one is also able to move them. It is absolutely essential that the pure actions of the Chief Cook shall come forth from his realisation of unity with all things and beings; having no prejudices himself, he must be able to see clearly into the minds and hearts of others. He must be so kaleidoscopic that, from only a stalk of cabbage, he seems to produce a sixteen-foot-long body of the Buddha. Even in this present day and age it is possible for him to develop a kaleidoscopic nature to such a degree that he helps all living things thereby.

All food, after being cooked, must be put away in a safe and suitable place: thereafter, when the Chief Cook hears the drums or gongs, he must go to do his Zazen in the Meditation Hall and listen to the words of the Abbot both morning and evening along with everyone else. On returning to his room, he must shut his eyes and think quietly of the number for whom he must make food, not forgetting the seniors in their private rooms, sick members of the community in the Infirmary, aged members of the community, those absent, guest monks in the Guest House and any other guests that may be present: should he be in any doubt as to the number within the temple, he must ask the Disciplinarian and other officers as well as the Chief Junior. When he is certain of the number, he should remember that, to whomsoever eats a grain of rice with True Mind another grain should be given, for this grain can be divided into two, three, four or more grains: even only half a grain is sometimes as good as one or two, and two halves, once they come together, become one—should one grain be divided into ten sections, and nine are given away, how many grains are left? When these same come together again, how many are there left? He who eats this grain with True Mind sees Daian and tames the pale blue cow; the pale blue cow also consumes Daian. It is important that the Chief Cook should think carefully about himself to see if he has fully understood the importance of a kaleidoscopic character: if he has done so he must teach all people according as he is able, making great efforts for religion everyday.

If someone offers money for food for the community, the Chief Cook must discuss the matter with the other officers—this is the traditional way of making all decisions concerning the distribution of offerings to the community—under no circumstances may the Chief Cook encroach upon the duties of others.

After the rice and soup have been prepared they are put upon the dining table. The Chief Cook burns incense, after putting on his kesa, spreads his mat and bows nine times towards the Meditation Hall before sending food to the Dining-Hall. He must always be diligent in preparing breakfast and lunch every day, under no circumstances whatsoever being idle: by being conscientious in all his work he will naturally awaken the seed of Buddhahood within himself for, should he meditate deeply, he will find that such action leads to ultimate bliss.

Although Buddhism was brought to Japan a long time ago, I have, as yet, never read anything written by any Zen teacher concerning the correct way of cooking, nor is it written anywhere that the Chief Cook must bow to the Meditation Hall before sending food to table. It is because people know nothing of the True Mind revealed within the correct meaning of the community's food, and their cooking methods, that it is said that such food is just the same as that of mere birds and animals: this is a great shame—let us examine the reason why it is so.

When I was staying in Tendōzan, the name of the Chief Cook was Lu. After lunch one day, when on my way to another part of the temple which was reached by means of the eastern corridor, I saw him busily drying mushrooms in front of the Butsuden, wearing no hat and using a bamboo stick: the sun was scorching both his head and the pavement but he continued to work hard, perspiring greatly. Feeling concern for the pain he was obviously enduring at so great an age, for his back was bent as taut as a bow, I said to him, "How old are you?" His big eyebrows were as white as the feathers of a crane. "I am sixty-eight," he replied. "Why do you not give such work to the junior trainees or servants?" I asked. "They are not me," he replied. "I know that you are very sincere, but the sun is now blazing hot. Why work so hard at such a time?" I asked. "What other time is there than now?" he replied. The conversation went no further than this but, as I continued on my way along the corridor, I suddenly understood intuitively why the position of Chief Cook is so very important.

During the May of the sixteenth year of Kia-ting, I was on board ship, speaking with the captain, when an old priest of about sixty came aboard to buy mushrooms: we took tea together and I found that he was the Chief Cook of a large temple. "I am from Shi-shu," he said, "and am sixty-one years old:

I left home forty years ago. In almost all the temples where I have lived, the life of the community was pure and truly religious: early last year I was in Ku-yung and had the opportunity of staying in Ayuwan-shan but did not make use of it at that time—luckily, however, I was later appointed Chief Cook there at the end of the summer. Tomorrow, being the fifth of May, I must make an offering of food to the entire community but there was nothing suitable in the temple. I originally wanted to give them vegetables and noodles but had no mushrooms so have come here." "When did you leave Ayuwan-shan?" "After lunch," he replied. "Did you have to come far?" I asked. "About thirty-four or thirty-five ri," was his answer. "When will you return?" "As soon as I have the mushrooms." "I am so glad we were able to meet and talk. I would like to offer you something," I said. "I am afraid that is impossible for, should I stay longer, who will do to-morrow's cooking?" he replied. "Surely, in a temple as big as Ayuwan-shan, someone else is capable of cooking food? I cannot believe that the absence of one Chief Cook could cause trouble." "Although I am old, I, as the Chief Cook, am in charge of cooking. Since this is the training of my old age, how is it possible for me to give such duties to others? It must also be remembered that I did not get permission to stay out for the night," was his reply. "Surely it would be better for you to do Zazen or study kōans," I said, "Whatever is the use of working so hard merely at the duties of a Chief Cook?" He laughed heartily when hearing my comment saying, "My good foreigner, you have no idea of the true meaning of Buddhist training, nor of its character." Feeling greatly ashamed and somewhat surprised at this comment, I said, "What are they?" "Remain still and quiet in the very depths of your own question and their meaning will manifest itself," he replied. I was unable to understand him and, realising this, he said, "If you cannot understand me, I suggest

you come to Ayuwan-shan, then we can talk of these matters."
He then rose to leave, saying, "It grows dark; I must get home
quickly: I have no time for idle chatter."

He came to see me the following July when I was in
Tendōzan and told me, "I am going to resign as Chief Cook
after this summer and go home. By accident I heard from a
fellow trainee that you were here and was anxious to see you."
I was overjoyed to see him and, in the course of discussing
many things, we touched upon the matters we had spoken of
on the ship. "If someone wishes to understand the true character of Buddhist training," he said, "its original meaning must
be thoroughly realised: if one undergoes Buddhist training, he
must understand the true meaning of that training." "What is
this true character?" I asked. "One, two, three, four, five," he
answered. "What is the discipline of Buddhism?" I asked. "The
whole universe manifests itself quite naturally," he answered.
I will not make mention of the other things of which we spoke
but, primarily because of him, I was able to understand, to a
considerable extent, what the character and discipline of
Buddhism are: on speaking of these matters to my late teacher,
Myozen, he happily agreed with my opinions. Some time later
I read the following verse by Setchō in the *Monastic Precepts*:–

> One, seven, three, five,
> Nothing may be depended upon by any universe;
> Night comes and the moon floods the water with light,
> Within the dragon's jaws I find many exquisite jewels.

This verse said exactly the same thing as had the Chief Cook
the year before; I know that he was a true seeker of Buddhahood.

In the beginning my characters were one, two, three,
four and five, and now they include six, seven, eight, nine and
ten. It is essential that we trainees study the true character of

Buddhism wholeheartedly, without attachment to any opposite whatsoever, for only then will the unity of Zen be understood in characters; should we do otherwise, innumerable varieties of Zen will ruin us to such an extent that we shall be unable to cook food for the community properly.

All Chief Cooks were diligent in their work and, within this fact, we can find the original meaning of Buddhist training and its true character for it is the very marrow of rightly Transmitted Buddhism.

The *Zen Temple Regulations* state that breakfast and dinner must be most carefully prepared bearing in mind the necessity for a sufficient supply of food at both: this is not only true of breakfast and dinner but also of all food and drink, as well as clothing, medicine and bed clothes. The Buddha gave forty-five years of His life for our benefit! So great is the light which He radiates that it is too great for us to appreciate fully: because of this, the Chief Cook must have no thought other than service to the community, having no concern for lack of wealth. Should he be completely unattached to the results of the work which he does, eternal bliss will be his; I believe that the same attitude of mind as that of the Chief Cook towards the community should also be adopted by the Abbot thereof.

The best way of handling food is for whoever is doing it to possess a sincere and appreciative opinion thereof, irrespective of its quality. Because of the sincerity of mind with which a woman offered the Buddha a bowl of milk it was foretold that she would become a Pratyekabuddha in the following life: because King Asoka, as his last good action, offered half of a piece of fruit to the priests attending him on his deathbed, he was free from all suffering at the moment of death: from this it may be seen that small acts of charity, made in a devotional spirit, are beneficial not only in the present but in the future also. However minute may be the offerings we make to

Buddha, they must be given in the spirit of true religion and sincerity; such deeds are the right action of all men.

The Chief Cook must never consider rich, creamy milk as superior food to soup or vegetables when choosing ingredients; whenever such a choice is involved it must be made with a mind free from defilement and in utter sincerity. Once a priest has entered the vast ocean of Buddhism he sees no difference whatsoever between rich, creamy milk and coarse soup and vegetables for then everything is identical with the ocean of Buddhism: it goes without saying that no Chief Cook sees any difference whatsoever between such things once he has truly awakened the seed of Buddhahood: it was once said by a great teacher that priests do not differentiate between various foods just as a fire does not differentiate between various sorts of firewood—if we are sincere when cooking, even the coarsest food can help us to exhibit the seed of Buddhahood—never make light of such things. However minute in quantity, or coarse in quality, food may be they who would lead both men and gods must be able to save all living things thereby.

Priests vary in age, being old or young; some have great merit whilst others have none; the Chief Cook must understand this quite clearly in its entirety. It is impossible for him to know what the future may hold and even more impossible for him to know the future of others; it would be thoroughly wicked of him to judge others by his own standards: all members of the priesthood are the treasure of Buddhism, whether senior or junior, clever or stupid—that which was wrong yesterday may be correct to-day; it is impossible to separate the sacred from the secular. The *Zen Temple Regulations* say that, whether priests are holy or unholy, they all have the potential of embracing and enfolding the universe; one must be entirely free from moral discrimination—strenuous training, of itself, is the True Way. Although Buddhism may be right before your eyes, you will be very far from the Truth should you make so much as one false step in the direction of moral discrimination: the true meaning of morality has been shown by the masters of old in their strenuous efforts to practice Buddhism—all future Chief Cooks must be very active when holding their office because of the above statement—there is no deception in the *Zen Temple Regulations* of Hyakujō.

When staying in Kenninji on my return to Japan, I was greatly surprised to find that the Chief Cook was completely unaware of the true way of preparing food: it was indeed unfortunate that he had no opportunity of learning from the great Chief Cooks of other temples for he spent much of his time in idleness which is so highly detrimental to Buddhism. He never personally took charge of the cooking or preparing of either breakfast or lunch, leaving all his work, whether important or otherwise, to a coarse servant who knew nothing, and cared less, about the correct way of cooking food. He never went to see if the man was doing anything correctly and saw no shame in visiting a woman who lived nearby: his only other occupations seemed to be gossiping with others and reciting Scriptures in his room—he did nothing more. He never went near the kitchen, however long he had been absent therefrom, and he would not buy any new utensils or consider the number of tastes to be relished in the food: obviously he did not consider that cooking was the work of Buddha—he had no notion of the fact that food could only be served after he had offered incense and bowed to the Meditation Hall: it is indeed a shame that he had no idea of how to lead his juniors during meals. Since he did not possess the Way Seeking Mind, he had never seen a True Seeker of Buddhahood; he was as one who returns from a mountain or ocean of treasures empty-handed. Even though he had not awakened to Buddhahood, he could still have behaved correctly as a Chief Cook, once given the chance to see a true teacher, one who was truly awakened to Buddhahood: since he neither awakened the Seed of Buddhahood, nor bothered to cook, what use was he?

The term of office of any temple officer in a Chinese Temple is one year; when special offerings are made by members of the laity, as sometimes happens at mealtimes, these priests have special duties. They must always make special efforts in their work, both for the benefit of themselves and others, as well as raise the standard of perfection of their own training by adhering strictly to the temple regulations and thus trying to reach the standards set by the old masters through copying their methods. If we compare this with the behaviour of the Chief Cook mentioned above we find that he thought of his training with as little interest as if it were belonging to someone else whilst those who followed the code of conduct outlined above considered others' training with as much care as if it were their own. There is an old poem which says:–

> Although he has already spent two-thirds of his life,
> He has not yet purified his mind;
> Being solely interested in fame and gain,
> He fails to heed the warning of my words.

It is clear from the above that, without true teachers, we would be engulfed in fame and gain: the Chief Cook I spoke of is as the stupid rich man's son, spoken of in the *Lotus Scripture*, who, on receiving a fortune bequeathed to him, ran away from home and threw it away as if it were worth nothing; it is a terrible situation for a Chief Cook.

When I think of the old Chief Cooks I realise that all were worthy of their posts: all were enlightened when performing their duties as Chief Cooks and Tōzan showed the Buddha to the entire community in three pounds of hemp.

There is nothing of greater value than enlightenment and no time more precious than now.

Let us now consider some examples of those who truly sought enlightenment. Because a child once handed its treasure of a handful of sand to Buddha it later became King Asoka; Shakyamuni Buddha once told King Udayama that, after His death, whosoever should make a statue of Buddha would be handsome, or beautiful, from one generation to another, no matter how many times he or she may be born; in addition to this, such a person will be born in heaven after death. Obviously both the office and name of Chief Cook will remain exactly as they are: since the actions of the old Chief Cooks have come down to us these priests can, if we truly train ourselves, be seen again in us.

Three attitudes of mind must be cultivated by all temple officers in addition to that of the Chief Cook; these are gratitude, love and generosity. The mind of ecstasy expresses gratitude: if we were to dwell in heaven our joy would be so excessive that there would be no time whatsoever for us to either train or awaken the Seed of Buddhahood within us and we would never prepare food for the Three Treasures. There is nothing of greater value, or excellence, than the Three Treasures; they far surpass the greatest deity in heaven, both in value and excellence, as well as equally surpassing the highest upon earth. The *Zen Temple Regulations* say that priests have far greater excellence than any other beings for their bodies and minds are pure and wholly free from earthly clinging: how wonderful it is that we have been fortunate enough to be born human and so can become Chief Cooks with the honour of preparing pure food for the superlative Three Treasures—than this, there is no greater delight. Were we to be born in one of the evil worlds, such as hell, that of the hungry ghosts, animals, Asuras or any of the other eight in which it is very hard to hear

Buddhist Truth, it would not be possible for us to personally make pure food for the Three Treasures, together with the great priesthood, for both body and mind would be subject to suffering: we are fortunate in that, in this life, we have the opportunity to offer pure food to the Three Treasures. How lucky we are: how blessed is this body: for all eternity there will be no greater opportunity than that offered to us now; its merit is undefileable. When we serve our fellow trainees purely, hundreds and thousands of lives are enfolded in one single day's, or hour's, work which will bear fruit for many lives to come: to grasp Truth thus clearly is to express gratitude. Even were we the highest in all the world such rank would be as useless as a bubble if we did not make pure food for the Three Treasures.

The mind of our parents expresses love and we must love the Three Treasures in the same way as our parents love us. However poor a person may be it is frequently possible to see the love he expresses towards his children; who is capable of understanding the extent of his loving mind other than he himself? All men, whether rich or poor, long for their children to grow strong and big, protecting them with unsparing devotion against inclement weather; this is the greatest of all sincerity: no one who does not possess this mind can understand it. A Chief Cook must love water and rice in the same way that parents love their children: the Buddha gave us forty-five years of His life because He wanted to teach us parental love by His example, not because He was eager for fame and gain.

A generous mind is one that is as firm as a rock and as limitless as the ocean, completely lacking in discrimination. One who possesses such a mind sees no difference between base metal and gold; he is not bewitched by beautiful voices, or ugly sounding ones, nor is he concerned with the changing of the seasons: we must make our own personal understanding of this mind clear by writing it down, fully comprehending and learning it in everything we do in our ordinary life.

Without a mind as above described, a former Chief Cook could not have taught his frivolous trainee, curing him of his wicked laughter, nor could Daii have shown his understanding to his master by blowing three times on a dead fire or Tōzan exhibit the Buddha in three pounds of hemp: you should understand from this that all the old teachers exhibited this mind in their everyday actions—even now they are showing us clearly the true meaning, and importance, of training, thus leading us to emancipation. The wide highway to enlightenment is our own training; whosoever we are, Abbot, Officers or any other trainees, all must constantly keep these three attitudes of mind in their thoughts.

GAKUDŌ-YŌJINSHŪ.

IMPORTANT ASPECTS OF ZAZEN.

1. *Necessity for a Desire for the Way.*

Although there are many names given to that which seeks the Way they all refer to the one, and same, Mind.[8]

Nagyaarajyuna said, "The universality of change, the arising and disappearing, when completely understood, is the seeing into the heart of all things, and the Mind that thus understands is the Mind that truly seeks the Way." As this is so, why is temporary dependence upon the ordinary mind of man called the Mind that seeks the Way? If one sees through the changeability of the universe, the ordinary, selfish mind is not in use; that which seeks for the sake of itself is nowhere to be found.

Time flies like an arrow from a bow and this fact should make us train with all our might, using the same energy we would employ if our hair were to catch fire. We must guard against weakness of body, our effort being as that of the Buddha when raising His foot. Sounds that flatter and distract, such as the call of the cuckoo and the voices of musical entertainers, should be thought of no more than as the sound of the evening breeze; the sight of beautiful courtesans should be regarded merely as dew touching the eyes. Once free from perceptual bondage, sound and colour, the Mind that seeks the Way is naturally in harmony with you. From ancient times there are those who have not heard Buddhist Truth, and some have had little opportunity of hearing or reading the Scriptures. Once trapped in the bonds forged by fame and gain, most people lose the Life of Buddha for eternity; such a fate is to be pitied and mourned. Just to read the Scriptures, thereby understanding Truth with the ordinary mind, and to transmit that which is clear and that which is hidden, is not to possess the Mind that seeks the Way if fame and gain are not forsaken.

There are those who believe that the Mind that seeks the Way is truly enlightened since there is no dependence upon fame and gain. There are those who say that the Mind that seeks the Way embraces three thousand worlds in a moment of thought as its meditation. There are those who say that the Mind that seeks the Way teaches the non-arising of any delusion. There are those who say that the Mind that seeks the Way enters straightway into the World of the Buddhas. None of these people yet know the Mind that seeks the Way and therefore devalue it; they are far from the Truth of the Buddhas. When one reflects upon the selfish mind, which concerns itself only with fame and gain, it is clear that it has no knowledge of the three thousand worlds within a thought moment and is also not non-delusional. Such a mind knows nothing other than delusion because of its immersion in fame and gain; it cannot be compared to the Mind that seeks the Way. Although many of the wise have used worldly methods to reach enlightenment it is certain that they had no misunderstanding in their own minds concerning fame and gain; they did not even have an attachment to Truth and no desire whatsoever for the world as most men know it.

The Mind that truly seeks the Way can be any one of those previously mentioned so long as it also clearly sees through the changeability of the universe, understanding utterly arising

The author with the Very Reverend Kohō Keidō Chisan Zenji after the ceremony of becoming his official, personal disciple.

and disappearing: the Mind is totally different to the mind of ordinary men. It is excellent to practice the meditations of the non-arising mind and the appearance of the three thousand worlds <u>after</u> you have gained the Mind that seeks the Way, but do not confuse the two by putting them in the wrong order.

Forget the selfish self for a little and allow the mind to remain natural for this is very close to the Mind that seeks the Way. Self is the basis for the sixty-two private opinions so, when you are beginning to become full of your own opinions, just sit quietly and watch how they arise. On what are they based, both within you and outside of you? Your body, hair and skin come from your parents: the seeds that came from your parents, however, are empty, both from the beginning of time and until the end of it. Within this there is no ego, the mind that is fettered by discrimination, knowledge and dualism of thought blinds us. After all, in the end, what is it that inhales and exhales? These two are not the self and there is no self to which to cling. They who live in delusion cling to all things whilst they who are enlightened are free of clinging and things: and still we measure the unreal self and grasp at worldly appearances, thus ignoring true Buddhist practice; by failing to sever the ties of the world, we are turning our backs upon the True teachings and chasing after false ones. Such mistakes must be carefully avoided.

2. The Necessity of Training for Truth.

When a loyal servant gives advice its power is frequently far-reaching; when the Buddhas and Ancestors give so much as only a single word, all living things will be converted. Only a wise king will take advice; only an exceptional trainee will truly hear the words of the Buddha. If the mind cannot change from one side to the other, the source of transmigration can never be severed; unless the loyal servant's advice is taken, the government of a country will show no virtue and wisdom in its policy.

3. The Necessity of Constantly Practicing the Way in Order to Realise Enlightenment.

Most people think that one must study in order to gain wealth but the Buddha teaches that training itself embraces enlightenment: as yet I have heard of no one who became wealthy without much study nor of anyone who became enlightened without undergoing training. There are, of course,

Above, the Crown Prince of Nepal (now King of Nepal) with the Very Reverend Kohō Keidō Chisan Zenji and the then Vice-Abbot of Dai Hon Zan Sōjiji together with other dignitaries and the author who was Foreign Guest Master at the temple.

Below, President Eisenhower and the Very Reverend Kohō Keidō Chisan Zenji at a reception at the White House.

differences in training methods; differences between faith and understanding—between sudden and gradual—but enlightenment can only be realised as a result of training. Some means of study are shallow, others deep, some are interesting and others boring, but treasure is derived from much study. None of these things depend upon the ability of rulers or just plain luck. If treasure is attainable without study, who is able to teach the way through which rulers learn to truly rule? If enlightenment can be realised without training, the teaching of the Buddhas cannot be perfected. Although you may be training in the world of delusion, it is still the world of enlightenment. If you can understand that ships and rafts are but a past dream, you will for ever leave behind the self-opinions which fettered you to the scriptures. The Buddhas do not force you; everything comes out of your own efforts in the Way. When you train, you are beckoning to enlightenment; your own treasure is within you, not outside; training and enlightenment are their own reward; enlightened action leaves no sign by which it can be traced. To look back upon one's training with enlightened eyes is to see no speck of dust: to look for such a thing is the same as trying to see a white cloud at a distance of ten thousand miles. When encompassing training and enlightenment, no single speck of dust can be trodden upon; should we do so heaven and earth would collapse but, in returning to our True Home, we are transcending the status of the Buddha.

4. *The Necessity of Selfless Training.*

The Truth of Buddhist Training has been handed on to us by our predecessors and, for this, it is impossible to use the selfish mind: we can gain the Truth of Buddhism neither with mind nor without mind. It must be remembered that, if the will to train and the Way of the Buddhas are not harmonised, neither body nor mind will know peace; if body and mind are not at peace they know only discomfort.

How do we harmonise the Way of the Buddhas with training? To do so the mind must neither grasp nor reject anything; it must be completely free from the fetters of fame and gain. Buddhist training is not undergone for the sake of others but, as in the case of the minds of most people nowadays, the minds of most Buddhist trainees are far from understanding the True Way. They do that which others praise although they know such action to be wrong; they do not follow the True Way because it is that which others heap scorn upon; this is indeed a great grief—such behaviour is no right use of the Mind of the Buddhas. The Buddhas and the Ancestors selflessly illuminated the universe with their all-penetrating eyes and it is our duty to copy them. Since Buddhist trainees do almost nothing for themselves, how is it possible that they should do anything for the sake of fame and gain? Only for Buddhism must one train in Buddhism. Out of their deep compassion for all living things, the Buddhas do absolutely nothing either for themselves or for others, merely doing all for the sake of Buddhism, and this is the True Tradition of Buddhism. Even insects and animals cherish their young, bearing any hardship for their sake and, when later they are full-grown, the parents seek no gain therefrom: just as compassion is strong in such small creatures, even so is compassion for all living creatures strong in the Buddhas. Compassion is not the only expression of the great teachings of the Buddhas; they appear in a myriad ways throughout the universe, thus exhibiting and being the True Spirit of Buddhism: since we are all already the children of Buddha, we have no alternative but to follow the path of Buddhism. You, as a Buddhist trainee, must not think of training as done for your own benefit and fame, nor must you train in Buddhism for the sake of getting results or performing miracles; you must just train in Buddhism for the sake of Buddhism, this being the True Way.

5. *The Necessity of Finding a True Teacher.*

A former Ancestor once said, "If the mind that seeks is untrue, training will be useless,"—this is utterly true and the quality of the training inevitably depends upon the quality of the teacher. The trainee is as a beautiful piece of wood which the teacher must fashion as does a skillful carpenter; even beautiful wood will show no graining unless the carpenter is an expert, but a warped piece of wood can show good results in the hands of a skilled craftsman. The truth or falsity of the teacher is in ratio to the truth or falsity of the enlightenment of his disciples; understand this clearly and become enlightened. For centuries there have been no good teachers in this country—how do we know? Just look at their words: they are as people who try to measure the source of flowing water from a scooped-up handful. Throughout the centuries this country's teachers have written books, taught trainees and given lectures to both men and gods, but their words were as green, unripe fruit for they had not reached the ultimate in training; they had not become one with true enlightenment. All that they transmitted were words, reciting names and sounds: day in and day out they counted in the treasury of others, contributing nothing whatsoever thereto of themselves. There is no doubt that this is the fault of the teachers of old, for some of them misled others into believing that enlightenment must be sought outside of the mind and some taught that rebirth in other lands was the goal; herein is to be found the source of both confusion and delusion. Unless one follows the prescription on the medicine-bottle, an illness may be made worse by taking medicine; it may even be the same as drinking poison. For centuries there have been no good doctors in this country who were capable of prescribing correctly, and of knowing the difference between, true medicine and poison, therefore it is extremely difficult to cure the sufferings and diseases of life: since this is so, how is it possible for us to escape from the sufferings brought on by old age and death? Only the teachers are to blame for this problem; it is certainly through no fault of the disciples. Why is this so? Because the teachers are leading others along the branches of the tree and ceasing to climb up the trunk to the source. They lure others into false paths before they have their own understanding based in certainty; they therefore fix their concentration solely upon their own selfish opinions: it is indeed terrible that teachers have no perception of their own delusions. Under these circumstances, how can disciples understand what is right and what is wrong? As yet Buddhism has not taken root in our tiny country and thus true teachers are still to be born: if you truly want to study the very best Buddhism you must visit the teachers in China, which is very far away, and you must think deeply upon the true road which is beyond the mind of delusion.

If a true teacher is not to be found, it is best not to study Buddhism at all: they who are called good teachers, however, are not necessarily either young or old but simple people who can make clear the true teaching and receive the seal of a genuine master. Neither learning nor knowledge are of much importance for such teachers have a characteristic in their extraordinary influence over others and their own will-power: they neither rely on their own selfish opinions nor do they cling to any obsession for training and understanding are perfectly harmonised within them. The above are the characteristics of a true teacher.

6. The Necessity of Being Aware During Zazen.

Zazen being of grave importance, neither neglect it nor regard it lightly. There have been magnificent examples of old masters in China who cut off their arms or fingers for the sake of the Truth: centuries ago the Buddha forsook both His home and His country—to do so are sure signs of true training. People of the present time say that they need only practice that which comes easily—this is very bad; such thinking is not at all akin to true Buddhism. If you concentrate only on one thing and consider it to be training then it is impossible to even lie down in peace: if one action is done with a bored or uneasy mind, all things become boring or uneasy; I know full well that they who seek things the easy way do not look for the True Way. Shakyamuni was able to give the teaching at present to be found in the world after undergoing very difficult training and thus He is the great teacher—His was the source: as this is so, how can the descendants of Shakyamuni gain anything by taking it easy? The Mind that seeks the Way does not search for easy training: should you look for an easy means of training, you will probably not reach the true realisation, and you can never find the treasure house. The most excellent of the old Ancestors said that training was hard to undergo for Buddhism is deep and immense: the great masters would never have spoken of the difficulty of Buddhism had it been easy. By comparison with the old Ancestors, people nowadays amount not even to so much as a single hair in a herd of nine cows: even if they do their best, pretending it is hard, they do not begin to attain the <u>easy</u> training and understanding of the Ancestors because of their lack of strength and knowledge. What is taught as easy training and beloved by present-day man? It is neither secular nor Buddhist for it cannot even be compared to the teachings of devils and evil gods, nor can it be compared to heresy and the two vehicles: the delusions of ordinary people have deep roots and they trap themselves in eternal transmigration by pretending to escape from the present world. It is difficult to break the bones and crush the marrow from outside, and to control the mind is more difficult still; it is of even greater difficulty to undergo true training and long austerity, whilst the greatest difficulty of all is the harmonising of the training of body and mind. Many, in olden times, underwent a training which required the crushing of their bones and, if this were valuable, they should have become enlightened but only a handful did. They who endured austerity, in like manner, should have become enlightened but, here again, few did: this is because, when undergoing such training, it is extremely difficult to harmonise body and mind. Neither a clear head nor a good knowledge of learning are of great importance any more than are mind, will, consciousness, thought, understanding or perception; all of them are useless; to enter the stream of Buddhism one must just simply harmonise the mind and the body—Shakyamuni said that one must turn the stream of compassion within and give up both knowledge and its recognition. Herein lies the full meaning of the above for in this neither movement nor stillness are in the ascendency and this is true harmony. If one could penetrate Buddhism as a result of intelligence and learning, certainly Shinshu could have done so: if it were difficult to penetrate Buddhism because of low birth and class, Daikan Enō could never have become the supreme Ancestor. The means by which Buddhism is Transmitted is far beyond normal intelligence and understanding; look carefully for all signs within yourself, meditate upon yourself and train hard.

The teachings of Zen make no choice between either old or young: Jōshu did not begin to train until he was over sixty but he was a very fine Ancestor: the priestess Teijō started her training at the age of twelve and became the finest of the priests in her monastery: it is the amount of effort made that conditions the understanding of Buddhism received, and this differs according to the training or lack thereof. They who have spent much time in worldly or Scriptural study should visit a Zen training centre; many have already done so: Bodhidharma taught the clever Eshi, known as Nangaku, whilst Daikan Enō taught Yōka Genkaku. To make the Truth clear and enter the Way, one must study with a Zen master: one must never try to bring a Zen master's teaching down to one's own level of understanding for, should one try to understand it from one's own self-opinionated view-point, one will never understand. Before asking for the Truth from a master, you must make your body and mind pure and quieten your perceptions so that both eyes and ears perceive and hear in peace; simply listen to the teaching and do not allow it to become soiled by your own thoughts: your body and mind must be at one with each other as water is poured from one bowl to another. If you can achieve such a state of body and mind, the Truth that the master teaches can be made one with yourself.

At the present time the unwise memorise the scriptures and cling to what they have heard; they try to equate such things with the master's teaching but actually only re-hear their own opinions and those of others which do not at all equate with the teaching they have just received; they are convinced that their own opinions are right and then memorise a few parts of the Scriptures calling this Buddhism. Should the teaching you hear from a Zen master go against your own opinions he is probably a good Zen master; if there is no clash of opinions in the beginning it is bad. People who are stuck with their own opinions frequently do not know how to get rid of them and so cannot use the teaching given to them: for a long time they suffer from grave confusion and must be regarded with great grief.

Presumption, discrimination, imagination, intellect, human understanding and the like have nothing to do with Buddhism when studying Zen—too many people are like children, playing with such things from their birth. You must awaken to Buddhism right now—above all, you must avoid presumption and choice; reflect carefully upon this. Only the Zen masters know the gateway to the Truth; professors have no knowledge thereof.

7. The Necessity for Zazen when Training to be Truly Free.

Because of its superiority Buddhism is sought by many people but, whilst Shakyamuni was alive, there was only one teaching and one teacher; by Himself, the Great Shakyamuni guided all living things to complete understanding. Since Makakashyo commenced the Transmission of the Truth, there have been twenty-eight Ancestors in India, six in China; the Ancestors of the five schools (churches) have, without interruption, Transmitted it to the present time: since the period of Ryokai, all really worthy persons have entered into Zen Buddhism whether they were in the priesthood or of royal blood. One should love the excellence of true Buddhism rather than what passes for Buddhism: it is wrong to love the dragon as did Sekkō. In some countries east of China a web of learning, rather than true Buddhism, has been spread across the seas and mountains; although it spreads over the mountains, the heart of the clouds is not within it; although it spreads across the seas the hearts of the waves are destroyed thereby, fools take pleasure herein; such people are as those who would treasure a fish-eye in the belief that it was a pearl, making a plaything thereof—to behave thus is to treasure a pebble from Gen as if it were a jewel. There are many who are ruined by falling into the hall of the demons.

In a country in which there is much bias, the Truth has difficulty in appearing because of the way in which it is beset by contrary winds. Although China has already taken refuge in the Truth of Buddhism neither our country nor Korea have, as yet, had any real contact therewith. Why? At least the Truth can be heard in Korea but here it is not; this is because those who went to China clung to erudition—they seem to have transmitted the Scriptures but they forgot to Transmit the Truth. What merit is there here? None whatsoever; their failure was due to their lack of understanding of true training. How unfortunate it is that the body should be thus vainly employed in hard work for all its natural life.

When learning the Way, listening to the teaching of the master and training after first entering the gate, there is something you should know. In the *Ryogonkyo* it says that external things control the self and that the self controls external things; should I control external things then I am strong and they are weak but, should the external things control me, then they are strong and I am weak; from the beginning these opposites have existed in Buddhism; unless someone has a true Transmission, this cannot be understood; unless a true master is found, even the names of these opposites are unheard of: those who have no knowledge of this can never study true Buddhism for how can they ever differentiate between right and wrong? They who practice true Zen by studying the Way naturally Transmit the meaning of these opposites; they make no mistakes such as are found in some teachings. It is not possible to understand the true Way without the training of Zen.

8. *How a Zen Trainee Should Behave.*

The Truth has been Transmitted directly to the present time from the time of the Buddhas and Ancestors; in all the twenty-eight Generations in India and the six in China no thread has been added to, or speck of dust taken away from, it. After the robe was given to Daikan Enō the Truth spread from one end of the world to the other and so the Buddha's Truth flourishes in China. Truth can never be sought and they who once see the Way forget all knowledge and fame for they transcend relative consciousness. Gunin was at Ōbai when Daikan Enō lost his face; Eka, the Second Ancestor, cut off his arm in front of Bodhidharma's cave thereby gaining the marrow of Buddhism by destroying the selfish mind: having gained the core of Buddhism, he gained vital freedom, dwelling neither in body nor mind and having no attachment, stagnation or grasping. A trainee asked Jōshu if a dog had Buddha Nature to which Jōshu replied, "Mu." How can "mu" be measured? There is nothing to hold on to; one must just let go. What are body and mind? What is Zen behaviour? What are birth and death, the affairs of the world, mountains, rivers, earth, men, animals, home? If you continue thus, neither action nor non-action arise as distinct of themselves, and so there is no inflexibility: few indeed understand this, most suffering from delusion. The Zen trainee can gain enlightenment if he reflects upon himself from the centre of his being; it is my sincere hope that you will not take pride in gaining the True Way.

9. The Necessity of Training in Order to Attain the Way of Buddhism.

They who would study the Way must first find out if they are looking in the right direction. Shakyamuni, who learned to control His self, saw the morning star whilst sitting beneath the Bodhi Tree, thereby becoming suddenly enlightened to the highest degree; because of this, His Way cannot be compared with that of the Shravakas and Pratyekabuddhas. Not only did the Buddha enlighten Himself, He Transmitted that enlightenment to the other Buddhas and Ancestors so that, even to the present day, the Transmission has not been interrupted. As this is so, how can they who are enlightened help but be Buddhas?

To face the Way squarely is to know the true source of Buddhism and make clear the approach thereto for it is beneath the feet of every living person: you find Buddhism in the very spot where you perceive the Way. The perfection of self comes with the penetration of enlightenment but, should you become proud of your enlightenment, you will only know the half thereof.

In such a frame of mind must you face the Way, but they who only study the Way do not know whether it is open or shut. Some greatly desire to perform miracles; these are gravely mistaken for they are as those who forsake their parents and escape, or give up treasure and just wander: they are as the only son of a rich father who becomes a beggar through seeking for external things; this indeed is a true picture.

To truly study the Way is to try to penetrate it and, in order to do this, one must forget even the slightest trace of enlightenment. One who would train in Buddhism must first believe completely therein and, in order to do so, one must believe that one has already found the Way, never having been lost, deluded, upside-down, increasing, decreasing or mistaken in the first place: one must train oneself thus, believing thus, in order to make the Way clear; this is the ground for Buddhist study. By this method one may cut the functioning of consciousness and turn one's back upon the road of learning; in such a way as herein described must trainees be guided. Only after such training can we be free of the opposites of body and mind, enlightenment and delusion.

They who believe that they are already within the Way are truly rare but, if you can truly believe it, the opening and closing of the Great Way are understood quite naturally and the root of delusion and enlightenment is seen as it is. If you try to cut the function of conscious discrimination you will almost see the Way.

10. The Receiving of Direct Teaching.

There are two ways in which to set body and mind right; one is to hear the teaching from a master and the other is to do pure Zazen yourself. If you HEAR the teachings the conscious mind is put to work whilst ZAZEN embraces both training and enlightenment; in order to understand the Truth you need both. All living beings possess both body and mind, irrespective of strong or weak behaviour, for behaviour itself is variable: it is by means of the body and mind that we become enlightened and this is the receiving of the teaching. There is no need to change the present body and mind; all one has to do is follow in the enlightened Way of a fine Zen master for this is the receiving of the teaching directly: to follow a Zen master is not to follow in old ways nor to create new ones, it is simply just to receive the teaching.

SHŌBŌGENZŌ.

THE TREASURY-EYE
OF THE TRUE TEACHING.

BENDŌWA.
LECTURE ON TRAINING.

The Buddhas have a very excellent means by which they may Transmit the Truth; when Transmitted from one Buddha to another it is the embodiment of meditation which is, of itself, utterly joyful: correct sitting is essential as the true gateway to entering naturally into this meditation. Every living being has a great store of Buddha Nature but it can never be seen unless practice is undertaken nor can it be evinced in daily life unless one becomes enlightened. If you do not cling to it, your hand will be full thereof for it transcends both all and nothing: if you speak of it, your mouth will be full thereof for its height and width are immeasureable; all Buddhas dwell therein eternally, clinging to no one-sided attachment whatsoever; all living beings work therein once they have transcended one-sided attachment. That which I now teach shows all things within original enlightenment, expressing unity in action; once this is thoroughly mastered, there is an end to clinging to trifles.

After the Way Seeking Mind was awakened within me, I visited many Buddhist teachers throughout the country, finally meeting Myozen at Kenninji: I served him for nine years and the time passed swiftly; from him I learned much about Rinzai. Myozen was the chief disciple of Eisai and Transmitted the highest Buddhism then available; none of the other disciples were able to bear any comparison to him. When visiting China, I visited Zen teachers, learning much about the five different churches of Buddhism represented there: I finally studied under Nyojō, in Tendōzan, thus completing my training. At the beginning of Shōtei I returned to Japan since I wished to rescue all living beings by spreading the Truth; I was as a man who carried a heavy burden. It then occurred to me to give up this idea of spreading the Truth so as to wait for a more suitable time for carrying out my purpose. I wandered in many places, sincerely trying to teach that which I had learned, for there are true trainees to be found; those who truly turn their backs on fame and gain in order to search for the True Way. It is a great grief that such trainees are often misled by untrue teachers since this results in the hiding of true understanding; such trainees become uselessly inebriated with the madness of self and eventually drown in the delusive world. Under such circumstances, how can the true seed of wisdom give forth shoots and the opportunity to gain enlightenment be made use of?

As, like a cloud or a reed, I wander from place to place, I ask myself what mountain or river I will visit. Because my sympathies lie with those who seek the Way I went to China and discovered the type of monastery there; I also received the Truth of Zen. I gathered all this, wrote down all that I saw and leave it as a legacy to all trainees in order that they may be able to find the Truth of Buddhism. This is the very core of Zen:– Shakyamuni Buddha Transmitted the Truth to Makakashyo on Mount Ryoju and, from him, the long line of Ancestors handed it down to Bodhidharma who, in turn, went to China and Transmitted the Truth to Taisō Eka.

By this means was started the eastern Transmission of Zen and it came naturally to the Sixth Ancestor, Daikan Enō, in all its original purity, thus true Buddhism was Transmitted to China completely free of all trivia. The Sixth Ancestor's two great disciples, Nangaku and Seigen, Transmitted the Buddha's Truth, being leaders of both men and gods; their two churches spread and the five styles of Zen emerged—these are Hōgen, Igyo, Sōtō, Unmon and Rinzai; at the present time only Rinzai flourishes in China. The five training styles differ somewhat but they are all part of the one Truth of the Buddha Mind.

From the end of the Han period until the present time all the Scriptures of the other churches were taught in each church but no one was able to decide which of them was the better. After Bodhidharma's arrival from India, however, this problem was solved and pure Buddhism could be spread; it is for us to try to do the same thing in this country. All the Buddhas and Ancestors have taught that the True Way to understanding was entered through simply sitting and meditating in a way which is, of itself, utterly joyful; all who have been enlightened did this because both masters and disciples Transmitted this method from one to the other and thereby received the Truth in all its purity.

Question 1. It is said that Zazen is superior to other methods of training but ordinary people will perhaps doubt this, saying that there are many gates to the Buddha's Way. As this is so, why do you advocate Zazen?

Answer. My answer to such persons is that Zazen is the only True Gateway to Buddhism.

Question 2. Why is Zazen the only True Gateway?

Answer. Shakyamuni, the Great master, gave us this unequalled way to understanding and all the Buddhas of past, present and future were enlightened by means of Zazen in the

same way as were also the Indian and Chinese Ancestors. This
is why I can tell you that this is the True Gate by which man
enters heaven.

Question 3. True Transmission and the unequalled Way of
the Buddhas, as well as following the Way of the Ancestors,
is beyond ordinary comprehension. For most people the natural way to enlightenment is to read the Scriptures and recite
the Nembutsu. Since you do nothing more than sit cross-legged,
how can this mere sitting be a means of gaining enlightenment?

Answer. Since you regard the meditation and Truth of the
Buddhas as just sitting and being idle, you are looking down
upon Mahayana Buddhism; such delusion is similar to that of
someone who, whilst being in the midst of a vast ocean, cries
out for water. We are lucky indeed that we are, even now, sitting comfortably in the Buddha's meditation which is, of itself,
utterly joyful. Is not this a great blessing? How piteous it is
that your eyes are closed and your mind inebriated. The world
of the Buddhas is nowhere to be found in either ordinary thinking or consciousness, nor can it be known through disbelief
or low knowledge for, in order to enter therein, one must have
true belief; however much an unbeliever may be taught, he
will still have trouble in finding it: when the Buddha was
preaching at Ryoju the unbelievers were allowed to depart.
In order to develop true belief in your own mind, you must
study and train yourself hard; if you cannot do so you should
give up for a little, at the same time regretting the fact that
you are uninfluenced in your search for Truth by former good
karma. Of what use is it to read the Scriptures and recite the
Nembutsu? It is useless to imagine that the merits of Buddhism
come merely from using one's tongue or voice; if you think
such things embrace all of Buddhism, the Truth is a long way
from you. You should only read the Scriptures so as to learn
that the Buddha was teaching the necessity of gradual and

sudden training and from this you can realise enlightenment; do not read them so as to pretend to be wise with useless intellection: to try to reach the goal of Buddhism by doing thus is the same as pointing to the north and then heading south: you are putting a square peg into a round hole. So long as you are seeing words and phrases, your way will remain dark; such behaviour is as useless as that of a doctor who forgets his prescriptions. Just to continually repeat the Nembutsu is equally useless for it is as a frog who croaks both day and night in some field. Those who suffer from the delusion of fame and gain find it extraordinarily difficult to give up Nembutsu for the fetters that bind them to such craving are deep-rooted, extending from the past right down to the present; such people are piteous to see. You need only understand this clearly:– if the Truth of the Seven Buddhas is truly Transmitted by both masters and disciples it manifests itself quite clearly and is experienced completely; they who do nothing more than study the Scriptures and their characters never understand this so stop it and thereby cure your delusions and doubts: follow the teachings of a true master and, through the power of Zazen, find the utterly joyful enlightenment of Buddha.

Question 4. Both the Tendai and Kegon teachings have been brought to Japan; they represent the highest form of Buddhism. The Shingon Church, which was Transmitted from Vairocana Buddha to Vajrasattva directly, teaches that no stain exists between master and disciple, maintaining that Buddha is this very mind—that this mind becomes Buddha: it gives no indication of any necessity for long and painstaking training, teaching simply the instantaneous enlightenment of the Five Buddhas; this teaching is unparalleled in all Buddhism. Bearing the above facts in mind, why do you regard Zazen as superior even to the extent of the exclusion of all other teachings?

Answer. The accent in Buddhism must always be placed on

the truth or inaccuracy of the actual training; the excellence, worthlessness, depth or shallowness of the teaching is of secondary importance. In olden times that which brought a man to Buddhism was the grass, flowers, mountains or streams; some received the Truth of the Buddha by taking dirt, stones, sand or grit in their hands: the Truth exceeds all forms so that even a speck of dust can preach a sermon. To say this mind is Buddha is like beholding the moon's reflection in water: to say that sitting cross-legged is, of itself, Buddhism is the same as seeing a figure in a mirror; do not become the victim of clever word manipulation. I advocate this training for instantaneous enlightenment because I wish to make a true being of you and so am showing you the highest Way that is Transmitted by the Buddhas and Ancestors. So as to Transmit the Buddha's Truth, you must find an enlightened teacher; do not simply follow some scholar who is concerned with the characters in which the Scriptures are written for this is the same as a blind man leading blind men; it is respect for those who are enlightened that sustains the Truth which is Transmitted by the Buddhas and Ancestors. When that which is worldly rejects the Zen master and the enlightened Arhats seek for the Way, the means of opening the Buddha Mind is provided, but the other teachings could not endure such a means of training. All that the followers of Buddhism have to do is study the Truth; understand clearly that the highest wisdom is to be found herein and that, although we may enjoy it for eternity, we will not always be in harmony therewith simply because we are self-opinionated and desirous of material gain; such things will hinder us in the Way. Ghosts arise as a result of being self-opinionated. Take, for example, the doctrine of dependent origination, the twenty-five worlds, the three vehicles, the five vehicles, the Buddha and no Buddha; all these things give rise to countless speculation but true training requires no knowledge whatsoever of these matters. Therefore, when sitting cross-legged allowing the Buddha Nature to manifest itself by giving up all opinions and cutting all ties, we enjoy great wisdom quite naturally for we instantly enter into the world which lies beyond both delusion and enlightenment wherein there is no difference between the wise and the foolish. It is impossible for anyone who clutches words to reach this height.

Question 5. Enlightenment is to be found within the three styles of training and the methods of meditation within the six stages of enlightenment which all Bodhisattvas study from the commencement of their training without discriminating between the clever and the stupid; perhaps this Zazen is part of such training. Why do you insist that the Truth is contained in its entirety in Zazen?

Answer. This question results from giving the name "Zen" to the treasury of the Truth to be found in the unequalled teachings of Buddha, but this name was given to it in China and the east (Japan and Korea), never having even been heard of in India. When Bodhidharma stared at the wall in Shōrinji for nine years neither the priests nor laity there understood the Truth of the Buddha, simply regarding Bodhidharma as a teacher who insisted on the importance of sitting cross-legged yet, after him, every Ancestor has devoted himself to this cross-legged sitting. Those members of the laity with no knowledge of these matters, when first seeing the practitioners of Zazen, spoke of them as members of the Zazen School (Church) in such a nonchalant manner as to prove their complete lack of understanding of the Truth. Nowadays the prefix "za" has been dropped from the word and they who practice Zazen are called members of the Zen School (Church) as is clear from all the writings of the Ancestors. Do not put Zazen into the same category as that of the six stages and the three training styles.

The spirit of the Transmission is very clearly expressed in the life and work of the Buddha: only to Makakashyo, on Ryoju, did the Buddha Transmit the Truth and this was seen by only a few of the gods in heaven. Never doubt that the heavenly deities protect Buddhism for eternity—even to-day this is a true fact; understand clearly that Zazen is the whole of the Buddhist Way and is utterly incomparable.

Question 6. There are four main types of action; since this is so, why does Buddhism select cross-legged sitting as the only means to enlightenment?

Answer. It is not for me to analyse the Buddha's training methods for the purpose of gaining enlightenment and neither should you. The Ancestors praised the method of sitting cross-legged and called it the comfortable way; I myself know that, of the four actions, this is the most comfortable. You should understand clearly that it is not merely the training method of one or two Buddhas but of all of them.

Question 7. For those who, as yet, know nothing of Buddhism, enlightenment must be obtained through the means of Zazen and training, but of what use is Zazen to someone who has already clearly reached enlightenment?

Answer. I may not speak of last night's dreams or give tools to a wood-cutter but I still have something which I can teach to you. It is heretical to believe that training and enlightenment are separable for, in Buddhism, the two are one and the same. Since training embraces enlightenment, the very beginning of training contains the whole of original enlightenment; as this is so, the teacher tells his disciples never to search for enlightenment outside of training since the latter mirrors enlightenment. Since training is already enlightenment, enlightenment is unending; since enlightenment is already training there can be no beginning (and no end) whatsoever to training. Both Shakyamuni and Makakashyo were used by training, which was enlightenment, and Bodhidharma and Daikan Enō were moved by it in the same way; such signs of Transmission are usual in Buddhism for training is inseparable from enlightenment. Since, from the very beginning, training Transmits enlightenment, original enlightenment is gained naturally. Both the Buddhas and Ancestors insisted upon the necessity of intense training in order that enlightenment may be kept pure, being identical with training itself. If you do not cling to training, your hand will be full of enlightenment; if you do not cling to enlightenment, your whole body will be filled with training. In many parts of China I saw Zen monasteries in which there were from five hundred to a thousand two hundred trainees practicing Zazen both day and night in their Meditation Halls. Whenever I asked those Zen teachers who had been entrusted with the Truth what the Truth of Buddhism was, they all said that training and enlightenment were inseparable and they urged their followers to continue in the path of their teachers since it was that which was taught by the Buddhas and Ancestors. They advocated Zazen for all seekers of the True Way, irrespective of whether or not they were advanced or just beginning, wise or foolish, and not merely taught it to their disciples. Nangaku once said that it is untrue that there is no training and no enlightenment but, should you cling to them, they will become sullied. Another Ancestor also said that anyone who sees the Way also trains in it, therefore it is essential that you train within enlightenment.

Question 8. Why did the former Japanese Ancestors, on returning from China, propagate teachings other than this one of Zen?

Answer. The former Ancestors did not propagate, or Transmit, Zen because the time for doing so had, as then, not yet arrived.

Question 9. Did the former Ancestors understand Zen?

Answer. Had they understood it, they would have propagated it.

Question 10. It was once said that one should not throw away delusion for, since the spirit is eternal, there is an easy way of becoming free of birth and death: this means that although the body may be condemned to birth and death, yet the spirit is immortal. Should this spirit, which has neither beginning nor end, reside within me, then it is the true original spirit and my body takes a physical, unmoving shape, dying here and resurrecting there; the spirit, being eternal, is unchanging from the past to the future; if one knows this, one is free of birth and death. When one knows this, birth and death vanish and the ocean of the spirit is entered; should you become one with this ocean, your virtue will be as that of Buddha. Since your body is the result of your former delusions, however, you will not be the same as the wise even should you know the above facts; should you not know them, you will be doomed to eternal transmigration. Because of this, it is essential to know nothing more than the eternity of the spirit; there is no hope for you even if you sit and waste your entire life in doing so. Is not this the opinion of the Buddhas and Ancestors?

Answer. This opinion is not Buddhist, being the Srenika heresy. This heresy teaches that there is knowledge of the spirit within our bodies and, because of this, we can differentiate between like and dislike, right and wrong, pleasure and suffering, pain and enjoyment. When the body dies this spiritual knowledge leaves it to be reborn in another one, therefore, although it may seem to die in one place, it is reborn elsewhere and thus, never dying, is eternal. If you believe in this heresy, believing it to be Buddhism, you are as stupid as someone who holds tiles and pebbles believing them to be gold: it is a shamefully foolish idea and not worthy of any serious thought. Echū gave a very grave warning about this heresy:

people who believe in it think that the mind is eternal whilst form is passing and they say that this is equal to the training of the Buddhas; by so doing they think they have freed themselves from birth and death but they are merely perpetuating it; such an opinion is not only untrue but piteous; you must not listen thereto. I should not say this, however, being sorry for you, I wish to cure your delusion:– Buddhism teaches that the body and mind are one as are spirit and form; this is known clearly throughout both India and China. When a teaching speaks of eternity, all is eternal, so body and mind must not be separated: when a teaching speaks of cessation, all things cease, so spirit and form must not be separated. It is contrary to the Truth to say that the body dies whilst the mind lives eternally; understand clearly that life and death are Nirvana itself and that we cannot speak of Nirvana without life and death. You are completely wrong if you think that the wisdom of the Buddhas is free from life and death: your mind knows and sees, comes and goes and is not eternal in any way; you must understand this completely for Buddhism has always maintained that body and mind are one. Taking this into consideration, why should the mind be released from birth and death whilst the body is fettered by it? Should you insist that body and mind are one at one time and not at another the teaching of the Buddha becomes unclear, and to think that birth and death should be avoided is clearly an error in Buddhism for they are truly the means by which Buddhism is taught. In the awakening of faith in Mahayana Buddhism the Buddha's treasury enfolds the causation of birth and death and does not divide reality and appearance or consider appearance and disappearance. Enlightenment is nothing other than the Buddha's treasury, being identical with, and containing, all things. All teachings are based upon that of the One Mind; make no mistake in this matter for this is to understand the Buddha Mind.

How is it possible to divide the Buddha Mind into mind and body, delusion and enlightenment? Already you are the child of Buddha so do not listen to the lunatics who teach heresy. *Question 11.* Must one who takes the practice of Zazen seriously keep the Precepts strictly and purify both body and mind?

Answer. The Buddhas and Ancestors have handed down the practice of strict observance of the Precepts and pure living as the rules governing Zen. Any who have not yet received the Precepts should do so at once, and they who have broken them should repent of their wrong doing; by so doing they may become one with the wisdom of the Buddhas.

Question 12. Is there any harm in a serious student of Zazen saying Shingon Mantras or practicing the peaceful illumination training of Tendai at the same time as doing Zazen?

Answer. When I was in China the teachers from whom I learned the Truth of Buddhism said that they had never heard of any Ancestor, either before or now, who had undergone such simultaneous training and then Transmitted the Truth of the Buddha. One should concentrate solely on one thing if one would understand the Truth.

Question 13. Can laymen practice Zazen or is it for priests alone?

Answer. All Ancestors who have clearly understood Buddhism have taught that there is no difference between the Zazen of a man or a woman, a rich person or a poor one.

Question 14. Since the priests have no ties there is nothing in the way of their practicing Zazen, but how can a busy layman do serious training in order to reach enlightenment?

Answer. The gates of compassion have been opened wide by the Buddhas and Ancestors out of their limitless love for all living things, whether they be men or gods; there are innumerable examples right from the beginning up to now. The state officials Tan-tsung and Sung-tsung were both extremely busy with affairs of government but they penetrated the Way of the Buddhas and Ancestors through the practice of Zazen; the prime minister Li, and the other prime minister Fang, did the same thing at the same time as being the emperor's counsellors: everything depends upon the will of the person involved and has nothing whatsoever to do with being either a layman or a priest. If one can distinguish between excellence and mundaneness, one can believe in Buddhism naturally. A person who believes that worldly work is a hindrance to Buddhism knows only that no Buddhism exists in the world for nothing whatsoever in Buddhism can be set apart as a worldly task. Prime minister P'ing, of China, wrote the following poem after becoming one with the Way of the Ancestors:–

> When not engaged in affairs of state, I practiced Zazen to such an extent that I hardly ever slept;
> My fame as a Zen master spread throughout the world in spite of the fact that I am prime minister.

P'ing was very busy with official business, but his determination to train was earnest and so he became one with enlightenment. Think of your own situation in the light of the situation of these people from the past. In China, even now, the emperor, ministers, soldiers and people, both men and women, are interested in the Way of the Ancestors; both warriors and scholars have the will to train themselves and many will understand the Truth; all these people's lives tell us clearly that worldly work is no hindrance whatsoever to Buddhism. Whenever true Buddhism is spread in any country the Buddhas and heavenly deities protect it and the whole world becomes peaceful; whenever the world is peaceful, Buddhism becomes strong. Even criminals, who heard the Buddha's

teaching whilst He lived, were enlightened, and those who
hunted or chopped wood were enlightened under the Ancestors; all you have to do to realise enlightenment is to hear the
instructions of a true teacher.

Question 15. Is it still possible to gain enlightenment through
Zazen in the present degenerate times of this evil world?

Answer. Most teachings concern themselves with the names
and styles of the doctrines but the true teaching sees no difference in the three five-hundred-year periods. Anyone who
truly trains must definitely realise enlightenment and, within
the correctly Transmitted Truth, you may always thoroughly
enjoy the rarest of treasures which is to be found within your
own house. Anyone who trains knows whether or not he has
reached enlightenment in the same way as someone drinking
water knows for himself whether or not it is hot or cold.

Question 16. There are those who say that one has only to
understand the fact that this mind itself is the Buddha in order
to understand Buddhism and that there is no need to recite the
Scriptures or undergo bodily training. If you understand that
Buddhism is inherent within yourself you are already fully
enlightened and there is no necessity to seek for anything
further from anywhere. If this is so, is there any sense in taking the trouble to practice Zazen?

Answer. This is a very grievous mistake and, even if it
should be true, and the sages teach it, it is impossible for you
to understand it: if you would truly study Buddhism, you must
transcend all opinions of subject and object. If it is possible
to be enlightened simply by knowing that the self is, in its self
nature, the Buddha, then there was no need for Shakyamuni
to try so diligently to teach the Way: this fact is proved by the
high standards maintained by the old teachers. Once a Zen
teacher named Hōgen asked his disciple, "How long have you
been in this temple?" "Three years," replied the disciple.

"Since you are younger than I, why do you never question me concerning Buddhism?" asked Hōgen. "I cannot lie to you," said the disciple, "but, whilst studying with my former master, I understood Buddhism." "From what words did you get your understanding?" Hōgen asked. "I asked, 'What is the True Self of a trainee?' and he answered, 'The god of fire is calling for fire.'" "That is excellent," said Hōgen, "but I doubt if you understood it." "Fire belongs to the god of fire," replied the disciple, "and fire needs fire; it is the same as saying that self needs self." "You obviously did not understand it at all," said Hōgen, "for, if Buddhism is thus, it could never have continued until the present time." The disciple was deeply perturbed and left the temple however, whilst on his way home, he thought, "Hōgen has five hundred disciples and is a very excellent teacher. Since he has pointed out my mistake, there must be some value in what he says." He returned to Hōgen's temple and, repenting his former behaviour, greeted Hōgen and asked, "What is the True Self of the trainee?" Hōgen replied, "The god of fire is calling for fire." The disciple became completely enlightened at hearing this. It is obvious that one cannot understand Buddhism simply by knowing that the self is the Buddha for, if this were Buddhism, Hōgen could never have shown the Way to his disciple in the way he did nor could he have given him the above advice. When you first visit a teacher, you should ask for the rules of training, then practice Zazen earnestly. Do not becloud your mind with useless knowledge; only then will the unequalled Way of Buddhism bear fruit.

Question 17. Both in India and China, from the beginning of time to the present day, some Zen teachers were enlightened by such things as the sound of stones striking bamboos whilst the colour of plum blossoms cleared the minds of others; the great Shakyamuni was enlightened at the sight of the morning star, whilst Ananda understood the Truth through seeing a stick fall. As well as these, many Zen teachers of the five churches after the Sixth Ancestor were enlightened by only so much as a word: did all of them practice Zazen?

Answer. From olden times down to the present day, all who were ever enlightened, either by colours or sounds, practiced Zazen without Zazen and became simultaneously enlightened.

Question 18. The men of India and China had integrity and, culture being universal, were able to understand Buddhism when they were taught. From early times in our country, how-ever, men have been wanting in fine intellect and so it has been difficult for the Truth to take root; this is indeed very unfortunate and is caused by the barbarianism amongst us— there is also the fact that the priests here are inferior to the laymen of other countries. Everyone in Japan, being foolish and narrow-minded, clings tightly to worldly rank and is hun-gry only for things that are superficial. Is it possible that such people can reach enlightenment quickly just by practicing Zazen?

Answer. All this is as you say for the people here have neither knowledge nor integrity and, even if they should see the Truth, they change its sweetness to poison: they look for fame and gain and have difficulty in freeing themselves from clinging. However, in order to become enlightened, it is not possible to rely upon the worldly knowledge of either men or gods. Whilst the Buddha lived there were various stupid and crazy persons who worked for enlightenment by various means and later found the True Way to freeing themselves from delu-sions as a result of True Faith. One female trainee, who waited with a cooked meal for a foolish old priest, was enlightened simply by observing his silent sitting. None of the above-mentioned enlightenments depended on knowledge, schol-arship, characters or sayings; every one of them points to the necessity of being helped by True Faith in Buddhism. Buddhism has spread to various countries during the last two thousand years and it appeals to other people besides the cultured, clever and rich, for Truth, with its inherent power for good, spreads naturally throughout the world when given the chance. Anyone who trains with True Faith will be enlightened equally with everybody else without differentiation between the clever or the stupid. Do not think that because Japan is a country of low culture and uneducated people it is unready for Buddhism; all beings have an abundance of the Seed of Truth but few people know this fact. They do not train with True Faith since they have no adequate recognition of Buddhist Truth and no experience in applying it.

Perhaps these questions and answers may seem unnecessary, however I have tried to help those with poor eyes to see blossoms where none were beforehand. As yet the core of Zazen has not been Transmitted in Japan and those who wish to know it are thereby made unhappy. Because of this, when in China, I collected all that I saw and heard, wrote down what the masters taught and, with all this, wish to help those who are in search of training; I also want to teach the rules and ceremonies to be found in the temples but have no time to do so for they cannot be described in simplified form. Buddhism came from the west (i.e. China) to Japan around the time of the emperors Kinmei and Yomei, although we are far from India, and its coming was indeed fortunate for us; however, as a result of names, forms, objects and relationships, many knots are created and the way of training is lost.

From now I will take my simple robe and bowl and dwell amongst the reed-clothed rocks: whilst I sit and train here true Zen Buddhism, which transcends even the Buddha, appears naturally and thus the end of training is brought to fulfillment— this is the teaching of the Buddha and the method bequeathed by Makakashyo. The rules for Zazen are to be found in the *Fukanzazengi* which I wrote during the Karoku period. In order to propagate Buddhism in any country, one must obtain the permission of the ruler thereof; many kings, ministers and generals appeared, as a result of the Buddha's Transmission on Mount Ryoju, and these were grateful for the Buddha's guidance as well as being mindful of the spirit which has always pervaded Buddhism since the beginning. Wherever the teachings have been spread is the Buddha's own country so there is no sense whatsoever in carefully choosing some special place, time or condition when propagating them: it is wrong to think that to-day is just the beginning. I have made and left this record for those True seekers of the Way, the True Trainees, who wander from place to place in search of the Truth.

SHŌJI.
LIFE AND DEATH.

There are no life and death when the Buddha is within them; when there is no Buddha within life and death we are not deluded by them. These sayings are those of two great Zen teachers, Gasan and Tōzan respectively, and they must be considered very seriously, as well as clearly understood, by all who wish to become free from birth and death. Should a man seek the Buddha outside of life and death he is as one who turns his cart to the north whilst heading for Esshū, or as one who tries to see the north star whilst looking southwards: by so doing, that which is the cause of life and death will be increased and the way to freedom lost sight of.

Should it be possible for us to understand that life and death are, of themselves, nothing more than Nirvana, there is obviously no need to either try to escape from life and death or to search for Nirvana and, for the first time, freedom from life and death becomes possible. Do not make the mistake of believing that a change takes place between life and death, for life is simply one position in time, already possessing both before and after: because of this Buddhism says that life, as we know it, is not life. Likewise, death is simply one position in time, with a before and an after, therefore death itself is not death. When called life, there is only life; when called death, there is only death; if life comes, it is life; if death comes, it is death: there is no reason whatsoever for a being to be controlled by either and hope should not be put within them. This very life and death is the Buddha's Own Life and, should you try to escape from them, you will lose the Life of the Buddha in escaping therefrom: should you do this all you will be doing is clutching at the apparition of Buddha but, if you neither refuse, nor search for, this life, you will enter immediately into the Buddha Mind.

Do not, under any circumstances, try to understand this intellectually or give it expression in words. If you allow your concern for, and attachment to, the body and mind to fall away naturally, you will precipitate yourself into the realm of Buddha. When the Buddha does all, and you follow this doing effortlessly and without worrying about it, you gain freedom from suffering and become, yourself, Buddha.

Since the above is so, what is there to hinder you within your own mind? The Way to Buddhahood is easy. They who do not perpetrate evil, they who do not try to grasp at life and death but work for the good of all living things with utter compassion, giving respect to those older, and loving understanding to those younger, than themselves, they who do not reject, search for, think on or worry about anything have the name of Buddha: you must look for nothing more.

UJI.
THE THEORY OF TIME.

It was Yakusan who said the following, "To stand upon a mountain-peak is existence, time, flow; to descend to the depth of the ocean is existence, time, flow; Avalokitesvara Bodhisattva is existence, time, flow; a Buddha who is ten or eight feet tall is existence, time, flow; the staff and the hossu are existence, time, flow; the post and the lantern are existence, time, flow; your next-door neighbour and yourself are existence, time, flow; the whole earth and the limitless sky are existence, time, flow." This existence, time, flow, means simply that time itself is existence and all existence itself is time. The golden body of the Buddha is time: since all is time, time is expressed in all things and they become, as it were, its ornamentation: it is, therefore, imperative that we study the twelve hours now in front of us. The body of Avalokitesvara Bodhisattva is exhibited through the aegis of time, and this body permeates the present twelve hours: although we have not yet measured this twelve hours, we still call it twelve hours; it is because the passing of time leaves behind the signs of its passage that we do not doubt its existence, even although we do not understand it. Since the average man is not in the habit of profound thought he doubts all things of which he has no full understanding; because of this his future doubts are out of harmony with his present ones but even doubt itself is only a part of time.

The author ringing the great bell of Dai Hon Zan Sōjiji when in training. The bell tells the hours of 11 A.M. and 3 P.M.; between these hours visitors may enter the monastery.

Outside of this doubting self no world exists for the world actually is this very self: all things in this world must be regarded as time and all things are in the same unhindered relationship, one with the other, as in each moment of time. Because of this the longing for enlightenment arises naturally as a result of time and, as a result of mind, time arises also; in addition to this, training and enlightenment also arise so, from this, it is clearly seen that the self itself is time itself.

Since the above is true it is important for us to learn that, upon this earth, many things appear and many forms of grass exist, and that each thing that appears, and each grass, is in no way separate from the whole earth. It is after reaching this viewpoint that we can commence training for, having reached this point in our journey's end, but one thing appears and one grass remains. Sometimes that which appears is recognised and again not always; there are times when the grass is recognised and again not always. Because there is only time of this description, *uji* is all of time, existence, flow and every single grass, and everything that appears, are also time, existence, flow; all existences, and all worlds, are present in each and every moment. Just think; is there any existence, or world, that is apart from time?

The average person, with no knowledge of Buddhism, thinks as follows when he hears the word *uji*, "There was a time when Buddha was active as Avalokitesvara Bodhisattva, and there was a time when he was ten or eight feet tall when crossing the rivers and climbing the mountains; we too have passed over these rivers and mountains and now dwell in this lordly mansion; mountains, rivers, heaven, earth and I are separate." Time is, however, far more than this for, when these mountains and rivers are passed over, not only I myself am present but so also is time. As I am now here time and I are one for, should time not include coming and departing, the eternal now is the very moment when the mountain is climbed. Should time include coming and departing then I am the eternal now and this, too, is *uji*. The time at which the mountain is climbed and the river crossed engulfs the time when I am within my lordly mansion; the time when I am within my lordly mansion is the time at which I cross the river and climb the mountain.

The three heads and eight arms of Avalokitesvara Bodhisattva are the time of yesterday whilst the time of being a Buddha eight or ten feet tall is that of to-day: yet what we say is yesterday and to-day is one and the same thing in the same way as, when looking at mountains, we see many peaks with only one glance. Time itself never flows for the Avalokitesvara Bodhisattva of yesterday passes on as our existence, time, flow; it appears to be elsewhere but it is actually here and now. The Buddha who is eight or ten feet tall, the one of to-day, passes on as our existence, time, flow, seeming again to be elsewhere but actually being here and now. Since the above is true, both the pine and the bamboo are time. Time does far more than merely fly away, there is much more to it than that: if all you can understand is that time flies you cannot understand *uji* for, by such understanding, what you have realised is something that is passing away.

In the end you will realise that all existences are joined together and are, themselves, time, my own, personal time; the chief trait of *uji* is continuity, going from to-day to to-morrow and from to-day to yesterday, from yesterday to to-day, to-day to to-day and from to-morrow to to-morrow. Since continuity is one of time's chief characteristics, neither past time nor present time accumulate: since there is no accumulation, Seigen, Ōbaku, Kōsei and Sekitō are all time. Since self and other are time, training and enlightenment are time also, as are the entering of mud and water. Although some say that the disinterested relationship of the views of the average person is what that person sees they are wrong for the Truth simply puts the average person into passing causal relationships. Since we learn that time and existence are not the Truth, we think that the golden body of the Buddha is not ours and we

try to free ourselves from this very fact of being the golden
body of the Buddha—and, even in this dire strait, we are still
uji as are also those who are not yet enlightened.

The hours of twelve and one follow each other in order
in the world as we know it and are made clear by the ascending and descending of seemingly fixed time: the hours of six
and eight are time as are also all living things and Buddhas.
The heavenly deities enlighten the world as Avalokitesvara
Bodhisattva through their three heads and eight arms; Buddhas do the same thing by means of their ten foot high golden
bodies. If one can transcend motion and rest, the world has
been fully entered; the signs of becoming a True Buddha are
shown whilst searching, attaining, knowing enlightenment and
experiencing Nirvana, and these are all existence, time, flow:
there is absolutely nothing more than the careful studying of
time as existence. Since delusion is delusion, existence, time,
flow, which is not properly studied, is the study of only half
existence, time, flow; even a body that is incorrectly seen is
existence, time, flow and, should you do nothing to remedy
the mistake, enfolding both the before and the after thereof,
it is still existence, time, flow: to work without restraint in
one's own environment is existence, time, flow. Do not waste
time believing the above to be trivial and, at the same time,
do not spend hours intellectualising about it. It is believed by
most that time passes however, in actual fact, it stays where
it is: this idea of passing may be called time but it is an incorrect one for, since one only sees it as passing, one cannot understand that it stays just where it is. However is it possible for
persons holding this view to find freedom? Who is able to give
expression to this freedom even supposing that they could
understand fully that time stays as it is? Even should you be
able to give expression to your understanding after many years
you will still be unaware of your original face for, should you

think of existence, time, flow in the usual way, both wisdom and enlightenment merely become things that simply appear in the arising and departing of time.

Free of all craving, existence, time, flow manifests itself sometimes here and sometimes there; the kings of heaven and their servants are not apart from the arising of existence, time, flow and all beings, whether on land or in the sea, come forth therefrom. Existence, time, flow gives rise to all things, whether they be good or evil, and their arising is the very process of time, nothing whatsoever being apart therefrom. It is wrong to think that continuity goes from east to west in the manner of a storm; words are neither unmoving nor standing still and this is an example of continuity. Spring, too, is the same as this for therein certain events take place which are spoken of as continuity; if you can understand that nothing whatsoever exists outside of this continuity, you can understand that spring is always spring. Understand that continuity is perfected in springtime as the actual continuity of spring: the average person thinks that continuity is a passing through many worlds and lives but this opinion is clearly obtained through inadequate training.

When advised by Sekitō, Yakusan visited Basō and said, "I have studied almost all of the teachings of the Three Vehicles. Why did the Ancestor come from the west?" "There are times when I make the Buddha raise His eyebrows and blink," replied Basō, "and there are times when I do not do so. There are times when it is good for Him to do these things and times when it is not. What do you think?" Yakusan was immediately enlightened and said, "When I was in Sekitō's temple I was as a mosquito who was trying to bite a bull made of iron." Basō is trying to say something rather different from what most others say for the raising of the eyebrows is the mountain and the ocean. Since the mountain and the ocean are the raising of the eyebrows, you must see truly the real mountain, in its actual form, if you would perform this act and, if you want to understand the meaning of the blink, the ocean must truly appear before your eyes. The opposites are familiar to each other; action and non-action are one. That which is not good is not necessarily of no use for all is existence, time, flow; if this were not so, there would be neither ocean nor mountain. It is impossible to say that time does not exist for the mountain and the ocean are in the absolute present: should time decay, so will the mountain and the ocean; if it does not do so then neither will they: because of this fact both eyes and picked flowers appear and this is existence, time, flow; if it were not so then all the above is not so.

Shōzan's disciple, Isan, once said to the trainees, "There are times when the will is adequate but words are not; there are times when words are adequate and the will is not; there are times when both words and will are adequate and times when neither are so." Both will and words are existence, time, flow; adequacy and inadequacy are existence, time, flow. When it is adequate, it is unfinished; when it is inadequate, it is already completed; will is (stubborn) like a donkey and words (jump and gallop about) like a horse; words, (to many, imply) horse (behaviour) and will, (to many, implies) donkey (behaviour); existence, time, flow is as this. They travel fastest who are not there since arrival is hindered by arrival but quite definitely not hindered whilst on the journey: the journey is hindered by non-arrival but not hindered by arrival. It is by means of the will that we understand the will; it is by means of words that we understand words: by being hindered we understand hindrance and hindrance is hindered by hindrance; this too is existence, time, flow. Other things may use hindrance and no hindrance whatsoever can use other things: people meet me; they meet each other; myself meets me and exit meets exit; these things could not be if existence, time, flow was not shared by all. The kōan in daily life is will; words are its key; adequacy is oneness; inadequacy is duality and each of these, will, words, adequacy and inadequacy, are themselves existence, time, flow. This must be both understood and experienced.

These things have been said many times by the Zen teachers of old but it is necessary for me to repeat them. Both will and words that go only half-way are existence, time, flow; those that do not even reach half-way are existence, time, flow: in such a way as this should study be undertaken. To make the Buddha raise His eyebrows and blink is half of existence, time, flow; to make the Buddha raise His eyebrows and blink is all of existence, time, flow; not to do so is half of existence, time, flow; not to do so is all of existence, time, flow: both to study and experience this, and not to study and experience this, are existence, time, flow.

GENJŌ-KŌAN.
THE PROBLEM OF EVERYDAY LIFE.

Delusion, enlightenment, training, life, death, Buddhas and all living things are in existence when there is Buddhism; none of the above exist when all is within the Truth; since the Way of the Buddha transcends unity and duality, all of the above exist; whilst we adore flowers they wither; weeds grow strong whilst we long for their destruction. When we wish to teach and enlighten all things by ourselves, we are deluded; when all things teach and enlighten us, we are enlightened: to enlighten delusion is to become Buddha; most living things are deluded within enlightenment—some are enlightened within enlightenment; others deluded within delusion. There is no need to know that one is identical with Buddha when Buddha is truly Buddha for a truly enlightened Buddha expresses his Buddhahood in his daily life: to observe objects and voices, with complete awareness of body and mind, is very different from seeing a reflection in a mirror or the moon reflected in water; even if you see one side of something the other will still be in shadow.

When one studies Buddhism, one studies oneself; when one studies oneself, one forgets oneself; when one forgets oneself one is enlightened by everything and this very enlightenment breaks the bonds of clinging to both body and mind not only for oneself but for all beings as well. If the enlightenment is True it even wipes out clinging to enlightenment, therefore it is imperative that we return to, and live in, the world of ordinary men. When a man first sees the Truth he automatically transcends the boundaries of truth; once the Truth has been awakened within a man he is simultaneously his own Original Face. It is normal for a man, whilst sailing and observing the shore, to think that the shore is moving instead of the boat but, should he look carefully, he will find that it is the boat which is doing the actual moving: in the same way as this, it is because man observes everything from a mistaken viewpoint of his body and mind that he comes to the conclusion that they are eternal however, should he learn to observe them correctly, as a result of penetrating Truth, he will discover that no form whatsoever attaches itself substantially to anything. The wood that is burnt upon a fire becomes ashes; it does not again become wood; you must not think that wood comes first and ashes afterwards. You must clearly understand that a piece of burning wood has both a before and an after; however, in spite of the fact that it has before and after, it is cut off therefrom: ashes, however, have before and after: in the same way that wood does not again become wood after becoming ashes so, in the very same way, man is not reborn again as man after dying; it is therefore correct for Buddhism to say that life does not become death and equally true to say that death does not become life—the Buddha Himself constantly preached this. The two above views are called non-life and non-death. The two, life and death, are simply positions in time as are spring and winter; winter no more becomes spring than spring becomes summer. The moon reflected in water is the same as the enlightenment that a man can reach; the moon is not wetted by the water and the water does not become disturbed: however much light the moon may radiate, its reflection can still be seen in a puddle; in the same way, the full moon and the limitless sky may be seen reflected in a single dewdrop suspended from a grass-blade. Man is not restrained by enlightenment and the moon is not restrained by the water; man puts nothing in the way of enlightenment and the dewdrop puts nothing in the way of either the moon or the limitless sky; in addition to this, the deeper the moon's reflection, the higher the moon—the length of time of the reflection is in ratio to the depth of the water and the fullness of the moon.

When a man has an incomplete knowledge of the Truth he feels that he already knows enough and when he has understood the Truth fully he feels sure that something is lacking. If you can see no land or mountains, when sailing, the ocean appears rounded but it is neither round nor square being in possession of a myriad characteristics. Some people regard it as a palace and others as a form of ornamentation but it is only for a very short time that it appears round owing to the distance we are able to see; this distance is constantly changing; we must view all things bearing this in mind. There are many things within the world of enlightenment but the Zen trainee can only see as far as his present understanding permits him.

If one would know the Truth, it is essential to know that the ocean and the mountains have many other attributes, in addition to being square or circular, and that there are many other worlds in addition to this. Our immediate surroundings are of no account: it is essential to know that the ocean is contained within a single drop of water and that the Truth is manifesting itself eternally on the very spot on which we are now standing.

The ocean is limitless no matter how far fish may swim therein; the sky is limitless no matter how far a bird may fly therein: from the very beginning of all things, both the fish and the birds have been one with the ocean and the sky respectively. Understand clearly that, when a great need appears, a great use appears also; when there is small need, there is small use; it is obvious, then, that full use is made of all things at all times according to the necessity thereof. When birds are out of unity with the sky, or fish out of unity with the ocean, they die, for the life of fish is lived in the ocean and the life of birds is lived in the sky: it is equally true that the life of the sky is lived in the birds and the life of the ocean is lived in the fish; birds are life and fish are life—it is easily possible to find many examples of the above idea. In spite of the facts of training and enlightenment, and variations in the length of a man's life span, all ways of living are the very personification of Truth: should a fish try to go beyond the limitations of the ocean, however, or a bird beyond the limitations of the sky there will be no resting-place for either.

Should you touch the Truth your every action will be vital and express the Way naturally for your every action will be fully understood and digested Truth performed in the ordinary daily activities of an ordinary man. This Truth can never be understood as a result of conceptual duality such as big and small or subject and object; the Way of Truth existed from the very beginning and makes no special appearance now,

The author being ordained in Malaysia by the Very Rev. Seck Kim Seng, Abbot of Cheng Hoon Teng Temple, a Rinzai monastery in Malacca. After this she went to study in Japan and became the disciple of the Very Rev. Kohō Keidō Chisan Zenji under whom she received the Transmission and the right to teach.

which is just as it should be. It is because the Way of Truth is as stated above that, after taking up one thing, you understand that one thing and, after finishing a practice, you understand that practice; this is the way in which Buddhism itself is practiced. It is not possible for us to know clearly when we are giving deep expression to the Way of Truth since it is an action which arises simultaneously and synonymously with Buddhist study.

It is wrong to believe that one is fully aware of being enlightened, as personal knowledge, even after enlightenment: that which is intuitive cannot necessarily be given easy expression and definite form even though enlightenment is already ours. One summer day a Zen teacher sat fanning himself when a monk asked, "Since the nature of wind is stationary and universally present, why do you use a fan?" The teacher replied, "Although you know its nature to be stationary, you do not know why it is universally present." "Why is it universally present?" asked the monk: for answer the teacher merely continued fanning himself and the monk bowed: the True Way of Transmission and enlightenment, which is the result of real experience, is the same as this. One who thinks that fanning is not needed, simply because wind is stationary by nature and requires no fan since it can be sensed, understands nothing whatsoever of its nature and its eternal presence: it is because it is eternally here that the wind of Buddhism makes the earth golden and the rivers run with ghee.

KYŌJUKAIMON.

GIVING AND RECEIVING THE
TEACHING OF THE PRECEPTS.

Preceptor:–

The Great Precepts of the Buddhas are kept carefully by the Buddhas; Buddhas give them to Buddhas, Ancestors give them to Ancestors. The Transmission of the Precepts is beyond the three existences of past, present and future; enlightenment ranges from time eternal and <u>is</u> even now. Shakyamuni Buddha, our Lord, Transmitted the Precepts to Makakashyo and he Transmitted them to Ananda; thus the Precepts have been Transmitted to me in the eighty-fifth generation. I am now going to give them to you, in order to show my gratitude for the compassion of the Buddhas, and thus make them the eyes of all sentient beings; this is the meaning of the Transmission of the Living Wisdom of the Buddhas. I am going to pray for the Buddha's guidance and you should make confession and be given the Precepts. Please recite this verse after me:–

Preceptor followed by congregation:–

All wrong actions, behaviour and karma, perpetrated by me from time immemorial, have been, and are, caused by greed, anger and delusion which have no beginning, born of my body, mouth and will; I now make full and open confession thereof.

Preceptor alone:–

Now, by the guidance of the Buddhas and Ancestors, we can discard and purify all our karma of body, mouth and will and obtain great immaculacy; this is by the power of confession.

You should now be converted to Buddha, Dharma and Sangha. In the Three Treasures there are three merits; the first is the true source of the Three Treasures; the second is the presence in the past of the Buddha; the third is His presence at the present time. The highest Truth is called the Buddha Treasure; immaculacy is called the Dharma Treasure; harmony is called the Sangha Treasure. The person who has realised the Truth really is called the Buddha Treasure; the Truth that is realised by Buddha is called the Dharma Treasure; the people who study the Dharma Treasure are called the Sangha Treasure. He who teaches devas and humans, appearing in the sky and in the world, is called the Buddha Treasure; that which appears in the world, in the Scriptures, and becomes good for others, is called the Dharma Treasure; he who is released from all suffering, and is beyond the world, is called the Sangha Treasure. This means that, when someone is converted to the Three Treasures, he can have the Precepts of the Buddhas completely: make the Buddha your teacher and do not follow wrong ways.

The Three Pure Precepts

Cease from evil.

This is the house of all the laws of Buddha; this is the source of all the laws of Buddha.

Do only good.

> The Dharma of the Samyaku Sambodai is the Dharma
> of all existence.

Do good for others.

> Be beyond both the holy and the unholy; let us rescue
> ourselves and others.

These three are called the Three Pure Precepts.

The Ten Great Precepts

Do not kill.

> No life can be cut off; the Life of Buddha is increas-
> ing; continue the Life of Buddha; do not kill Buddha.

Do not steal.

> The mind and its object are one; the gateway to enlight-
> enment stands open wide.

Do not covet.

> The doer, the doing and that which has the doing done
> to it are immaculate therefore there is no desire; it is
> the same doing as that of the Buddhas.

Do not say that which is not true.

> The wheel of the Dharma rolls constantly, lacks for noth-
> ing and needs something; the sweet dew covers the
> whole world and within it lies the Truth.

Do not sell the wine of delusion.

> There is nothing to be deluded about; if we realise this
> we are enlightenment itself.

Do not speak against others.

> In Buddhism the Truth, and everything, are the same; the
> same law, the same enlightenment and the same behav-
> iour. Do not allow any one to speak of another's faults;
> do not allow any one to make a mistake in Buddhism.

Do not be proud of yourself and devalue others.

> Every Buddha and every Ancestor realises that he is the
> same as the limitless sky and as great as the universe:
> when they realise their true body, there is nothing with-
> in or without; when they realise their true body, they are
> nowhere upon the earth.

Do not be mean in giving either Dharma or wealth.

> There is nothing to be mean with; one phrase, one verse,
> the hundred grasses, one Dharma, one enlightenment,
> every Buddha, every Ancestor.

Do not be angry.

> There is no retiring, no going, no Truth, no lie; there is
> a brilliant sea of clouds, there is a dignified sea of clouds.

Do not defame the Three Treasures.

> To do something by ourselves, without copying others,
> is to become an example to the world and the merit of
> doing such a thing becomes the source of all wisdom:
> do not criticise; accept everything.

These sixteen Precepts are thus.
Be obedient to the teaching and its giving; accept it with bows.

BOOK THREE.

THE TEACHINGS OF
KEIZAN ZENJI.

INTRODUCTION
TO THE TRANSLATIONS.

Keizan Zenji was born in Fukui Prefecture, in 1267, and entered Eiheiji, under Koun Ejō, at the age of twelve; thereafter he studied under Tetsu Gikai of the same temple. Much of his life was spent in establishing temples, in different parts of Japan, until he became Chief Abbot of Daijōji, in Ishikawa Prefecture, where he spent ten years teaching. In 1321, at the request of Jōken-risshi, he became Chief Abbot of Shōgakuji; he renamed this temple Shōgaku-zan Sōjiji. Sōjiji, which was made an Imperial Prayer Temple under Emperor Gō-Daigo (1318–1339), became one of the two head temples of the Sōtō Zen Church of Japan, ranking as equal with Eiheiji, and Keizan Zenji became the greatest of the Sōtō Zen Ancestors after Dōgen Zenji. The main ikon of the Sōtō Zen Church shows Shakyamuni Buddha at the top, in the centre, with Dōgen Zenji on His right hand and Keizan Zenji on His left, both being slightly below Him. Dōgen is regarded as the father of Sōtō Zen and Keizan as its mother.

Before Keizan's advent, Sōtō Zen had been confined to a few small monasteries, none of which were to be found in Kyoto, the spiritual centre of Japan at that time. As a result of Keizan's genius, Sōtō not only flourished but became the largest of all the Buddhist churches, eventually rivalling the Shin Church in later centuries.

Keizan Zenji's writings are highly intuitive. Whereas Dōgen was sometimes somewhat like a puritanical father, constantly exhorting his children to the utmost sincerity in their meditation, Keizan, as will be seen from the following translations, was an intuitive genius. Dōgen was also very intuitive but expressed it less directly.

Keizan's works include the *Denkōroku* and the *Sankonzazen-setsu*, as well as the majority, if not the entirety, of the ceremonies presently used in the Sōtō Zen Church. From the point of view of understanding Buddhism, however, his most important work, by far, is the *Denkōroku*, or *Transmission of the Light* (translated in *Selling Water by the River* under the title of, *Book of the Transmission*). This consists of fifty-two chapters, each one describing the particular kōan, and its solution, of each of the Ancestors from the time of, and including, Shakyamuni Buddha to the time of Dōgen. The chapters are very short and succinct: each commences with a description of the actual moment of solving the kōan, together with the kōan itself: then follows a short history of the Ancestor.

The most valuable asset of this book is the feeling of flowing movement that it inspires in the reader. In the original, past, present and future were always indicated by a *manji*, the symbol of movement that is beyond time and space. Thus, the feeling of flow, which is expressed in Dōgen's "Uji," is mystically, and practically, felt to exist within the whole being of the reader of Keizan's *Denkōroku* rather than understood with the head: to understand the *Denkōroku* you must know that time and space do not exist. Shakyamuni Buddha was, is and will be enlightened at all times and IS even now. The encompassing of past, present and future IS within the winking of an eye and, in Keizan's brilliant writing, it is possible for us to be one with the Lord of the House without the use of the intellect. In addition to getting us out of fixed time, by making it clear that everything is taking place in past, present and future at all times, every sentence (much of which may seem long to the American mind) was deliberately constructed so as to be both voice and echo. "One calls and one answers," say the Scriptures; in each sentence one half calls and the other half answers so that the sound of the voice of Buddha is always heard. It is not enough to know the voice; we must know the echo. It is not enough to know the now; we must know that this is the past and future as well and that all is contained within all. Further, we must be disturbed by the movement within the past, present and future, the constant going on, going on, going on which is not only made clear by the thread running through the kōan at the beginning of each chapter, but also by the thread running through the explanation in each chapter and that running through the poem at the end of each chapter. This book moves; if it does not cause you to move within your spirit, if it does not cause you to be disturbed by the Truth, you cannot understand it. It is the disturbance in stillness, and the stillness within disturbance, the blinking of the eyes and the raising of the eyebrows of Shakyamuni Buddha at all times from the beginning of all things to the end of eternity. You cannot know that you are turning a wheel from the far past to the present and to the future, so that there is nothing but the turning, you cannot understand the first kōan, "I was, am and will be enlightened simultaneously with the universe," unless you move in your heart at the very beginning and right through your life and eternity. Under no circumstances try to understand this book with your head.

Kohō Zenji asked that I work hard to bring out the meaning of the *Denkōroku* in English rather than make an academic translation. In many respects it is a lot easier to write such a book in a pictorial language such as Japanese rather than in western, alphabetised words but if, instead of reading to intellectualise about this, you just get into the flow and flow along with it, having first moved the wheel (manji) in the beginning, your heart will hear the voice and know the echo in each sentence. The book, as it is here presented, is in the form in which it was originally translated rather than as it was first published. (It took a long time to find a publisher that would print what was written rather than what they wanted to hear.) It is hoped that the reader will be able to find an affinity with one of the problems, or facets, of the eternal kōan which each of the Ancestors deals with in both the same, and different, ways: it is equally hoped that the reader will discover from this book that his problems, or kōans, are no different from those of the ancients and are but facets of the one eternal kōan.

The *Sankon-zazen-setsu* is a short work describing the three types of mind that result from the three types of meditation practice. It was many years before this manuscript was unearthed and, apart from one very poor translation, it has never before, as far as I know, appeared in the English language.

The ceremonies, formerly in Book Four, are now published separately. Many ceremonies were created by Keizan simply as an alternative form of meditation, i.e. meditation in activity. In order to bring home to the trainees of the time that all activity, of whatever form, was actually meditation if done with the correct mind, Keizan Zenji worked on perfecting ceremonial in daily life; however he achieved far more than merely teaching his trainees that all life's activities can be one with meditation. Through the magnificence of public ceremonies he was also able to reach the poorer classes who, having very little beauty in their lives, could nevertheless come to the temple and see something beautiful. Many of them were able to sublimate their work in the world and go beyond it, making every activity of their lives a meditative practice in the same way as did the trainees.

The details of the lives of Shakyamuni Buddha and the Ancestors, as presented by Keizan Zenji in the *Denkōroku*, are not historically accurate.

The following notes refer only to the *Denkōroku* and not to *Sankon-zazen-setsu*.

1. In order to help the reader to know intuitively the all is one and all is different of both before and after enlightenment and thus obtain the maximum help from this book, I am taking the unusual step of using different type styles here and there throughout it. For example, the name of the Buddha prior to enlightenment was Siddhartha Gautama: in the first chapter the word "Gautama" will always be in ordinary style type; the name "Shakyamuni," which refers only to the Buddha after enlightenment, will always be in italics in this chapter. One would think that the difference in the words would be sufficient to make this distinction clear but experience has shown me that this is not so.

2. Verbs, when referring to the state of enlightenment, appear in bold italics and are used in past, present and future form thus:– "When S*hakyamuni **saw, sees and will see** the morning star." Whenever these three tenses are used in any verb the reader should understand that what is being spoken of here is eternity as it is understood in Buddhism. Buddhist eternity, although it is the same as the eternity of other religions, is looked at from a slightly different viewpoint; I have laboured long to try and find how to put this viewpoint into words and have come to the conclusion that Keizan has done it (as above) in the best way I know. Past, present and future are eternity but be careful of getting stuck with the word "eternity."

3. In Chapter 1 of the *Denkōroku* when the word "I" appears in ordinary type face it refers to the old, egocentric "I;" the

apparent relationship of this "I" to the universe prior to enlightenment is expressed by "with." When both "I" and "with" appear in italics they refer to the non-egocentric state and an "at oneness" *with* the universe; I hesitate to say an "old I" and a "new I" because one immediately gets into opposites. The word "I," appearing in one form and then in another, somehow helps me to understand the change that takes place in a person as a result of Buddhist training.

4. When small capitals only are used, such as in the phrase "the Lord IS," those capitals imply absolute certainty of which there can be no shadow of the possibility of the shadow of the thought of a possibility of doubt; it implies a certainty so totally absolute that that certainty can only have come forth from the Lord of the House. In any sentence in which a word (or words) in this type occurs, that word (or words) should be understood as the most important word (or words) and any word (or words) in the same sentence that is underlined should be understood as the next most important word (or words), thus I am attempting to bring forth both meaning and emphasis. When one sees these small capitals, one should realise and know something that is beyond the opposites and for which there really is no suitable, one word. When "truth" is capitalised, for example, such TRUTH does not imply something that has an opposite but something beyond itself and its opposite (i.e. in a flowing, third position).

5. Only in the *Denkōroku* will books, scriptures, foreign terms, et cetera not be italicised. They will always be between single quotes.

6. I have used the term "the Lord" in such a way as would make it appear ambiguous; the reader should know that, whenever it is used, it is intended to imply not only identification of the Ancestor being spoken of with Shakyamuni

Buddha <u>but</u> also with the Unborn, Undying, Uncreated and Unchanging, thus making all one through the Transmission of the Light. Keizan is attempting, through the use of the words "the Lord," to show the all is one and all is different. The only way I know to try to make this clear to the reader is by making the term "the Lord" deliberately ambiguous as to who is being referred to in the text.

7. The poem at the end of each chapter should, at some time, be read in sequence with all the others; they will then be perceived as one long, Rolling of the Wheel of the Eternal.

DENKŌROKU.
TRANSMISSION OF THE LIGHT.

CHAPTER 1.

SHAKYAMUNI BUDDHA.

When *Shakyamuni **saw, sees and will see*** the morning star and ***was, is and will be enlightened***, He ***said, says and will say***, "***I was, am and will be enlightened*** instantaneously *with* the universe."

Shakyamuni Buddha belonged to the Nisshu race which is known in India as the Race of the Sun. At nineteen years of age He escaped from His castle, at midnight, and fled to Mount Dandokusen where He cut His hair; He then practiced asceticism for six years. For six years He sat still in one place with spiders' webs upon His brow and birds' nests in His hair; reeds grew between His legs and round Him, but He sat still for six years.

As the morning star rose on December eighth, He knew spiritual enlightenment and, for the first time, spoke the words quoted above; He was thirty years of age.

After that, for forty-nine years, He was never alone: there was never a day when He was not lecturing to His disciples nor was there a day when He had no begging bowl and robe. He lectured to as many as three hundred and sixty groups.

The last time He Transmitted the TRUTH was to Maka-kashyo and this Transmission has continued to the present time: indeed, all over India, China and Japan the training for TRUTH has come down to this day.

His sayings, actions and behaviour are the rule of His disciples. Even though He had the thirty-two marks of a Buddha, the good aspects and eighty appearances, He always had the form and appearance of an old monk; His form was no different from our own. Because of this, after Him, in the three five-hundred-year periods since His death known respectively as Shō, Zō and Matsu (i.e. in the three consecutive five-hundred-year periods), everyone who yearns for Him takes the same form as He; they take the Lord's way of life and do not set themselves up as better than He. Since *Shakyamuni Buddha's* time, every Buddha and every Ancestor has continued to Transmit the TRUTH constantly, this fact is very clear.

Although the various illustrations, facts and words which were pointed out, and lectured on, to the three hundred and sixty groups of people for forty-nine years were different, none were outside this TRUTH. The so-called egocentric "I" is not *Shakyamuni Buddha*; He is born out of this "I"—not only He is born out of it, the whole world and animate things are outside of it also. When *Shakyamuni **was, is and will be enlightened**,* the whole world and animate things ***were, are and will be enlightened*** just as the main rope has every branch rope connected with it: not only the whole world and animate things ***were, are and will be enlightened***, all Buddhas in the Triple Universe ***did apprehend, apprehend and will apprehend*** the TRUTH.

Although this is so, *Shakyamuni Buddha* is not conscious of being enlightened: do not look for the Lord outside the whole world, the ground and animate things. Everything in the universe is within the LORD'S EYES; you too are standing within them—not only are you within them, they <u>are</u> you: the LORD'S

EYES become a globule of your flesh and all is within all, standing straight, unruled by anything. Therefore, do not think that the LORD'S EYES are the LORD'S EYES and that you are you, constantly, unchanging. You *were, are and will be* the LORD'S EYES: the LORD is all of you. As this is so, what is the principle of enlightenment?

I ask of you this question:–

Were, are and will you *be enlightened* with *Shakyamuni Buddha* or *was, is and will Shakyamuni be enlightened* with you?

If it is said that you *were, are and will be enlightened* with *Shakyamuni*, or *Shakyamuni was, is and will be enlightened* with you, then this is not *Shakyamuni's* enlightenment and this cannot be the principle of enlightenment. If you want to understand the principle of enlightenment in detail, throw away *Shakyamuni* and you at the same time and know that they are "I." The *"I"* and *"with"* in *Shakyamuni's* first utterance *was, is and will be* the whole world, the universe and animate things; this *"I"* is not the old Gautama.

Study in detail, think fully and understand *"I"* and *"with."* Even if you can understand *"I,"* and you cannot realise *"with,"* you cannot understand fully; you see with only one eye.

The *"I"* and *"with"* are not one and two; your skin, flesh, bones and marrow are all *"with."* The LORD OF THE HOUSE is *"I;"* if you want to know the ETERNAL LORD OF THE HOUSE, you must not think of it as the whole world and animate things.

Although the LORD OF THE HOUSE is represented in spring, summer, autumn and winter, and although mountains, rivers and the ground are different in time, the LORD is represented fully in the world in the raising of the eyebrows and winking of the eyes of old *Shakyamuni*.

The LORD neither discards everything worldly nor does not discard it; Reverend Hōgen said, "There is no need to speak," and Reverend Jizō said, "WHAT is called everything?" Therefore practice in detail, realise fully and understand the enlightenment of *Shakyamuni* and that of yourself; understand this kōan fully: speak from your own heart without borrowing the words of the Ancestors and your contemporaries: the answer should be shown to me at our next meeting.

Do you want to hear my humble words?

> The branch of an old plum tree grows straight;
> Its thorns spread with time.

CHAPTER 2.

THE FIRST ANCESTOR, SAINT MAKAKASHYO.

Then the Sainted Shakyamuni, the most respectable Person in this whole world, took a flower and winked; Makakashyo smiled. Shakyamuni said that the Truth was within him and Transmitted Makakashyo.

Saint Makakashyo, the respectable, belonged to the Brahmin race; his Indian name was Kashapa which means "Light-Drinker."

When he was born the room was filled with golden light and the light entered his mouth; because of this he was called the Light-Drinker. His body was golden and had thirty of the good aspects; only the cupola on the top of his head, and the white hair curling to the right on his brow, were missing.

He met the Sainted Shakyamuni, for the first time, before Tashi Tower, that is, the Tower of Many Sons. The Sainted One said, "Welcome, monk," and immediately

Makakashyo's hair and beard fell out and a kesa was placed upon his body.

Having received the Transmission of the TRUTH, Makakashyo practiced the Twelve Zuda, the ways by which we can control worldly desire and let the MIND OF TRUTH show itself; he never passed a day idly or in vain, but so haggard was his shape, and so coarse were his clothes, that everyone wondered what he was. Therefore, whenever Shakyamuni, the Sainted One, lectured, He gave half of His seat to Makakashyo to sit upon; from that time he was always the highest senior: he was thus at all times—not only at the lecture meetings of Shakyamuni but also at the ones of the past Buddhas; you should know he was an excellent Buddha; do not let him be among the shōmon who are beneath the Bodhisattvas.

At the meeting on Mount Ryoju, before eighty thousand people, Shakyamuni took a flower and winked: most people cannot realise the meaning of this and are silent; only Makakashyo smiled. Shakyamuni said, "I have the RIGHT LAW; the EXCELLENT NIRVANA, MIND, the round and clear LAW which has no aspects. Now I have Transmitted IT to great Makakashyo."

The so-called "taking of a flower" has come down to this time, being Transmitted from one Ancestor to another: those who are not Transmitted cannot understand it nor can the teachers of Scriptures and logic; I KNOW they have no understanding that is real—as this is so, this is not the kōan at the Ryozen meeting but the one at the Tashi Tower; it is wrong to say that this is the kōan at the Ryozen meeting as it does in the 'Dentōroku' and 'Futoroku.' When Buddhism was Transmitted for the first time there was the ceremony described above.

Leave the "taking of a flower" as it is; you should understand Shakyamuni's wink clearly. There is no difference between your ordinary wink and Shakyamuni's; further, there is no difference between your talking and smiling and Makakashyo's talking and smiling: however, if you do not really understand WHAT raised its brow and winked, you are thinking that there is a difference between Shakyamuni and Makakashyo in India and you, and that you are in a restricted body: the flower is beclouding your eyes, like vapour from the summer sun, both from the far past to the limitless future. If you can really catch the LORD, Makakashyo will live in you; did you know that when Shakyamuni raised His brow and winked He had disappeared? Further, did you know that when Makakashyo smiled he had been enlightened? Then is this fact not universal? In the same way as this, the TRUTH has been Transmitted to us, therefore we can call it neither Makakashyo nor Shakyamuni.

There is nothing to give or to be given; this is called the Right Law. By taking a flower Shakyamuni showed that TRUTH *was, is and will be* eternal and by smiling He pointed out that it *was, is and will be* endless: because of this, in seeing each other face to face, the LIFE OF THE TRUTH has come down from master to disciple to this time.

So, having perfect wisdom without worldly knowledge, and cutting off his intellection, Makakashyo entered Mount Kukkutapada where he *was, is and will be waiting* for Miroku; therefore Makakashyo is not dead.

If you can really understand, and practice, the TRUTH, not only Makakashyo is eternal but Shakyamuni is eternal also; therefore the TRUTH, which *was, is and will be Transmitted* from the far past when no one was born, is spreading constantly all over the past, present and future.

Do not yearn for two thousand years ago; at the present time, if you practice the TRUTH wholeheartedly, Makakashyo will not enter Mount Kukkutapada; he can come here.

Therefore the warm flesh of Shakyamuni is now and always here and the smiling of Makakashyo is now and always new; if you can find this spiritual place, you can accept the Truth directly from Makakashyo and Makakashyo will accept it from you: not only can the VERY TRUTH pass through to you from the Seven Buddhas—you will discover that you *were, are and will be* the ancestor of the Seven Buddhas. The VERY TRUTH is now here, eternally, beyond all ages: therefore SHAKYAMUNI ACCEPTED MAKAKASHYO'S TRANSMISSION and is now in Tosotsuten; YOU are now at the Ryozen meeting and unchangeable. Do you not know the poem:–

> Constantly I am at the Ryozen meeting throughout endless ages;
> Even should there be a great fire, my heart is always safe and calm and filled with angels.

India, China, Japan and the whole world must be included in the Ryozen meeting; the TRUTH OF THE LORD comes to us unchanged—since this is so, this meeting must be the Ryozen meeting and the Ryozen meeting must be this one; only when you concentrate your mind will Buddhas appear. Because of your ignorance about yourself, Shakyamuni died long ago; you are the children of Buddha; why do you kill Buddha?

If you are in a hurry to practice the Truth, soon you can meet Buddha; in daily life Shakyamuni *was, is and will be walking, stopping, sitting, lying down, talking and seeing* by, in, through and with you and is not separate from you even for a moment, being all of you.

If you cannot see Him all through your life, you must be an undutiful being—already you *were, are and will be* the children of Buddha but, if you are undutiful, a thousand Buddhas cannot help you.

To-day, do you want to hear my humble words?

Did you not know that, at the edge of a deep valley,
    there is an excellent pine tree
Growing up straight in spite of the many years of cold?

CHAPTER 3.

THE SECOND ANCESTOR,
SAINT ANANDA.

Ananda asked Makakashyo, "My dear senior, what did
Shakyamuni Transmit to you besides His kesa of gold brocade?" Makakashyo called, "Ananda." Ananda replied,
"Yes?" Makakashyo said, "Chop down the flagpole." Ananda
was enlightened.

Saint Ananda was born in Osha Castle; he belonged to
the Kshatriya race: his father was King Kokubon, a cousin of
Shakyamuni; he was named Ananda which means "Joy." He
was born on the same night that Gautama was enlightened;
he had classical features and no one in the sixteen neighbouring countries could be compared with him for looks: everyone who saw him was pleased; because of this he was so named.
He was the cleverest, and the most learned, among the disciples of Shakyamuni and, because of this, he passed twenty
years as Buddha's jiisha; there was not one of the Buddha's
lectures at which he did not act as interpreter; there was not
one of the Buddha's ways that he did not learn. At the same
time that Shakyamuni Transmitted the TRUTH to Makakashyo
He ordered Ananda to help him; Ananda therefore obeyed
Makakashyo for a further twenty years; there was no TRUTH

in him that was not Transmitted. Here is the proof that the TRUTH of our Ancestors is different from the truth of others; Ananda was already the cleverest, and most erudite, among the disciples; there were many spiritual prizes that Buddha had awarded him, but still he did not hold the TRUTH and was not enlightened.

When Makakashyo was going to collect the doctrines that had been left by Buddha at Hiparakutsu Ananda was not permitted to go to the meeting because he was not enlightened. Ananda had obtained Arhat rank however, and Makakashyo said, "You have obtained Arhat rank; you can enter by supernatural means." Changing his body to a small one, Ananda entered Hiparakutsu. All the disciples said, "Ananda was the jiisha of Buddha and is the cleverest and most erudite among us; there are no sayings that have not been transmitted to him in the same way as the water from one cup is poured into another. We hope that Ananda will repeat the sayings of Buddha again."

Then Ananda, who had been ordered by Buddha Himself to help Makakashyo, agreed to Makakashyo's request, worshipped at the feet of the disciples and stood on the lecture platform. He repeated all the lectures of Buddha with the following as an opening:– "Thus have I heard, once the Lord lived in. . ." Makakashyo asked many of the disciples if there were any mistakes and they replied that there were none; Ananda's words were no different from the Buddha's. They who said this were the great Arhats who had the Three Wisdoms and the six supernatural powers; there was nothing they had not heard from Buddha. They all said, "We are wondering if the Lord has come back again or if these are the lectures of Ananda: the waters of the Sea of Buddhism have flowed into Ananda." Through Ananda's efforts, the sayings of Buddha were able to be handed down to us.

I know well that the REAL TRUTH is not in the clever and erudite nor is it in those who gain worldly rank; this is the proof. Ananda followed Makakashyo for twenty years and was enlightened in the way described earlier; he was born on the same night that the Lord was enlightened. He did not hear the 'Kegon' and other scriptures, however he could repeat the sayings of Buddha because of 'kakusammai' (capacity given by a Buddha); this is not the same as entering into the Truth of our Ancestors.

Ananda had had the wish for the TRUTH when he was with Shakyamuni under Kūō Buddha but he liked erudition and, because of this, was not enlightened; Shakyamuni Buddha concentrated His mind and so was enlightened. I know well that erudition disturbs enlightenment; this is the proof. The following saying is in the 'Kegon Scripture,' "A poor man who counts another's treasure cannot have his own: erudition is as this." If you wish to understand the TRUTH really, you should not like erudition; concentrate your mind hard.

Ananda was always thinking that there must be something other than the kesa of gold brocade. Because of this he asked one day, "My dear senior, what did Shakyamuni Transmit to you other than the kesa of gold brocade?" Knowing the time was right, Makakashyo called, "Ananda." Ananda replied, "Yes?" Immediately Makakashyo said, "Chop down the flagpole by the gate." Ananda was enlightened by the tone of his voice and the clothes of Buddha came and hung themselves naturally on his body. This kesa of gold brocade is the very one that *was, is and will be Transmitted* from the time of the Seven Buddhas.

> Manzan's Commentary. There are three theories about this kesa. The first is that Shakyamuni wore it in the interior of His mother's womb; the second is that it was

offered by Jōgōten (the world); the third is that a hunter offered it, and there are several kinds of Buddha's kesa other than this. The kesa given by Bodhidharma to Sōkei is made of kutsujun cloth which is blue-black in colour: in China the kesa was lined with blue cloth and this one is preserved in the tower of Daikan Enō Zenji being an important national treasure; in the 'Chidoron' it is said that Shakyamuni wore a coarse kesa. It is the brocade kesa, mentioned above, that, in one of the scriptures, is said to have been offered to Buddha by His aunt and woven personally by her. These are a few among several kesas. The miracle of the kesa can be found in many scriptures: once Saint Bashyashita got into trouble with an evil king who took the kesa and threw it in the fire. The kesa shone, radiating five-coloured light and, after the fire had been extinguished, it was still safe. This kesa was believed to have been Buddha's and will later be given to Maitreya.

The TRUTH was not Transmitted to both Makakashyo and Ananda; only Makakashyo had the Lord's permission: Ananda held the TRUTH after spending twenty years as a jiisha; we should know, therefore, that there is something other than the Scriptures. At the present time, however, most people think that the TRUTH and the Scriptures are one; if both are one, Ananda could be called the First Ancestor, for he was the Arhat who had the Three Wisdoms and the six supernatural powers. Is there anyone who can understand the meaning of the Scriptures better than Ananda? If there is such a person, we can allow that the TRUTH and the meaning of the Scriptures are one. If we simply say both are one, why did Ananda spend twenty years as a jiisha and become enlightened by the chopping down of the flagpole? We should know the meaning of the

Scriptures and doctrines as different from the TRUTH of our Ancestors; we are not saying that Buddha is not true Buddha. Although Ananda was the Lord's jiisha he could not have the TRUTH Transmitted to him for he had not the TRUE understanding of the Real Mind (i.e. TRUTH) of Buddha.

The TRUTH cannot be gained by erudition; although a person is clever, and has sharp ears and can understand every (Chinese) character in the Scriptures and doctrines, he is counting another's treasure if he cannot understand their real meaning: it is not because there is no meaning in the Scriptures and doctrines; it is because the person concerned, as in this case of Ananda, has not been enlightened. Therefore, in Japan, they understand the meaning of the Scriptures by words and thus cannot understand fully. Of course the TRUTH should be thought of sincerely; if Ananda, who was the disciple of Buddha, could have been enlightened by understanding the Scriptures and doctrines of the Lord in words, all would be able to do so; however, it was only after spending many years as the jiisha of Makakashyo, and being enlightened, that he was TRULY able to repeat the Scriptures and doctrines; we should know this. If you want to become one with the TRUTH, as one fire combines with another fire, throw away selfish opinions, old emotions, arrogance and obstinacy and learn the TRUE MIND OF THE LORD with the naïve mind of a child.

Generally, most people think that there is nothing more than the kesa of gold brocade; but they should know that, after being the jiisha of Makakashyo, Ananda obtained something else. Knowing the time had come, Makakashyo called, "Ananda." Ananda replied, "Yes?" It was as if an echo replied to a voice and one fire sprang up between two stones.

Although Makakashyo called "Ananda," he was not calling Ananda; although Ananda replied "Yes," he was not replying to Makakashyo's call. "Chopping down the flagpole" means the following:– In India, when the disciples of Buddha and others wanted to argue, they set up a pole on each side of the place of debate; when either side was defeated they chopped down their pole: if they lost, they rang no bells and beat no drums. Both Makakashyo and Ananda set up their poles; if Ananda wins, Makakashyo is beaten: if one wins, the other is beaten; however, in this case, it is not so. Makakashyo is one flagpole and Ananda is another; if we are thinking they are flag-poles, the TRUTH does not manifest itself: when the flagpole *was, is and will be chopped* down, the TRUTH manifests it-self. Makakashyo said, "Chop down the flagpole;" Ananda was enlightened because he understood the TRUTH that *was, is and will be existing* from master to disciple. After enlightenment, Makakashyo was chopped down, along with nature and every-thing else; therefore the clothes of Buddha descended naturally onto Ananda's head: but do not stay with the flesh of Ananda; do not stay with cleanness: we should know the echo; there is only this point; many Buddhas came here in turn, many Ancestors pointed for ages.

Mind is being Transmitted with Mind; others cannot know this. Although both Makakashyo and Ananda are the repre-sentations of the TRUTH we should not make them the TRUTH; YOU, YOURSELF, ARE the manifestation of TRUTH: if you can realise TRUTH, you disappear at once; as this is so, we should not look for it outside ourselves.

Do you want to hear my humble words?

> The wistaria has withered and the trees have fallen
>   down,
> But the water in the valley has increased and from
>   the very stones fire has gushed forth.

CHAPTER 4.

THE THIRD ANCESTOR, SAINT SHŌNAWASHYU.

Shōnawashyu asked Ananda, "What is the Unborn in all things?" Ananda pointed to the corner of Shōnawashyu's kesa. Shōnawashyu asked again, "What is the fundamental nature, or characteristic, of the Truth of the Buddhas?" Ananda pulled the corner of Shōnawashyu's kesa; Shōnawashyu was enlightened.

Shōnawashyu came from Matora in India, he was named Shodaka which means "Natural Clothes" since he was born with clothes on; these clothes were warm in winter and cool in summer. When he became a monk, his worldly clothes instantaneously became the kesa; the same thing happened to the girl trainee Rengeshiki during the Lord's lifetime. In Shōnawashyu's previous life he had been a merchant and had offered a hundred blankets to a hundred Buddhas; since that time, he had been born with natural clothes on.

> Manzan's Commentary. The middle existence is the time after a person's death when he has not yet been born into the next existence; at this time he has no clothes on his body: Shōnawashyu was wearing clothes during the middle existence. The name Shōnawashyu is also the name of a plant, 'kushishu,' 'ku' means "nine," 'shi' means "branch," and 'shu' means "excellence:" kushishu is a kind of grass and people believe that, when a saint is born, it grows in virgin soil. When Shōnawashyu was born this grass grew and he was named after it.

He spent six years in his mother's womb; long ago Shakya-muni Buddha pointed to a forest and said to Ananda, "I call this forest Urada. A hundred years after My death a saint, whose name is Shōnawashyu, will appear and roll the WHEEL OF TRUTH." At the end of a hundred years Shōnawashyu was born; he received the Transmission of the TRUTH from Ananda and stayed in the forest of Urada; he rolled the WHEEL OF TRUTH and the fire-dragon surrendered to him. The fire-dragon offered this forest to the Buddha for this purpose so that the prophecy of the Lord was fulfilled.

Shōnawashyu was the saint of the Snow Mountain. Be-tween Ananda and Shōnawashyu there was this:– no one had ever asked, "What is the Unborn in all things?" Only Shō-nawashyu asked it; all people have the same nature, but no one knew, so no one asked about it. Why is it called "THE UNBORN" nature? All things appear therefrom but there is nothing that can produce it; therefore it is called "THE UNBORN." Every-thing is UNBORN; a mountain is not a mountain and water is not water; because of this, Ananda pointed to the corner of Shōnawashyu's kesa.

> Manzan's Commentary. The word 'kesa' is Indian; ke-
> sas have "broken," or "UNBORN," colour. From Buddhas
> above to ants below, and even horseflies, all creatures
> and their circumstances take form or shape; they are seen
> as they are from a one-sided viewpoint—in another
> sense, they do not belong to the world that can be seen.

There are no worlds that are to be thrown away and no TRUTH that is to be caught; thus Shōnawashyu understood: however, Shōnawashyu asked again, "What is the FUNDAMENTAL NATURE of the Buddha's TRUTH?" Although this NATURE is clear from the limitless past, we are misled if we do not realise it: therefore, in order to be clear as to the place from whence Buddhas come, Shōnawashyu asked his question again. So that he should <u>know</u> the TRUTH, everyone called and the TRUTH answered; all knocked and the TRUTH appeared: Ananda pulled the corner of Shōnawashyu's kesa to let him know and Shōnawashyu was enlightened. Although the foregoing is clear from the limitless past, we cannot understand that we are the very source of Buddhas if we do not experience it at least once; therefore Buddhas appear in turn and Ancestors explain for generations.

Although there is no TRUTH which is to be accepted from others, and to be given to others, we should understand it as exactly as we know our noses by touching them. We must REALLY understand the TRUTH by REALLY studying Zen: after understanding it, we must be tested in our understanding by the most excellent person we can find; if we do not do this, we will go badly astray. We must understand from this the importance of making every minute count; we should not allow our natural feelings and emotions to become uppermost and put our own opinions first. In addition to this we should not think that the Way of the Buddhas and Ancestors is for anyone other than ourselves; this opinion is the most useless of all useless opinions. All of the Ancestors were born, they had parents, feelings of filial love, honour and a desire for the good things of life however, when once they had studied Zen, they were all enlightened; because of this, there were plenty of wise and excellent people all over India, China and Japan although they lived at different times in the past, present and future.

We should know that we ourselves are the very persons who have the capacity for understanding the TRUTH for we have the same body and heart as the ancients; we have the same body and heart as Makakashyo and Ananda. Why are we different from the ancients? Because we do not study the TRUTH <u>sincerely</u>; we let the body go on, oblivious to the passing of time, and do not know the REAL SELF. In order to let us know this fact Ananda took Makakashyo as his master and then taught Shōnawashyu and the Way of TRUTH was Transmitted from master to disciple; thus the TRUTH now is no different from the TRUTH during the Lord's lifetime: we should not complain that we were not born in the Lord's country and did not meet Him (in the historical sense).

You have gathered together at this meeting because you sowed good seed, and came in contact with prajna, in ancient times, therefore you rank with Makakashyo and talk familiarly with Ananda. Although one is master and the other disciple they are the same Buddha; do not be muddled by the thought of old and new; do not remain with the thought of forms; do not waste time either by day or night. Study in detail; become one with the ancients and accept the approval of the master now.

So that you may make sense of the meaning of this, I will tell you my humble words.

> Although there is limitless water gushing from the
>   high rocks,
> Washing out the stones and scattering the clouds,
> Watering the snows and crushing the flowers,
> Yet is there an immaculate kesa above the dirt.

CHAPTER 5.

THE FOURTH ANCESTOR, SAINT UBAKIKUTA.

Ubakikuta served Saint Shōnawashyu for three years and, at the end of that time, shaved his head and became a monk.

Shōnawashyu asked him, "Are you a monk of body or a monk of mind?" Ubakikuta answered, "I am a monk of body." Shōnawashyu said, "The excellent LAW of Buddha has nothing to do with either mind or body." Ubakikuta was enlightened.

Ubakikuta hailed from the country of Dali and belonged to the Suda race; he was taught from the age of fifteen, became a monk at seventeen and was enlightened at twenty-two; he then went to Matsala to teach others. Because there were many people who were ordained by him, devils were afraid of him. Every time he ordained someone he put a numbered piece of bamboo, the length of four fingers, into a stone room: the size of this room was eighteen chū in length and twenty chū in width,

> Manzan's Commentary. A 'chū' is roughly equivalent to a foot.

and the room was filled with them: he was cremated with these bamboo sticks because there were so many people ordained during (his) the Lord's lifetime.

Although people called him the Buddha who had no good aspects, the devils feared him and were angry. When he was meditating they wanted to disturb him but he knew what was happening. One devil came and offered him a necklace; Ubakikuta, wanting to conquer him, stood up, took the dead bodies of a man, a dog and a snake, and changed them into a necklace. He then said sweetly to the devil, "You gave me a wonderful necklace. I have one for you too." The devil was pleased at this and accepted the necklace with outstretched neck; at once it changed back into three badly-smelling dead bodies which were rotting and had maggots wriggling in them. The devil disliked this necklace greatly and was much worried but, although he did his best, he could not throw it away, destroy it or remove it; he went up to the six heavens and told the lords thereof and then went to Bonten and asked to be released from the necklace. The lords told him that the power of the Disciple of the Ten Forces (that is, Buddha) was most excellent and that their powers were very poor and therefore they could not help him. The devil then said, "What ought I to do?" and Bonten answered, "You should be converted by Saint Ubakikuta. If you are, he will remove the necklace." Then Bonten recited the following poem:–

> If someone falls on the ground
> He can stand up again;
> If he wants to stand above the ground
> He cannot do so.

All the lords said, "You should ask the Disciple of Buddha to remove the necklace."

Accepting this teaching, the devil came down from Bonten and worshipped at the feet of Ubakikuta, confessing himself to be in the wrong.

Ubakikuta said, "Now, will you continue to disturb the Lord's TRUTH?" The devil replied, "Upon my word, I will be converted to the TRUTH and cease from my wickedness."

Ubakikuta said, "If that is so, you should say, with your own lips, 'I am converted to the Three Treasures.'" The devil recited the words three times and the necklace was removed. Thus Ubakikuta showed the authority of the TRUTH in the same way as it was during the Lord's lifetime.

When Ubakikuta shaved his head at the age of seventeen Shōnawashyu asked him, "Are you a monk of body or a monk of mind?" There are two kinds of monks; monks of body and monks of mind. The so-called monk of body severs family ties, lives away from home, shaves his head, changes the colour of his clothes, has no servants, becomes a trainee and seeks for the TRUTH throughout his life; therefore he wastes no time and has no desire: he is pleased with neither life nor death, his mind is as pure as the moon in autumn and his eyes as clear as an immaculate mirror. He does not look for the "Real Self," seeking only the TRUTH; because of this he stays neither in delusion nor enlightenment and thus he is a REAL man—this is a monk of body.

> Manzan's Commentary. The so-called monk of mind does not shave his head and change the colour of his clothes; although he lives among his family and attends to worldly affairs, he is as pure as a lotus untouched by dirt or as a jewel that accepts no dust. Even if he has a family, as a result of karmic relations, he thinks of it only as dust and has no love for, or concern with, it. As the moon in the sky, or a bowl rolling on a tray, he has leisure in a crowd; he goes beyond limitation, on reaching limitation, knowing that worldly desire is a disease to be discarded and that it is wrong to look for the TRUTH: he knows that Nirvana, birth and death are illusions in the sky and has no attachment to truth and delusion (as opposites, J.K.). This is a monk of mind.

So, Shōnawashyu asked his question. If Ubakikuta is a monk outside of these two kinds he is not a real monk; because of this the question was so framed. Ubakikuta answered, "I am a monk of body." It was obvious that he was not a monk of mind, nature or anything else but a monk of body: he could reach this understanding naturally and knew it, and with this he was completely satisfied: he got this far without looking and so understood that everything he could not understand was as it was; therefore he said he was a monk of body.

The excellent TRUTH of Buddha should not be understood
as above as Shōnawashyu pointed out; Buddha should not be
a monk of body or a monk of mind and be seen as a material
or mental existence. He who knows the TRUTH is beyond both
the holy and the unholy and has conquered both body and mind:
he is like the sky with neither inside nor outside; like sea-
water with neither an obverse nor a reverse. Although Shōnawashyu taught many doctrines he pointed out the TRUE FACT
that enlightenment had nothing to do with body or mind: we
should not say that he was Buddha because he was the most
excellent person in the world—Buddha should not be spoken
of as non-coming and non-going—nor should we speak of existence before parents were born and before the world existed;
the TRUTH of Buddha is beyond both birth and no-birth and is
outside the argument of mind and no-mind: it is like water
within vessels or the emptiness of the sky; we cannot catch it
with our hands and we cannot see its mark: thus, Ubakikuta
does not exist and Shōnawashyu does not appear. We cannot
understand this TRUTH from their actions and movements: although there are neither "he" and "I," nor "good" and "bad,"
between them, they sound as an echo and are as the endless sky.
If one does not experience the TRUTH with his own body, the
TRUTH may become delusion; when this was pointed out,
Ubakikuta was enlightened: this was as thunder in a clear sky
or a great fire on the ground. When the thunder beat on
Ubakikuta's ears he lost his previous life; fire burned the
Law of Buddha and the Teachings of the Ancestors to ashes:
these ashes became Ubakikuta and they were as hard as
stones and as black as lacquer. Ubakikuta threw away the
dirty surface of others and took many disciples; in vain he
threw bamboos into a room and counted emptiness, then
burned emptiness and left the mark in emptiness.

Now I, a disciple in Daijō Temple, want to look for the mark beyond the clouds and to write my words in emptiness. Do you want to hear?

> The house is broken, the man has disappeared.
> There is neither inside nor outside
> So where can body and mind hide themselves?

CHAPTER 6.

THE FIFTH ANCESTOR, SAINT DAITAKA.

The Fifth Ancestor, Daitaka, said, "A monk has no self and, because of this, he has no selfish thing, therefore his mind is unchanging:– this is called constant TRUTH. Buddhas are thus; neither their minds nor their bodies have aspects." Ubakikuta said, "You must understand fully from your own experience." Daitaka understood completely.

Daitaka was from Makada and, when he was born, his father dreamed that the golden sun shone from his house upon the world; there was a great hill, decorated with many jewels and, from a fountain at the top of it, much water gushed forth.

When Daitaka met Ubakikuta he told him about this. Ubakikuta said, "I am the hill; the fountain means that your wisdom can make the TRUTH endless. The shining of the sun from your father's house means your entering my way; this shining shows that your wisdom is most excellent." Daitaka was named "Perfumed Elephant" before becoming a monk; after ordination his name was changed to its present form. In

India he was called Daitaka which means "UNDERSTANDER OF THE TRUTH."

After Daitaka heard his master's teaching he sang a poem:–

> Lofty mountain of Seven Treasures
> From whence constantly gush out the plentiful waters
>   of wisdom;
> Changing into the real taste of TRUTH,
> It does the best for everyone.

Ubakikuta sang a poem also:–

> My LAW has been Transmitted to you;
> You should manifest your great wisdom.
> As the sun shining from a house
> So should you shine all over the world.

From that time Daitaka followed Ubakikuta and wished to become a monk.

Ubakikuta said, "You wish to become a monk; do you wish to be a monk of body or mind?" Daitaka replied, "I have come here to become a monk; it is neither for body nor mind." Ubakikuta said, "Who can be a monk other than in body and mind?" then he spoke the words quoted above and Daitaka was enlightened.

The REAL MONK should manifest the REAL SELF without self or selfish things therefore we must not argue about body and mind. The REAL SELF, without self and selfish things, should be called the REAL WAY, BUDDHA NATURE; we should not understand the REAL WAY from the viewpoint of birth and death, Buddha and Sattva, the four elements and the five skandhas, the Three Worlds and the Six Lokas. There is no form in BUDDHA NATURE; although we have senses and understanding BUDDHA

NATURE is beyond them: one who understands thus should still be called one who understands intellectually.

Although Daitaka understood, Ubakikuta said again, "Understand the TRUTH fully." This saying is as the seal of a king on trade goods; if the king guarantees, by the use of his seal, that the goods are not poisonous, of doubtful quality or commonplace, everyone can, and will, use them; in such a way the disciple is guaranteed by his master. Although there are neither disciplines that one can undergo nor ways that one cannot understand fully, one should still be truly enlightened; if one is not so, one becomes a person who understands intellectually and cannot understand the TRUTH completely. Such a one is always being disturbed by the thought of the existence of both Buddha and Teaching; he cannot be released from either his own, or others', bondage so, although there is neither a (Chinese) character in the Lord's lectures which one does not remember, nor a teaching in the three dhyanas or the five dhyanas which one does not keep, still one cannot be permitted to be a REAL MONK; even if one can lecture on many Scriptures, make Buddha appear in this place, shake the earth and make flowers fall from the sky, still one only ranks with lecturers; one is not a REAL MONK.

We must not understand the Truth as follows:– The whole world comes from the Buddha Nature, everything exists as it is; everything has the Buddha Nature; anyway everything is void. The opinion "everything is void" is equal to the wrong opinion that everything is empty: we are apt to have a constant self in ourselves if we hold the opinion that "everything has the Buddha Nature,"—the opinion that "everything exists as it is" has some sharp edges. The first opinion, "The whole world comes from the mind," seems somewhat sensible however, if you want to look for the Truth, you must not seek for it in the myriad Scriptures; should you do so, you are like the man who ran away from his father (an illustration from the 'Lotus Scripture'). We must open the door of our own treasure and then we can have the TRUTH as our own; if you do not understand this, the Buddhas and Ancestors will become your enemy. I pray that you do not hear the saying, "What devil let you become a monk? What demon let you wander among teachers?" Both when you can, and when you cannot, teach, you should be beaten to death; because of this, one does not become a monk for either body, mind or both: it was this that Daitaka understood. In spite of this, he was still not a REAL MONK; only when Ubakikuta again pointed the Way was he enlightened.

Study hard and in detail; you cannot understand the TRUE MEANING through the meaning of words. Throw away heaven, earth, the holy, the mean, subject and object; wherever you go, you should be disturbed by nothing, completely free.

Make a hole in emptiness; make waves on the barren earth. You should be in contact with the FACE OF THE BUDDHA and realise the TRUTH fully; TRUTH is as the gourd-vine twining round the gourd, as jewels shining brilliantly. Do you want to hear my humble words?

> The TRUE WISDOM should be caught exactly;
> The TURNING WHEEL still has a secret which cannot be
>   explained;
> Do not understand a constant self within the senses.

CHAPTER 7.

THE SIXTH ANCESTOR, SAINT MISHAKA.

The Fifth Ancestor, Daitaka, told the following teaching of the Lord to Mishaka:– "If one practices a supernatural art, or studies Hinayana, one will be bound with <u>rope</u>; one should know oneself. If one turns away from Hinayana and enters the great sea, which is Mahayana, one can realise the UNBORN." Mishaka was enlightened.

Mishaka came from the centre of India; he was the head genius of eight thousand genii. One day he worshipped Daitaka with them saying, "In olden times I was born in Bonten, as you were, and I studied the supernatural arts with the genius Ashida whilst you practiced dhyana, thus following the disciple of Buddha. Since then, our ways have been separate and six kalpas have passed." Daitaka said, "We spent a long time in separation and it is true what you say; now you should give up the wrong way and be converted to the RIGHT ONE." Mishaka said, "Long ago the genius Ashida made a prophecy that, after six kalpas, I would meet a classmate and be enlightened, thus reaching Arhatship; now we meet. Is it not destiny? Please let me be released." Daitaka then made him a monk and he accepted the Precepts. Unfortunately the eight thousand genii were proud of themselves so Daitaka manifested a great supernatural happening, which caused the genii to have a longing for salvation, and they all became monks at the same time: when the eight thousand genii became eight thousand monks Daitaka gave them the teaching quoted above.

Even if one could lengthen one's life and have extraordinary powers through the supernatural arts, the term of eighty thousand kalpas from the past is still only eighty thousand kalpas to the future; such arts have no power either after or before this term. Even if one could be born in the heaven of no-thought, lengthen one's life and have no concrete body as a result of practicing no-thought samadhi, or not-no-thought samadhi, one would still be in delusion; one could not meet Buddha and realise the TRUTH. When one's accumulated good

karma comes to an end, one has to enter constant hell, therefore one is bound by rope and cannot be released.

Although one who has studied Hinayana can apprehend
the first stage of enlightenment, the second, third, fourth, and
alone enlightenments, such a one still practices within body
and mind and learns within delusion and enlightenment. In the
first enlightenment, one can become a first-mind Bodhisattva
after eighty thousand kalpas; in the second, one can do so after
sixty thousand kalpas; in the third, one can do so after forty
thousand kalpas and one in the alone enlightenment can
become a first-mind Bodhisattva after a thousand kalpas.
Although good seeds will grow according to their nature, wandering karma is still not cut off: one is held by ropes, one is
not really released. Although one is entirely transparent after
cutting off the eighty-eight opinions and unlimited delusion,
one still looks for something; this is not real Buddhahood—
both to want to return to the fundamental and to look for enlightenment are as this.

You! Do not look for anything; you may go the wrong
way and that leads only to emptiness: do not stay beyond
unlimited kalpas otherwise you are like the dead in which the
soul remains; do not desire to apprehend real nature and
remain, like floating flowers, in wrong understanding. You
are still as the saint who cuts through no-wisdom and appre-
hends the Middle Way; do not make clouds in a clear sky; do
not injure a healthy body: you are as a poor son, wandering
about in foreign countries, or a poor man becoming intoxi-
cated with the dark. Meditate sincerely; is there before-birth
or after-death? Are there the past, the future and the present?
Everything is always THUS from birth to death; if one is not
in real contact with this condition, one is muddled by the senses
and their objects and cannot understand the REAL SELF. One
should not neglect one's daily life; we do not know from where

our bodies, minds and everything else come; therefore we should give up all vain desire to look <u>uselessly</u> for the TRUTH. Buddhas appear troublesomely; Ancestors teach in detail. Although Buddhas and Ancestors are kind to us, we say we do not know, or we do not understand, because we are disturbed by our selfish opinions; we are neither in real darkness, nor in real contact, with TRUTH—we understand vainly the right, or the wrong, only in our thoughts.

You! One calls and one replies; one points and one appears: this means 'no deliberate thought, no natural thought:'— THIS IS YOUR REAL LORD. The LORD has neither face nor form; the LORD moves always and unceasingly: our senses make the LORD manifest; our actions are termed bodily: the four elements, five skandhas, eighty-four thousand pores and three hundred and sixty bones gather together and make a body; this is as brilliant jewels and a sounding voice. Change, impermanence— birth and death—have nothing to do with the REAL LORD; this change, impermanence, has no beginning and no end. The waves of the sea leave no mark after subsiding yet they do not disappear; they go on without going to a different place: and still the form of the sea has big and small waves—your mind is as this—it moves always without ceasing. The LORD manifests HIMSELF as skin, flesh, bones and marrow and uses HIMSELF as the four elements and the five skandhas; HE manifests HIMSELF as peach blossoms and green bamboos and as the apprehension of the TRUTH and ENLIGHTENMENT. The LORD works in different voices and forms, seeing and hearing, clothing and eating, words and actions; the LORD is separate and does not belong to differentiation. The LORD manifests HIMSELF in differentiation and does not stop in forms; a genius exhibits many supernatural arts, or many figures, in dreams. Although many forms appear in a mirror, the mirror is one; if one does not know this fact, merely learning Hinayana and practicing supernatural arts, one cannot be permanently re-leased from suffering. No one binds you so there is no need to be released; there is no delusion and no enlightenment; we are apart from being bound. Is not this the UNBORN? Is not this the great sea? Where are the brooks? Every place belongs to the SEA OF THE LAW (TRUTH); brooks, falls and rivers are works of the great sea. There are neither brooks to be thrown away nor the sea to be picked up; therefore Mishaka threw away every detail and changed his old opinions; he became a monk instead of a genius and still he may have to bear the consequences of his former karma.

You! If you study hard and sincerely, you can be in real contact with the TRUTH as one meets an intimate friend, and as self nods at itself: you can swim always in the SEA of this REAL NATURE and there is no time when you are apart from IT. Hear the saying of Ba, the great master:–

> Every Sattva is always within the REAL NATURE,
> Wears clothes and eats food in it, talks and works,
> For these are the REAL NATURE.

However, when hearing this, do not understand that all Sattvas are in the REAL NATURE: the REAL NATURE and every Sattva are as the water and the waves; there is no difference. Do you want to hear my humble words?

> There is clearness in autumn waters ranging to the sky;
> There is a most excellent vision of the moon on a spring
>   night.

Most houses need to be clean and pure and even a thousand sweepings cannot clear the dust away completely.

CHAPTER 8.

THE SEVENTH ANCESTOR, SAINT BASHUMITSU.

The Seventh Ancestor, Saint Bashumitsu, put a vessel of wine in front of Saint Mishaka and stood and worshipped him. Mishaka asked, "Is this vessel mine or yours?" Bashumitsu thought about it. Mishaka said, "If this belongs to me, this is your REAL NATURE; if it belongs to you, the LAW in me should be Transmitted to you." Bashumitsu heard this teaching and realised the TRUE MEANING OF THE UNBORN.

Bashumitsu came from the northern part of India; he belonged to the Harada race. He wandered about the streets with a vessel of wine in his hand, singing and chanting; people said he was mad and no one knew his name. When Mishaka went to the northern part of India he saw a golden cloud over a fence and said to his pupils, "This cloud is the mark of a sincere seeker; there must be an excellent person here who can accept the Truth and become my disciple." As soon as Mishaka said these words Bashumitsu appeared and asked Mishaka, "Do you know what I am carrying?" Mishaka replied, "It is an unclean vessel; it is apart from immaculacy." Bashumitsu put the vessel in front of Mishaka and they exchanged the questions and answers quoted above; suddenly the vessel disappeared. Mishaka said, "Tell me your name." Bashumitsu answered in verse:–

> From the unlimited past to the time
> When I was born in this country
> My family name was Harada and I am called
> Bashumitsu.

Mishaka said, "My master said, 'Once, when the Lord was in the northern part of India, He told Ananda that, three hundred years after His death, there would be a saint whose family name was Harada and who would be called Bashumitsu:' " Mishaka then said that Bashumitsu would be the Seventh Ancestor and added, "The Lord made this prophecy for you; you should become a monk."

On hearing these words, Bashumitsu said to Mishaka, "In olden times there was one who studied dhyana and offered a beautiful seat covering to a Buddha. This Buddha made a prophecy to me, saying that you would become an Ancestor in the age of Shakyamuni." Bashumitsu then became the Seventh Ancestor.

Before he went to Mishaka, Bashumitsu always had a vessel of wine with him and never threw it away; he thought it most excellent—he wanted it in the morning as well as in the evening, using it freely—indeed, his very life <u>was</u> the vessel! Because of this, his first question was, "Do you know what I am carrying?"

Even if one understands (intellectually, J.K.) that mind is the very truth, or that body is the very truth, such understanding is clouded; if it is clouded, such understanding will be defeated by clarity. Even such understanding as future, past and present is clouded; also, <u>What</u> is called the past? <u>What</u> is called present? <u>What</u> is called beginning? <u>What</u> is called end? Such understanding will be shattered by clarity. Bashumitsu realised this and so put down the vessel of wine; this was the proof that he was converted by Mishaka. Because of this Mishaka asked, "Is this my vessel or is it yours?"

THE VERY TRUTH is not in such understanding as the past and the present, or in going and coming; it is not me; it is not you; the TRUTH is apart from both. Because this is so Mishaka taught, "If this belongs to me, this is your REAL NATURE (and the vessel is not Mishaka's personal property); if this belongs to you, you should be Transmitted by my LAW (DHARMA) (when this happens, the vessel is not Bashumitsu's personal property either)." The vessel belongs neither to me nor to you so the vessel is non-existent in the REAL sense; for this reason the vessel disappeared: it is very difficult to know the TRUE MEANING of this. Even if one could reach a state inaccessible to many Buddhas and Ancestors, in spite of their abilities, still one would be as a clouded vessel; surely this could be overcome by immaculacy? REAL IMMACULACY, however, does not insist on immaculacy, therefore the vessel does not do so. The disciple is in REAL contact with his master because there is no disturbance between them. My LAW (TRUTH) should be Transmitted to you because it is your REAL NATURE; there are neither things one can give to others nor things others can give to one; when we understand this, we can no longer speak of master and disciple; because of this, the disciple stands upon his master's head and the master stands beneath his disciple's feet, there is neither duality nor separation: because of this the vessel cannot be called a vessel and, therefore, it disappeared. This is the FACT of Transmission between Mishaka and Bashumitsu.

If one can realise such a thing as this body and mind are not the same as before such realisation.

One cannot say, "This has nothing to do with the present, past, birth, going and coming—this has no skin, flesh, bones and marrow."

THIS is the complete clarity itself; IT has no surface, no reverse, no inside and no outside.

Do you want to hear my humble words?

Just as the bell rings according to the way it is struck
So there is no need to want any empty vessel at all.

CHAPTER 9.

THE EIGHTH ANCESTOR, SAINT BUTSUDANANDAI.

When the Eighth Ancestor, Butsudanandai, met the Seventh Ancestor, Bashumitsu, he said, "I want to argue with you."

Bashumitsu replied, "You! Argument cannot be about the REAL TRUTH; the REAL TRUTH cannot be proved by argument. If we want to argue about something it will not be an argument about the REAL TRUTH." Butsudanandai understood that what Bashumitsu said was more excellent than his own theory and realised the reason for the UNBORN.

Butsudanandai came from Kamala; his family name was Gautama and he had a fleshy projection on the top of his head; he was very clever at arguing.

When Bashumitsu went to Kamala to spread the teaching of Buddhism Butsudanandai stood in front of his seat and said, "I am Butsudanandai; I want to argue with you." Bashumitsu replied, "If you want to argue you cannot know the TRUTH; the REAL TRUTH has nothing to do with argument."

Indeed the REAL TRUTH cannot be explained by argument and real argument has no shadow of TRUTH: if there is an argument, or a truth, that can be taken notice of, in the real sense, then it is neither the REAL TRUTH nor a real argument: because of this Bashumitsu said that, if one <u>wanted</u> to argue, the argument could not be about the REAL TRUTH. There are neither things to be called truth nor things to be called argument; the Lord did not have two kinds of words: one who can hear the Lord's words TRULY can see the Lord's BODY; one who can see the Lord's BODY can understand the Lord's TONGUE.

Although one may explain that the mind and the object are not two this explanation is not a real argument; even though one may explain that there is no change, one is not stating the TRUTH. Should one explain that there are neither words to explain with, nor reasons to be manifested, still the TRUTH will not appear; even though one explains that the Real Nature is true and the Mind right, that both the light and the world disappear, that both the light and the world do not disappear, that sometimes we are the host and sometimes the guest, the same and the one, yet no explanation is the real argument. Although Manjusri said, "No words, no explaining," this saying cannot be true; although Yuima sat on his seat and said nothing his silence cannot be an argument about the TRUTH: thus both Manjusri and Yuima were wrong. Sharihotsu, who was exceptionally clever, and Mokkenren, who was possessed of supernatural powers, were both unable to understand this TRUTH even in their dreams just as a blind man can see nothing. The Lord said, "Shōmon and Engaku (the two lower ranks in Hinayana) cannot understand the BUDDHA NATURE even in dreams:" even Bodhisattvas in the ten jū (the ten ranks in the last and highest class) made mistakes in distinguishing between water and cranes from afar: although they could <u>understand</u>, after thinking for a long time, that what they saw were cranes, still they were not sure. These Bodhisattvas also could not understand the BUDDHA NATURE clearly from the Lord's explanation and they said, with pleasure, "It is because we have been muddled by no-self that we have been unable to understand the eternal rolling of birth and death from ages past. Even if one can forget what one sees and hears, both with body and mind, and is beyond enlightenment, delusion, cloud and clarity, one cannot understand the TRUTH even in dreams."

Do not seek for TRUTH in the void; do not look for IT in form: even more, do not seek for IT in Buddhas and Ancestors. You! Everyone has passed through birth and death many times and, from long ago to the present time, has had mind and body endlessly. One may think of birth and death, coming and going, as floating delusion but such thoughts should be laughed at. Is there anything being born, or dying, or coming, or going? What can be said to be the REAL EXISTENCE of a person? What can be said to be floating delusion? One must not understand the Truth as real or delusive; if one does, such understanding is all wrong. Study in detail; do not fall into a thought-void. Although one realises the truth as clarity, as clear water or as the sky without dust, one cannot understand <u>really</u>.

The priest Tōzan, who followed Isan and Ungan, could do everything instantaneously: he could lecture with his whole body but there was something missing in him so Ungan said to him, "In order to understand the TRUTH, study in detail." Tōzan then left Ungan and went elsewhere. Suddenly he was enlightened and uttered the following verse:–

> Truly I should not seek for the TRUTH from others
> For then it will be far from me;
> Now I am going alone.
> Everywhere I am able to meet HIM;
> HE IS ME NOW;
> I am not HIM.
> When we understand this,
> We are instantaneously with the TRUTH.

He became the core of the Sōtō Church in China; before his enlightenment he could not only understand the full reason why every part of his body lectured, he could also understand that a naked pillar (round pillar in a temple) and a garden lantern lecture too, and everything, in every place, lectures throughout the three ages of past, present and future, and still he was lacking in full understanding.

It is very strange that one can understand the truth by intellection, understand a mind as a Buddha and a body as a Buddha, and not understand what Buddhism is, thinking vaguely that the Truth is simply that blossoms come out in spring and leaves fall in autumn. If Buddhism is thus, why did Shakyamuni appear and Bodhidharma come to China? There were no Buddhas and no Ancestors from Shakyamuni to this time who were not enlightened.

If one insists that what one gets from words and sentences is right and the truth itself, there will be no Buddha and no Ancestor. Give up this type of understanding; study this one, important point and you will be a Buddha: one who is not enlightened cannot be called real; do not stay in clarity or in the void.

The priest Sensu said, "The place where one can stay eternally is unmarked; do not stay eternally in this unmarked place. After following the priest Yakusan for thirty years, I understood only this one thing; clarity is not the place to stay in eternally. Do not stay in such a place for there is no operation of the senses and no object to it." So said he.

There is no time when it is present or past; there is nothing which is enlightenment or delusion: if one is enlightened in this way, there is no obstruction, no disturbance; one is completely free. Study in detail; do not think hastily. Do you want to hear my humble words?

> The sayings of Subhuti and Vimalakirti are not complete;
> Mangalama and Shariputra are like the blind;
> If one wants to understand the meaning of this truly,
> Salt is suitable for all food.

CHAPTER 10.

THE NINTH ANCESTOR, SAINT FUDAMITTA.

The Ninth Ancestor, Fudamitta, heard the following words from Butsudanandai,—"Your words are more in tune with your BUDDHA NATURE than are those of your parents; your behaviour is in contact with the TRUTH. Thus are Buddhas. If you seek outside yourself for a Buddha who has form that which you will find will be other than TRUE: if you want to know your TRUE NATURE you should neither be in contact with it nor apart from it."

Fudamitta came from Daigya; his family name was Bishara. When Butsudanandai went to Bishara's house, which was the castle of Daigya, he saw a white light rising therefrom and said to his followers, "There is a REAL saint here; his mouth has spoken no words because he is a REAL Buddhist of the Mahayana, and his feet have never walked upon the ground for he knows that, if they do, they will get dirty. Perhaps he will become my heir."

Soon the master of the house came out and, worshipping Butsudanandai, asked, "What do you need?" Butsudanandai replied, "I need a jiisha." The other said, "I have a son who is fifty years old; he has spoken no words and has never walked upon the ground." Butsudanandai said, "If he is thus, he will be my real disciple." Hearing Butsudanandai's words Fudamitta stood up and worshipped him; he then asked Butsudanandai the following in verse:–

> Even my parents are not in tune with me;
> What is in tune with me?

Even the teaching of Buddhas is not real for me;
<u>What</u> is real for me?

Butsudanandai replied with the words quoted above.

Hearing these excellent words, Fudamitta took seven steps. Butsudanandai said, "When this man followed the Lord he earnestly made his prayers: until now he has spoken no words and has never walked upon the ground because he believed it to be very difficult to cast off his filial ties."

Usually our parents are not the most in tune with us and the teaching of the Buddhas is not the most REAL thing for us. Therefore, if we want to understand that which is most in tune with us we should not compare it to our parents; also, if we want to realise the REAL TRUTH we should not learn it from Buddhas. The reason for this is that we can see, hear and work without the assistance of others; we are thus; Buddhas are thus also. We study from Buddhas and Buddhas study from us; we are not, however, as much in tune with this relationship, because of lack of training, as we could be. Can it be the TRUTH? Fudamitta spent fifty years without speaking a word, or walking on the ground, for this reason. Because of this Fudamitta was the very person who should belong to Mahayana; he should not remain among worldly persons. He said his parents were not in tune with him and this saying is similar to his nature. He said the teaching of Buddha was not the real truth and he did not walk on the ground; this was his behaviour and he was in contact with the TRUTH. If he wanted a Buddha who appeared as he thought a Buddha should appear, his behaviour was wrong; because they understand this, TRUE MONKS have Transmitted the TRUTH. At Transmission they represent the TRUTH without words, point out the TRUTH directly and understand their own TRUE NATURE without worrying about their external appearance. In order to let one understand this direct pointing, and let the TRUTH pass simply, they use no special means such as changing their own form; they simply allow one to cut off one's delusion by sitting and permitting mould to grow up around their mouths. This does not mean that they dislike words and value silence; in order to let one know that one's BUDDHA NATURE is thus, they teach thus.

Our TRUE NATURE is as clean water and the sky; it is clarity itself and, staying in peace, has no disturbance. There is no form to manifest outside our NATURES and there is nothing dirty in these NATURES; we cannot compare them to other jewels. We should not compare the light of these NATURES to the light of the sun or the moon; we should not compare THEM to the light of shining jewels. Do you not see that the light of our NATURES is as a thousand suns shining in the sky? One who does not understand completely is seeking for the TRUTH outside himself; one who understands completely does not seek the TRUTH even inside himself. Reflect quietly; do not think that inside is in tune and outside unharmonious; the TRUTH is the same at all times but do not be selfish. Every Ancestor met the next one honestly; they cared nothing for their form and only thus do they meet; there is no other reason for their meeting and we should know this from the foregoing.

Butsudanandai did not say that the TRUTH could be understood through training, enlightenment or study; he said, "Your MIND is in tune with you and you yourself are the TRUTH ITSELF." Butsudanandai also suggested that we should not seek to become Buddha, either with or without special form, therefore we can understand that there is nothing with which we ought to be in contact or from which we ought to be apart:

the TRUTH is beyond contact and separation. Even though it can be explained by the word body it cannot be separated from anything; even though it can be explained by the word mind (nature) it cannot be in contact with it: even if you understand the TRUTH in this way, do not seek for the BUDDHA NATURE outside of the body. Body and mind belong to change and change is not the working of mind and body. Many Buddhas hold the TRUTH thus at all times and are always enlightened; all Ancestors hold the TRUTH thus and are always appearing in the countries of India, China, Japan and elsewhere: you too should hold the TRUTH thus and not work outside it; these things are eternal. The twelve aspects of life are explained by Shakyamuni and are the ROLLING WHEEL OF TRUTH; wandering from one Loka to another is the manifestation of TRUTH in Mahayana.

Life in the four lives is the TRUE LIFE; even if one explains the TRUTH as animate or inanimate this explanation is the same as saying that our eyes have two different names, 'me' and 'manko' (both words mean "eyes" in Japanese). Although one explains the truth as a living thing it is only a different name for mind and will. Do not let the mind be excellent and the will non-excellent; can we despise our 'me' and respect our 'manko'? There are neither senses nor their objects therefore everyone is the TRUTH ITSELF. There is nothing outside BUDDHA NATURE. Do you want to hear my humble words?

> Do not think we can explain
> TRUE NATURE with words and silence;
> Can the senses and their objects
> Make TRUE NATURE dusty?

CHAPTER 11.

THE TENTH ANCESTOR, SAINT BARISHIBA.

The Tenth Ancestor, Barishiba, followed Fudamitta for three years and, during that time, never slept. One day Fudamitta explained the meaning of no-birth after reciting Scriptures and Barishiba was instantaneously enlightened.

Barishiba was born in central India and his name was Nanshō meaning "Difficult Birth." At his birth his father dreamed of a white elephant with a beautiful saddle upon its back; there was a brilliant jewel on this saddle which shone in all directions. When Fudamitta went to central India there lived a rich man there named Kōgai who came to Fudamitta with his son and, after worshipping him, said, "This son was in his mother's womb for sixty years and, because of this, he was named 'Difficult Birth;' when a genius met him he said that he was not ordinary and would become a REAL MONK. Now we have met you, I will let him become a monk." Fudamitta then shaved the son's head and ordained him.

Barishiba spent sixty years in his mother's womb and lived eighty years after his birth, he was, therefore, very old. When he wanted to become a monk people warned him that, as he was old and therefore not strong, it would be useless for him to enter the monks' circle. They told him there were two kinds of monks, one studying Zen and the other reciting Scriptures, and that he could not manage either: when he heard this he vowed to himself that, when he became a monk, he would not lie down until he could realise the TRUTH, so he studied Zen and recited Scriptures in the daytime and sat in

Zazen during the night, never sleeping. When he first became a monk, a portentous light fell upon his seat and he could feel that the bones of Shakyamuni Buddha were close to him; from then on he worked very hard, without tiring, for three years and was able to realise the TRUTH. This realisation came when he heard Fudamitta reciting Scriptures and explaining the meaning of no-birth however, only those Scriptures were recited that are <u>real</u> Mahayana ones, such as the 'Ryogikyo,' for such Scriptures have full meaning: these Scriptures do not say that we need to get <u>rid</u> of delusion. The 'Ryogikyo' not only explains doctrine, it explains actual things; merely to explain the doctrine that all is one and all things have the Buddha Nature is not good enough. Buddhas have a mind that penetrates the TRUTH; they study and train themselves so as to realise the TRUTH. In <u>real</u> Scriptures there are many things such as the five degrees of human, angel, unsui, those who have been Transmitted and Bodhisattva, the length of time of training, the names of places such as Jōdō, the place of immaculacy; these things the 'Ryogikyo' explains fully; we should know that <u>real</u> Scriptures make such explanations.

Even if one realises the full meaning of one verse or one doctrine he cannot be allowed to be an Ancestor unless he realises the whole TRUTH. We should work hard, forgetting tiredness, have excellent wills, train ourselves strictly, study everything in detail day and night, realise the <u>true</u> wish of the Buddhas and what we are, and understand both the doctrine and actual things; only thus can we become Ancestors. In recent years the WAY of the Ancestors has been forgotten and there is no real training; most monks think they are good enough if they understand just one verse or one doctrine: they are self-opinionated: be careful of this. The TRUTH is like mountains; the farther we climb the higher they become:

VIRTUE is like the sea; the farther we swim the deeper it becomes: when we fathom the sea's depth and climb to the top
of the mountain, we become the REAL CHILDREN of Buddha.
Treat both your bodies and your minds with care; everyone
is the vessel of the TRUTH; every day is a good day.

Understanding and ignorance come from training and
from the failure to train; the TRUTH has no preference for any
person or any time. Barishiba was a hundred and forty years
old, very aged; he realised the TRUTH because of his excellent will, forgetting all tiredness; he became the jiisha of his
master for three years and never slept. Nowadays the old are
often lazy. Think of the saints of ancient times; do not think
that when you work hard in hot or cold weather you will die.
Do not think that you are unsuccessful; if you think positive-
ly you can become excellent: everyone who can think thus is
an Ancestor. Barishiba recited Scriptures but this does not
mean that he only recited them with his mouth or opened the
book only with his hands; we should know what is the work
in the house of the Buddha. We should neither be controlled
by delusion nor plant any seeds that can become a cause for
greed, anger or delusion; every place is itself a Scripture therefore we can acquire wisdom in all places and at any time. When
we live thus, we depend upon nothing and we realise the TRUE
MEANING OF NO-BIRTH; we do not know whence we come or
where we go: born here, die there, always appearing and disappearing: birth is not birth and death is not death.

As a seeker for TRUTH, do not think of birth and death:
we should know that our knowledge and our bodies are the
TRUTH ITSELF. We can make light radiate from our eyes so
that all may see its glory; we can radiate light from our ears
so that all may hear the sounds of Buddha: we can radiate light
from our hands and make both others and ourselves happy and
we can walk with the glorious light for ever under our feet.

Now I will give you my humble words, listen!

How many Scriptures do we recite?
We die here and are born there;
All is different
And all is one.

CHAPTER 12.

THE ELEVENTH ANCESTOR,
SAINT FUNAYASHYA.

The Eleventh Ancestor, Funayashya, stood in front of Saint Barishiba, making gasshō, and Barishiba asked him, "From where have you come?"

"My mind (nature) is not going anywhere," Funayashya answered. Barishiba asked him, "Where do you stay?"

"My mind (nature) stays nowhere," Funayashya replied.

"Then are you wandering (floating)?" asked Barishiba.

"Every Buddha is as I," answered Funayashya.

"You are not Buddha," said Barishiba. "To call something Buddha is wrong."

On hearing this saying, Funayashya trained himself for twenty-one days and realised no-self. He then told Barishiba, "It is wrong to call something Buddha and to call you Saint."

Barishiba allowed him to Transmit the TRUTH.

Funayashya came from Kashikoku; his family name was Gautama and his father's name was Hōshin. When Saint Barishiba came to Kashikoku he rested under a tree and, pointing at the ground, said to the people, "When this ground becomes golden, a saint will appear."

At that moment the ground turned golden and someone called Funayashya, the son of a rich man, appeared. The conversation quoted above took place and Barishiba recited the following verse:–

> This ground turned golden;
> I have known for some time that a saint would come.
> You, Funayashya, are to become Buddha
> So you should sit under the Bodhi tree,
> As did Shakyamuni Buddha, and realise the TRUTH.

Funayashya replied with the following verse:–

> You sit on the golden ground,
> Teaching the radiating light,
> Thus allowing me to enter samadhi.

Barishiba knew his secret wish and ordained him, giving him the Precepts.

Funayashya was a saint from the beginning and so he said that his mind was beyond going and staying, being as Buddha, but still he felt himself to be in dualism; he thought that both his mind and the Buddha Mind were beyond going and staying: Barishiba took the most important things he had away from him as a cow takes food from the hungry. Even a person who realises the TRUTH is still imperfect and so Barishiba told him that there should be no Buddha; because of this he said, "You are not Buddha." The above cannot be realised through reasoning and cannot be understood without form; the TRUTH cannot be understood with the Wisdom of the Buddhas nor can it be understood with our ordinary knowledge. Funayashya, after hearing this comment, trained himself for twenty-one days:

finally he touched the TRUTH and let go of his individual mind, going beyond Buddhas; this is called no-birth. He realised what TRUTH is and spoke it:– "To call something Buddha, or Saint, is wrong."

The WAY of the Ancestors cannot be understood with either reasoning or mind; we cannot call the Dharma and the One Mind of the world the deepest TRUTH; we cannot understand IT as eternity, immaculacy or emptiness. Because of this, when many saints got to this stage, they changed their minds, opened the gate to the TRUTH and ceased to be self-opinionated. Funayashya was a saint from the beginning therefore, when he came forward, the ground turned golden and there was something about him which frightened others, but he trained himself for twenty-one days and understood the TRUTH; as this is so, you, the disciple, must study much more deeply. I want you to hear my humble verse.

> The MIND is neither Buddha nor you;
> Coming and going are in this.

CHAPTER 13.

THE TWELFTH ANCESTOR, SAINT ANABOTEI MEMYŌ.

The Twelfth Ancestor, Saint Anabotei Memyō, asked Funayashya, "What is BUDDHA?"

"You want to know that! It is BUDDHA itself that asks," replied Funayashya.

"I do not know BUDDHA so how can I know that I am BUDDHA?" asked Anabotei.

"You do not know BUDDHA so how can you know that you are not BUDDHA?" said Funayashya.

"This argument is like a saw," said Anabotei.

"No, it is like a tree. What do you mean when you say that it is like a saw?" replied Funayashya.

"We are standing up in a straight line like a saw's teeth. What do you mean when you say it is like a tree?" asked Anabotei.

"You have been cut down by me," replied Funayashya. Anabotei understood the TRUTH.

Anabotei came from Harana and was named Kōshō, being excellent in many virtues; desire can be made a virtue; non-desire can also be made a virtue: therefore he was named Kōshō. He went to Funayashya and asked the first question:– "What is BUDDHA?" Funayashya replied, "You want to <u>know</u> BUDDHA! It is BUDDHA itself that is asking."

This is the first question to be asked by someone entering Buddhism. The Buddhas in the three generations, and all the Ancestors, were trying to understand BUDDHA; if a person does not study what Buddhism is he walks in the wrong direction. We cannot make a BUDDHA from forms nor can we make one from the thirty-two good aspects or eighty marks; because of this Anabotei asked the first question and Funayashya gave the first answer, "You want to know what BUDDHA is! The BUDDHA is the very person who is asking the question"—that is, ANABOTEI HIMSELF (i.e. Anabotei's TRUE SELF).

There is no difference in a person when he knows he is BUDDHA and when he does not; there is nothing special between before and after; BUDDHA was the same in ancient times as IT is now: sometimes HE has thirty-two good aspects and eighty marks and these show what a Buddha is supposed to look like; sometimes BUDDHA has three heads and eight arms; sometimes HE lives in heaven and suffers from the five discomforts; sometimes HE appears in the form of a human being and suffers from the eight miseries; sometimes HE has the aspects of animals and sometimes HE is in hell. HE is always in the Three Worlds with the same NATURE and behaves in HIS own world of BUDDHA NATURE but with different aspects. No one knows what is being born or what is dying; no one can give HIM a definite form; no one can give HIM a definite name and no one can ever realise fully what HE is. Most people misunderstand this and, when they say they know what a BUDDHA is, they just do not know; when they say they know that BUDDHA cannot be known and recognised they know the TRUE BUDDHA.

If the TRUE meaning of the conversation above is thus, why did Funayashya need to say such things? People go from darkness to darkness and do not behave as Buddhas, therefore Funayashya said that BUDDHA is the very person who does not know BUDDHA and is thus asking; Anabotei did not understand this and showed his misunderstanding by saying, "If we do not know what BUDDHA is, how can we show our BUDDHA NATURE?" Funayashya replied, "If we do not know what BUDDHA is, how can we show anything other than BUDDHA NATURE? We must not look for BUDDHA NATURE outside ourselves; the person who asks what BUDDHA is is the BUDDHA ITSELF. How can we say it is not so?" "This is chop-logic," said Anabotei. "No," said Funayashya, "this logic is as wood. What is the meaning of 'chop-logic?'" "You and I are standing in the same line," replied Anabotei; "why is this logic as wood?" Funayashya said, "I know (THE REAL) YOU completely." Anabotei suddenly understood the TRUTH.

You and I have the same BUDDHA NATURE; there is no difference between you and I; both our hands are full of BUDDHA

NATURE: you and I can never be more than we are; you and I borrow nothing from others. Within this the master and disciple stand in the same line as the teeth of a saw; Funayashya said that the meaning of "wood" was that no one can know anything when in darkness; in the dark there is nothing to be taken away or added: the head of a wooden stick has no mind but functions as a head; this is the meaning of "wood." Anabotei could not well understand what his master meant and Funayashya replied with compassion, "What is the meaning of the 'saw?' " Anabotei said, "You and I are in the same line," and then asked his master, "What is the meaning of the 'wood?' " Funayashya put his hand on Anabotei's shoulder and said, "YOU (the REAL YOU) are known completely by me." The way between master and disciple was opened and they became One in the BUDDHA NATURE; they could walk both in dreams and in heaven so Funayashya said, "You are known to me." Anabotei was enlightened completely and became the Twelfth Ancestor.

Funayashya said, "This great one was the king of Bishari; in this country there is a group of people who wear no clothes. The king turned himself into many silkworms so that they could have clothes and, at a later date, he was born in central India and the group cried with great feeling; because of this he was named Anabotei which means "Crying Horse" (the group were like a horse in being without clothes). Shakyamuni Buddha said that, about six hundred years after His death, there would be a wise person called Anabotei Memyō, in Harana, who would teach the Truth. This was foretold by Shakyamuni Buddha; Funayashya Transmitted the Truth to Anabotei Memyō.

Thinking that we are BUDDHA because we do not know we are BUDDHA, and that the TRUTH is Transmitted without being known, does not mean that we should not think that we are BUDDHA because we do not know what IT is; although we do not know what BUDDHA is we should enquire deeply concerning IT at the time before our parents were conceived; with the knowledge that we have after we are born, we cannot know IT: we cannot understand what face Buddhas, Ancestors, human beings or devils have.

The TRUTH is changing or not changing, is empty or not empty, is beyond within and without, beyond absolute and non-absolute; IT is indeed our TRUE EXISTENCE. Within this TRUTH the average person and the saint, all things, subject and object appear and disappear as the waves of the sea and nothing is added: we call things Buddhas or devils but they are the facets of ONE THING. When we call something Buddha we are wrong; when we call it devil we are wrong. When we teach the TRUTH to others everything finds the REAL WAY therefore we perform TRUE actions as if in a dream. The ways of teaching and the supernatural powers of India have come down to the present; if we train ourselves well and accept everything, being beyond birth and death, we are TRUE monks. Now I want to tell you my humble verse.

> The peach tree does not know that its blossoms are red
> But it leads Rei-un to the TRUTH.

CHAPTER 14.

THE THIRTEENTH ANCESTOR,
SAINT KABIMORA.

One day when Saint Anabotei explained the SEA OF BUDDHA NATURE saying, "Mountains, rivers and the earth are all made thereof; the Three Wisdoms and the six extraordinary senses also," Saint Kabimora realised the TRUTH.

Kabimora was born in India, in Kashikoku; before he learned Buddhism he had about three thousand disciples and knew various teachings. Once, when Saint Anabotei Memyō was giving a good lecture in that area, an old man collapsed in front of him; Saint Anabotei told the audience that this was not an ordinary person and must have an excellent appearance. The old man suddenly disappeared and a golden one manifested itself from the bosom of the earth and changed into a woman; she pointed to Anabotei saying in verse:–

> I worship you, the great one,
> You should accept the prediction of Shakyamuni
>   Buddha;
> Please spread the TRUTH throughout the world.

She then disappeared. Saint Anabotei said, "There is a devil who wants to fight with me." A storm arose and Saint Anabotei said, "This is proof that the devil has come; I will get rid of it." He pointed to the sky and a big, golden dragon appeared and showed its power by shaking the mountains; Saint Anabotei sat still and the devil disappeared. After seven days there appeared a small worm, like a large Shōmei; Saint Anabotei took it from beneath his seat and showed it to the audience saying, "This is what the devil has changed into; it wants to steal my DHARMA." Saint Anabotei freed it from his finger but it could not move; he told it that, if it were converted to the THREE TREASURES OF THE DHARMA, it would have the extraordinary senses. The devil then appeared as he truly was, bowed to Saint Anabotei and confessed his wrong doing. Saint Anabotei said, "What are you? How many followers do you have?" The devil replied, "My name is Kabimora; I have three thousand followers." Saint Anabotei said, "Why do you change so often?" The devil replied, "It is a very easy thing for me to change the great sea into something else." Saint Anabotei said, "Can you change the SEA OF THE TRUTH into something else?" The devil said, "What is the SEA OF THE TRUTH? I have never heard of such a thing." Saint Anabotei explained it to him saying, "Mountains, rivers and the earth are all made of IT; the Three Wisdoms and the six extraordinary senses come therefrom." Kabimora realised the TRUTH.

From the time when an old man collapsed until the time when a small worm appeared, the devil changed often; it was a small thing for it to change a great sea into a mountain and a mountain into a great sea but since it did not even know the name of the SEA OF THE TRUTH how could it change that? Though he did not know WHAT changed into a mountain and other things Saint Anabotei Memyō explained that they were the SEA OF THE TRUTH and that the Three Wisdoms and six extraordinary senses came out of IT. The following are some of the many samadhis:– shuryogon-zammai, the samadhi which exterminates all delusions; tengentsu, wherein one is all-seeing; tennitsu, wherein one has supernatural hearing, and many others: these have neither beginning nor end and this world is full of them—it is, in fact, them themselves.

When mountains, rivers and the earth are made, the samadhi changes into the earth, water, fire, wind, grass, wood, skin, flesh, bones and all parts of our bodies; there is nothing outside it: there is nothing to be abandoned: birth and death continue and both are within samadhi; there is endless sight and sound: even the wisdom of Buddhas cannot understand these things; all are part of the constant movement of THE SEA OF TRUTH. Everything in the world is endless; it is not a problem of comparison. When we see our bodies we see our minds;

when we know the BUDDHA NATURE, we <u>know</u> the body: body and mind are not two separate things; form and matter are not different. Even though one is in another world than that of humans, still one is in samadhi; one does not, however, know it and doubts both oneself and others. If someone does not know that everything is in samadhi he cannot understand the fundamental TRUTH; because of this the power of the devil was destroyed: it abandoned selfishness and came to Saint Anabotei Memyō, ceased to fight with him and manifested HIS LIGHT.

Even when you understand your own TRUE NATURE do not stay in the realm of the senses however, the senses are still facets of the BUDDHA, as are the fence, wall and stones; the TRUE NATURE is beyond seeing, hearing, touching, movement and stillness. When THE SEA OF THE TRUTH is established, movement and stillness arise—skin, flesh and bones appear with time: think of the TRUE MEANING of this; IT appears as senses and sights but not necessarily for others; we can make sound by beating the sky and, when the sky is changed into many things, they have various forms. We should not think that the sky has no form and no voice; we should realise that there is nothing to be called 'emptiness' or 'existence;' such 'existence' is neither visible nor invisible.

There is nothing separate: what is "other"? What is "I"? In the sky there is nothing and in the sea there is water; this is true at all times, past, present and future. When it is visible, there is nothing to be added to it: when it is invisible, there is nothing to be hidden. Our bodies are made up of many facets; beyond existence, there is something which we call ONE MIND, BUDDHA NATURE. When you want to be enlightened do not look for IT outside yourself; when the TRUTH manifests ITSELF others call IT human beings and animals. Seppō said, "If we want to understand, we should realise that we are as an excellent mirror; when foreigners come they appear in it; when our own relations come they appear in it." There is no beginning and no end; mountains, rivers and the earth come from THIS: the Three Wisdoms and six supernatural powers come from THIS. There is nothing outside BUDDHA NATURE: please listen to my humble verse.

> Even when great waves rise up to heaven,
> The PURE WATER does not change at all.

CHAPTER 15.

THE FOURTEENTH ANCESTOR, SAINT NAGYAARAJYUNA.

When the Thirteenth Ancestor went to the King of the Dragons he was given a Nyoi jewel. Nagyaarajyuna asked him, "Since this jewel is the most excellent thing in all the world how can it benefit me?" Kabimora replied, "You know only of apparent benefits: you do not realise that this jewel is beyond them, nor do you know that this is not a jewel." Nagyaarajyuna realised the TRUTH deeply.

Saint Nagyaarajyuna came from the western part of India; he was named Ryunnyo or Ryushō. The Thirteenth Ancestor went to the western part of India after he was enlightened and there a prince, named Unjizai, invited him to his palace and offered him many gifts. He told the prince, "There is a teaching of Shakyamuni Buddha that says no monk can be near a king, nobles and the powerful." The prince said, "There is a great hill behind my castle; on it there is a stone hall. Would you like to meditate there?" The Thirteenth Ancestor said,

"Yes." He went to the hill and, on the way to the stone hall, saw a large python; he took no notice of it but it came and encircled his body and he gave it the Three Treasures: after hearing them, the python left him. When he arrived at the stone hall, an old man, in poor clothes, came out and made gasshō. Saint Kabimora said to him, "Where do you live?" He replied, "When I was a monk, I liked to live alone in a peaceful forest or on a mountain, but someone who wanted to learn from me came often. I found this very troublesome and got angry with him and, for this, I was reborn as a python and spent a thousand years in this stone hall. Fortunately I met you and heard the Three Treasures; now I want to thank you for them." Saint Kabimora asked him, "What people are there on this hill?" He replied, "About ten ri from here, there is a great one who teaches five hundred great dragons; I listen to him also." Saint Kabimora went to Nagyaarajyuna, who came out to welcome him, saying, "This place is lonely and deep in the mountains; there are many dragons and pythons. Why has the great monk come?" Saint Kabimora replied, "I am not great; I have just come to see a wise man." Nagyaarajyuna considered silently whether or not the Thirteenth Ancestor was a great monk and had the Transmission from Shakyamuni Buddha. Saint Kabimora said, "You are wondering about me; I know well what you are thinking. Just become a monk; you do not need to worry as to whether I am great." After hearing this comment, Nagyaarajyuna apologised and became a monk, and the five hundred dragons accepted the Precepts: he followed the Thirteenth Ancestor for four years. When the latter went to the King of the Dragons and was given the Nyoi jewel, Nagyaarajyuna asked him, "Is this the most excellent jewel in the world or not?" Although he asked other questions he was enlightened by this one thereby becoming the Fourteenth Ancestor.

Nagyaarajyuna had learned from several religions; he had also learned supernatural arts: he used to go to the palace beneath the sea to see the Scriptures of the Seven Buddhas; on just seeing the titles, he understood the contents, and used to teach them to the five hundred dragons. (The so-called Manda Ryu-ō and Butsudanda Ryo-ō are called Bodhi-sattvas: they keep many Scriptures in a safe place beneath the sea because they were asked to do so by the ancient Buddhas. When the teachings and Scriptures of Shakyamuni Buddha cease to be useful for others they will be put in this same palace beneath the sea.) Although Nagyaarajyuna had such power that he could talk with the great King of the Dragons he was still not a REAL monk; all he did was learn other religions.

From the time he belonged to the Thirteenth Ancestor, he was truly enlightened, however people thought he was not only the Fourteenth Ancestor but the founder of many churches of Buddhism as well; the Shingon Church made him its true founder as did also Tendai; the sorcerers and weavers made him their founder also. Many other people learned many things from him but, after he became the Fourteenth Ancestor, he took no notice of the sorcerers although they still thought he was their founder. They were as animals and devils which cannot recognise the difference between jewels and stones; only Kanadaiba could be given his TRUTH: he took no notice of others. Because he had five hundred excellent people when Saint Kabimora came to see him, he went out, bowed and desired to test Kabimora; Saint Kabimora, however, did not show his TRUE MIND. Nagyaarajyuna silently wondered whether Kabimora was a TRUE monk; Saint Kabimora said, "Become a monk. Why do you need to wonder whether I am a saint or not?" Nagyaarajyuna apologised and followed him. Nagyaarajyuna said, "This jewel is the most excellent in the world; of what use is it?" Possessing dual thought, he could not understand the TRUTH: Kabimora's reply was, "Even though this jewel is the most excellent in the whole world, we should know that TRUTH is beyond worldly benefit and appearance." This is just a jewel. A jewel that is in the hair of a wrestler, a jewel that is in the middle of the forehead of a worldly noble, a jewel of the King of the Dragons, a jewel in the pocket of a drunkard—these may or may not have worldly benefits and appearances however they are all worldly jewels and not within the TRUTH. No one knows these jewels are not jewels so you must study carefully; you have to go into such things in minute detail.

Your whole body is the JEWEL of the teaching; you must know that all the ten worlds <u>are</u> THIS ONE BRIGHT JEWEL. Although TRUTH is like a jewel of the world it does not come from outside—it appears in one's own heart; if you are ill, and hold this JEWEL, the illness will be cured: if you have this JEWEL when you are afraid, the anguish will be swept away. Divine appearances are all traceable to this JEWEL; among the seven jewels of the king of the Tomoe, there is a wonderful JEWEL from which all rare jewels are born; THIS is infinity. In the world of men there are victor and vanquished—distinctions; the jewel of the world of humans may be called a grain of rice, a jewel stone. This however, compared with the HEAVENLY JEWEL, is as something manufactured or produced which is thereafter called a jewel; the Buddha's bones and the Dharma are THE JEWEL. IT brings everything and becomes a grain of rice; IT rescues living beings: sometimes IT appears as the Buddha Body, sometimes as a grain of rice; IT manifests all Dharma; IT manifests as One; IT manifests as one's own heart; IT becomes a body five shaku high; IT becomes a body with three heads; IT becomes all things in the universe.

Like the monks of old you must not search for tranquil-
lity by retiring to forests and mountains; this is truly not the
Way: it is a mistake. You must take the arm of all who still
hesitate and come and go together with them; to secrete yourself in forests, mountains and valleys, and do Zazen alone, is
to be one who trains without any purpose: such a one walks
the wrong road and does not know the TRUTH; in all things
he is self first. Daibaijō Zenji sat in the pine-smoke and Isan
Zenji sat under clouds in the fog with the tigers and the
wolves; one should not laugh because the ancients took this
road and became TRUE masters: we must do the same. If we
do not train with purity we will for ever be waiting for an opportunity to do so; we must know this. Daibai received Basō's
certification as well as Isan's and Hyakujō's; the old masters,
like Inzan and Rasan, did not live alone. Having gained merit once, their names remain for future generations; such persons have clear vision. To live in mountains and valleys, and
never go where one should, is one-sided; such a person is the
personification of training that is done only out of desire for
one's own moral perfection.

If the eye is not pure and clean, and yet one trains oneself alone, one becomes only an unsui and not a SEED of
Buddha; one who is a SEED of Buddha does not cut himself
off from the SEEDS of Buddha. One who stays with others,
trains and realises the SELF, deepens himself and follows the
former Ancestors; two former Ancestors said that their disciples could not sit alone—they had to train and work with
others. No one must sit apart from his fellow trainees; one
who does not take this principle to heart will never be a LEAF
OF THE FIVE GATES. Enō Zenji said, "The ancients went to
the mountains and their best food was rice; they forgot about
the human world for ten or twenty years, thus they could
realise ETERNAL GRATITUDE." Ōryunan said, "We preserve

the WAY for ourselves; some go to mountains and forests and do not draw monks into the Shūryo. No teacher of this generation, however, likes to live alone." We are weaker than the men of old; we are only in the Shūryo so we must do training as the ancients did. If we prefer solitude, because of some lack of understanding, and a monk should come, his coming could cause resentment; to behave thus is to have no understanding. You must break with attachment to body and mind; you must not live alone and apart. You must not be like Nagyaarajyuna in the mountains, even though he was lecturing, since he was only speaking about his own learning; only through deeds of charity, when living together with others, can BUDDHA'S RIGHT LAW be heard. If one trains without preference for solitude, and makes progress in training, one will extract the VERY SOURCE of the Dharma and become the MOUTH OF BUDDHA. Do you want to hear my humble words?

One ray of light does not cause blindness;
The NYOI radiates brilliantly in all directions.

CHAPTER 16.

THE FIFTEENTH ANCESTOR,
SAINT KANADAIBA.

Kanadaiba came to see Nagyaarajyuna; as he came through the door, the latter realised that he, Kanadaiba, was a wise man. Nagyaarajyuna sent away the jiisha and put a bowl of water in front of his seat: staring at the water Nagyaarajyuna held up a needle and plunged it into the bowl whilst looking into Kanadaiba's eyes. Joyfully Kanadaiba understood.

Kanadaiba was from southern India being of the Bishala clan; first he devoted himself to good deeds but later enjoyed debating also. When Nagyaarajyuna had attained understanding and was beginning to teach, he went to southern India; many men in that area had faith in good deeds so, when they heard that Nagyaarajyuna was going to give a lecture on the WONDERFUL DHARMA, they began to debate with him saying, "The most important thing in the world is for a man to do good deeds. It is vain to speak of BUDDHA NATURE for who can experience it?"

"If you wish to see the BUDDHA NATURE, you must first throw away the idea of self," said Nagyaarajyuna.

Someone said, "How big is the BUDDHA NATURE?"

"BUDDHA NATURE has nothing to do with bigness or smallness, wideness or narrowness; IT has no good or bad effect, IT does not die, IT is not born," replied Nagyaarajyuna.

When they heard this, the FUNDAMENTAL TRUTH triumphed and they completely reversed their earlier way of thinking; one of those who realised GREAT WISDOM was Kanadaiba. He went to visit Nagyaarajyuna and, as stated above, joyfully understood. Because of this Nagyaarajyuna gave him half his seat to sit on just as Shakyamuni Buddha gave half of His seat to Makakashyo on Vulture Peak.

Once, when Nagyaarajyuna was to give a lecture on the DHARMA, he did not rise from his seat: at this time his appearance was as the full moon and Kanadaiba said to the crowd, "Nagyaarajyuna is now showing the sign of the BUDDHA NATURE; he is pointing to the UNIVERSAL NATURE of (THE TRUE) SELF. How can one know this? Because his featureless samadhi, his face, is as the full moon; it is supremely vain to intellectualise the meaning of BUDDHA NATURE." When he ceased speaking, the full moon could no longer be seen.

Kanadaiba went back to his original seat and recited this verse:–

> By showing the appearance of the full moon,
> He exhibits the substance of all BUDDHAHOOD.
> To speak of the DHARMA is to lose its FACE:
> Intellectual thought is far from ITS sound and shape.

In this way master and disciple are completely one, and the very pulsing THREAD OF LIFE, which is the THREAD OF BUDDHISM, is Transmitted. This is no ordinary Transmission; right from the start, both master and disciple are ONE with the WAY. Nagyaarajyuna did not say a word; Kanadaiba did not ask a single question: the master and disciple see as one; this is the way Kanadaiba teaches and, in the five regions of India, the Kanadaiba School (Church) was spoken of.

Snow on the silver plate; the heron hiding in the bright moon: when Nagyaarajyuna and Kanadaiba meet for the first time, Nagyaarajyuna places a bowl full of water in front of Kanadaiba; when looking at the water, you can see the bottom of the bowl: there is no top, bottom or sides to the water— the TRUE SELF is as this. The full bowl is free from defilement, the water clear and pure; the needle is put in the water and penetrates both top and bottom—here there is no right or wrong. Master and disciple are inseparable; when comparing them, there is nothing which is not pure, there is no stain: when mixed together, blended, there is no trace. By raising the eyebrows and winking, this *was, is and will be made manifest, expressed;* IT *was, is and will be demonstrated* by seeing and hearing: IT does not discard seeing and hearing. Formless and empty as clear water, IT penetrates the spirit beyond the reason; IT is as a miraculous lance which passes through the heart. Flowing water excavates a hole in a mountain, soaking heaven;

the needle can pierce even the smallest mustard seed. Water can be torn by nothing; water leaves no trace; the needle is hard as a diamond. When talking about the needle and the water, what is being spoken of is your body and mind; when all the water is consumed, the needle remains alone: there is clear water when we cleanse our karma. The WAY of master and disciple is the same; there is no self or other; THE LIFE BLOOD OF BUDDHISM is passed on from master to disciple: this LIFE, open and bright, cannot be hidden in the ten quarters. Just as the vines of the wistaria entwine and climb together, so the master and disciple are one.

Those who know the clear water should study in detail and see the needle clearly in the bottom; if a mistake is made, surely the throat will be torn: do not think of the water and the needle as two; drink the water entirely or spit it out entirely. Consider the following in detail:– even should you become empty and immaculate, you must still stand firm and straight: you have to stand firm in water, fire and wind, the three disasters. Do not refute this.

> A single needle penetrates the waters of the ocean;
> When fierce dragons reach your secret place, you can
>   no longer hide.

CHAPTER 17.

THE SIXTEENTH ANCESTOR, SAINT RAGORATA.

When serving as jiisha to Kanadaiba, Ragorata heard the meaning of Karma and suddenly understood the TRUTH.

Ragorata came from Kapilavastu. The following is what is meant by "causes from a previous life," that is 'karma,' in the above kōan:– When Kanadaiba reached understanding he went to teach in Kapilavastu. There he found a rich man named Rama Ching Te in whose garden a large tree-fungus began to grow one morning: it tasted like a marvellous mushroom, however only the rich man and his second son, Ragorata, could pick and eat it: the more they picked it the more it grew; when they had eaten it all, it would again start growing: when they had had enough, they offered some to their friends, but no one else could even see it. Kanadaiba, knowing what had caused the mushroom to grow, went to Rama Ching Te's house. Rama Ching Te asked him why the mushroom had grown and Kanadaiba said, "Long ago this family provided food for a monk but he had not received the Transmission of the LIGHT; he received your gifts in vain and so these tree-mushrooms have come to you as repayment. Although others also gave him alms, it was actually only you and Ragorata who gave food with TRUE faith, thus only the two of you can see the mushrooms. Continue to eat them until they no longer appear." He then asked the rich man his age and the latter said that he was seventy-nine. Kanadaiba said in verse:–

> He has entered the WAY but not yet reached
>   enlightenment
> So has come back to repay the gifts of the faithful.
> When you are eighty-one years old
> The tree will grow no more mushrooms.

When Rama Ching Te heard these words he was very moved and said, "I am old and cannot follow you but I would like to give you my second son," so, following Kanadaiba, Ragorata left home. Kanadaiba said, "Formerly the Tathagata prophesied that you, Ragorata, would be a great teacher in the second five hundred year period: our meeting now must surely be the result of some karmic cause in a previous life." Ragorata cut off his hair and was numbered as the Sixteenth Ancestor.

Now, as in ancient times, members of the priesthood and Followers of the WAY are forbidden to accept alms without illuminating their minds; to accept alms without illuminating one's mind is shameless. A trainee gives up his home and thus has no place to call his own; his food does not belong to him and the robes he makes and wears are not his: not even a drop of water or a blade of grass is his to be used idly; you are all sustained by the land of the country in which you live and this land belongs to the ruler of the country. If you are a layman, you serve your parents and country at home, thus you have the divine grace of both heaven and earth and the blessing of the sunlight and moonshade; if you are a homeless trainee and serve neither your parents nor your country—<u>what</u> do you do if you are thus half-hearted in the DHARMA? You cannot repay your parents for raising you or the ruler for the sustenance of his land. If you enter the WAY and do not receive the Transmission of the LIGHT, it could be said that you are a traitor; to be thus is to abandon responsibility and enter upon idleness: by so doing you will give rise to the three worlds of desire, form and emptiness. After leaving home to become a trainee, you bow to neither parents nor ruler; if you take the form of a disciple of Buddha and enter the pure assembly, you do not receive alms in the same way that you would if you were completely in the world, even if they come from your former wife or child, for such alms are all given in faith.

The ancients said, "As long as the Transmission of the LIGHT has not taken place you are not worthy of receiving one grain of rice but, once the Transmission has taken place, the universe is your begging bowl and you can eat MOUNT SUMERU: even if you beg all day and all night, you will not be at fault for receiving the alms of the faithful."

It is impossible to become a TRUE trainee and to try to receive alms, when alms are scarce, without first considering whether you have received the Transmission of the LIGHT; all disciples must reflect upon this very carefully. When you discarded your home and left your birthplace, not one single grain of rice had you stored nor had you a thread to wear; you went out alone, begging, despising the body for the sake of the DHARMA and even throwing away life itself for the sake of the DHARMA. In the beginning, you did not act from a desire for fame, robes or food nor did you suffer from ambition. Do not turn to others; only reflect upon your initial intention, where you are now and where you are not; there is a saying, "It is hard to keep the initial humility to the end." If you do not keep the INITIAL MIND (NATURE) that you had at the time of ordination, you are not a FOLLOWER OF THE WAY; those of either sex who forget this, even though becoming trainees, are nothing but traitors to their country.

The trainee of old in this story, although he did not receive the Transmission of the LIGHT, did not give up his training; he became a mushroom in order to repay the alms he had received. The untrue trainees of to-day, when their lives end, will not be pardoned by Yama; the rice gruel they accept now will become molten lead or a red hot iron ball, which will make their body and mind red and inflamed when it is swallowed, if they are still unworthy, at the time of death, of the alms they have received.

Yun P'eng-huai Zenji said, "The old man did not understand what the Ancestor said: the words, 'He has entered the WAY, but not yet reached enlightenment, so has come back to repay the gifts of the faithful' are definitely the root of the matter; here there is no mistake. Trainees, do not waste time; time does not wait for man; do not wait until the time of your death; there is no merit whatsoever in simply wearing the robes of a trainee; the ties of worldly attachments will cause you to suffer the pangs of a hundred tortures; speak only in accord with the WAY."

To encounter the TATHAGATA'S WHEEL OF THE DHARMA with humility and gratitude is rarer than meeting with a tiger in the city; it is even rarer than the flowering of the Udumbara. As this is so, always take care that you practice; make the Transmission of the LIGHT clear. Do you not understand? You say that this or that state of life has feeling or non-feeling but we must not separate the two: the trainee of yesterday is the mushroom of to-day; at the time of being a mushroom the mushroom does not know that it was once a trainee: at the time of being a trainee the trainee did not know that his TRUE SELF manifested naturally in all Dharmas. Because you now have feeling you have a little wisdom and, to a certain extent, can distinguish between pain and itching: because of your delusion, the mushroom does not know you; due to your delusion, you do not know the mushroom. You distinguish between that which feels and that which does not, between animate and inanimate things; if you see your TRUE NATURE, what is it that you call feeling, what is it that you call non-feeling? IT is not past, present or future, not the sense organs, not the objects of cognition, not consciousness, neither active nor inactive, not self-made, not other-made. If you are proud of your monkish appearance, you have not yet left behind the dust of your home-life; although you escape a flood you should not be anxious because of possible disaster by fire: even if you tear delusion and become a Buddha, it is still hard to be saved from fire.

To what can this be likened? Men become deluded by things; blown like dust in the breeze, they run east and west—

they rise and fall in society and their feet do not touch the ground of reality; if their hearts do not find the REAL PLACE, their lives are nothing but an empty waste. Do you not know? If you still do not realise that, from long ago until now, many have unmistakably found the TRUE SELF, you are as drifting dust. If to-day you have exhausted kalpas, what time are you waiting for? To express this, I offer you these humble words:—

> It is sad when the Seeking Eye is not purest white;
> With the illusion of repaying others,
>> karma goes on unending.

CHAPTER 18.

THE SEVENTEENTH ANCESTOR, SAINT SŌGYANANDAI.

Ragorata said the following, "Because I already have no 'I,' you must see my *I*;[9] because you have taken me as your teacher, understand that *I* am not any 'I.'" Sōgyanandai's MIND (NATURE) awakened abruptly and he sought release.

Sōgyanandai was the son of King Baujuangyen of Sravasti; he could already speak when he was born and often praised Buddhism. By the age of seven he had had enough of worldly pleasure and said to his parents, "With a deep bow to you, my great, kind father, and homage to you, mother of my flesh and blood, I now wish to leave home in order to take vows of compassion." His parents vigorously opposed him so he refused to eat all day; they then allowed him to become a monk on condition that he lived at home so he took the name of Sōgyanandai and made the Sramanera Chanlido his novice master. He practiced without ceasing until he was nineteen but never forgot the inconsistency of being a monk and still living in the royal palace. One evening a light came down from the sky and a road appeared; without thinking, he followed it. After about four miles he reached the foot of a cliff with caves in it and settled there alone; when his parents missed him they banished Chanlido to look for him but he could not find him. Ten years passed.

At that time Ragorata came to teach in Sravasti and, one day, the water in the river there, called the Golden Waters, had a marvellous taste; the shapes of the five Buddhas appeared in mid-stream and Ragorata said to his followers, "At the source of this river, about a hundred and seventy miles away, the sage Sōgyanandai is living. Buddha predicted that, after a thousand years, Sōgyanandai would become a sage." After saying this, he took all the trainees upstream with him; eventually they came upon Sōgyanandai sitting quietly in samadhi. Ragorata and his followers went up to him and waited three weeks; only then did he come out of samadhi. Ragorata asked him, "Is it body or mind that is in samadhi?"

Sōgyanandai replied, "Both body and mind are in samadhi as one."

Ragorata said, "If both body and mind are in samadhi as one, how can there be going into, and coming out of, it?"

This is true. What can there be to go into, and come out of, if they are both one and in it? If there is still an idea that there are body and mind that you have to train, then you still do not understand the REAL samadhi: if it is not REAL samadhi then, of course, there will be going into, and coming out of, it; if there is going into, and coming out of, samadhi such samadhi cannot be REAL samadhi. When you apply yourself to samadhi, the purpose is not for body or mind or the training of body or mind. Right from the very start, practicing Zen means the dropping of both body and mind. What do you call body? What do you call mind?

Sōgyanandai said, "Though there is going into, and coming out of, it, one does not lose the state of samadhi. Samadhi is as gold in a well; always it remains still."

Ragorata said, "Whether the gold is in the well, or comes out of the well, it has neither movement nor rest. So what is it that goes in and comes out?"

If you say that whether the gold is in or out it has neither movement nor rest, what is it that goes in and comes out? If there is going in and coming out, it cannot be REAL gold. This is not something that reason will understand.

Sōgyanandai said, "By saying, 'What is it that goes in and comes out?' you have granted that the gold goes in and comes out without movement or rest."

Gold has no movement or non-movement; you cannot apply going in and coming out; these are two differing viewpoints.

Ragorata said, "If the gold is in the well, what comes out is not the gold; if the gold comes out of the well, what is it that is in the well?"

From the outside nothing goes in and from the inside nothing comes out; going in is absolute and coming out is absolute. What goes in and what comes out? What is the gold? If you say going or coming, your argument has no reason.

Sōgyanandai said, "If the gold comes out of the well, what is in it is indeed not gold. What is in the well cannot be something that has come out."

These words show that he has not understood the TRUE NATURE of the gold.

Ragorata said, "This reasoning is false."

It looks as <u>if</u> Sōgyanandai entered TRUE samadhi and understands but actually he is still in duality for he sees self and other.

Sōgyanandai said, "Your argument is not clear."

Sōgyanandai does not understand the TRUTH; he is vacillating.

Ragorata said, "This reasoning should be dropped."

Sōgyanandai said, "Your reasoning is not complete."

Ragorata, out of the depths of his great compassion, added emphatically, "You say my reasoning is not complete but it is complete."

Sōgyanandai is misinterpreting "NO-SELF."

Sōgyanandai said, "Even if your reasoning is complete, the DHARMA has nothing to do with a self."

Ragorata said, "My reasoning is already complete; I have no self."

He has heard that all Dharmas are selfless but he does not <u>really</u> know the TRUTH of selflessness; thus is the state of Sōgyanandai.

Sōgyanandai said, "I have no self so there is no need to complete the reasoning."

Ragorata said, "As *I* am selfless in TRUTH, earth, water, fire and wind are SELFLESS; the five skandhas originally are VOID; assuming a self where there is no self is discriminatory thinking."

Because he was discriminating, Sōgyanandai asked, "Sir, how can it be that your master was a sage?"

He asked this to discover whether there was any fault in the line of succession.

Ragorata said, "My master, Kanadaiba, realised the state of NO-SELF."

Sōgyanandai said, "I pay my respects to Kanadaiba and become your disciple. You have NO-SELF; I would like to follow you."

Ragorata replied, "Because I already have no 'I,' you must see my *I*; since you take me as your teacher, understand that *I* am not my 'I.'"

If you see the TRUE SELF, you have no ego so no thing will disturb your eyes; it will simply be seeing, hearing, consciousness, understanding and nothing more: there will be no division into things and Dharmas. There will be nothing such as "sage" and "worldly man;" the way of master and disciple will be one. When you see this, you will see eye to eye with the Buddhas and Ancestors; the *I* will be your master and the master will be your *I*: even should you cut this with a sword or an axe, there will be no division into two. Because of the TRUTH of this reasoning, Sōgyanandai's MIND (NATURE) awakened abruptly and he sought release.

Ragorata said, "Of itself your mind IS; its awakening is not connected to the words I said to you."

Ragorata picked up his golden bowl with his right hand and they went to a temple: Sōgyanandai took incense and food and offered the crowd some but they were shocked and critical. Ragorata said, "This has got nothing to do with me; you do as you wish." He then ordered Sōgyanandai to take half of his seat and they shared the food; the crowd exclaimed in surprise. Ragorata said, "The reason you could not eat is simply this: you have not yet realised your BUDDHAHOOD. Understand that he who is sharing my seat is an incarnation of the BUDDHA HIMSELF; out of sympathy for all creatures we give external signs: all of you will, in the middle of the Chuang-yen kalpa, reach the stage of non-returning to mortality but not the state of being outside the stream of transmigratory suffering."

The crowd said, "How can we believe in his spiritual power? You say he is a Buddha from the past but we doubt it."

Sōgyanandai, understanding the arrogance of the crowd, said, "When the World Honoured One was alive, the world was flat without any hillocks, the waters of the ditches and rivers were all sweet and beautiful, grass and trees flourished, the land was very prosperous, there was no suffering, the ten good actions were practiced and the tree of wisdom pointed to the destruction of self. Now, after just over eight hundred years, the world is mountainous and waste and the trees are withered, men do not have complete faith, TRUE thinking they treat lightly, they do not believe in TRUE SUCHNESS and only look for spiritual powers." He stopped speaking and, gradually pushing his right hand down into the earth to the limit of the lowest hell, brought nectar therefrom to the meeting place in a vessel of green vaidurya stone. The great crowd, on seeing this, took REFUGE and repented their sins.

This is very sad; as early as eight hundred years after the Buddha was in the world those who heard the DHARMA did not search. Then, as now, even if the DOCTRINE is only heard slightly, it is not retained; even when people understand the teachings intellectually they have no TRUE understanding; if there are no TRUE FOLLOWERS OF THE WAY, there is no one who has awakened the WAY-SEEKING MIND. Because of the corruption of the last generations, we have these terrible times; there is much shame and regret. Not being born in the first one thousand years after the Buddha's death is sad for both teacher and disciple but, when we think about it, even though we have been born within the five hundred years thereafter, we have been hearing the RIGHT DHARMA for five hundred and sixty years since Buddhism came to Japan from the West (i.e. India and China) so we can say it is only the start and there is no place where BUDDHISM will not grow. If we persevere dauntlessly and the will appears, we can understand NO-SELF and we will reach NO-MIND; there will be no limit to the working of body and mind; there will be no attachment to delusion or enlightenment. You will not dwell in either life or death; you will not be caught in the net of either Buddha or sentient being: uncountable kalpas come; in the endless future the unchanging SELF is there. This you should know:–

> The intellectual mind plausibly feigns phenomena of mind;
> Past my 'I,' what proportion of my REAL SELF comes into the open?

SANKON ZAZEN SETSU.
THE THREE TYPES OF PERSONALITIES RESULTING FROM TRAINING.

The person who does Zazen of the highest type has no interest in such matters as how Buddhas appear in this present world nor does he consider Truths which are untransmittable by even the Buddhas and Ancestors. He does not doctrinalise about all things being expressions of the self for he is beyond enlightenment and delusion. Since he never considers anything from a dualistic angle, nothing whatsoever enslaves him even when differences show themselves; he just eats when he is hungry and sleeps when he is tired.

The person who does Zazen of the less high type gives up everything and cuts all ties. Since, throughout the entire day, he is never idle, every moment of his life, every breath, is a meditation upon Truth; as an alternative to this, he may concentrate on a kōan with his eyes fixed in one place such as the tip of his nose. The considerations of life and death, or going and staying, are not to be seen upon his face: the discriminatory mind can never perceive the highest Truth of the Eternal nor can it comprehend the Buddha Mind; since there is no dualism in his thought, he is enlightened. From the far past to the present day, wisdom is always shining clearly and brightly; the whole universe, in all the ten directions, is permeated suddenly by the illumination from his head; all phenomena are seen separately within his body.

The person who does ordinary Zazen considers everything from all angles before freeing himself from good and evil
karma: the mind expresses naturally the True Nature of all the
Buddhas for the feet of man stand where the Buddha stands;
thus are evil ways avoided. The hands are in the position for
meditation, holding no Scripture; the mouth, being tightly shut,
is as if a seal were upon the lips for no word of any doctrine is
ever uttered; the eyes are neither wide open nor half shut; in
no way is anything considered from the point of view of differentiation for the voice of good and evil is not listened to;
the nose takes no cognisance of smells as either good or bad;
the body relies upon nothing whatsoever for all delusion is suddenly ended. Since there is no delusion to disturb the mind,
neither sorrow nor joy are to be found: as in the case of a wood-
en Buddha, both material and form are one with the Truth. Although worldly thoughts may arise they are not disturbing for
the mind is as a bright mirror in which no shadows move. From
Zazen, the Precepts arise eternally, whether they are the five,
the eight, the Great Precepts of the Bodhisattvas, the Precepts
of the priesthood, the three thousand manners, the eighty thousand beliefs or the Highest Law of the Buddhas and Ancestors; in all training, nothing whatsoever compares with Zazen.

Even if only one merit is gained from doing Zazen it is
greater than the building of a hundred, a thousand or an uncountable number of temples. Just do Zazen for ever without
ceasing for, by so doing, we are free of birth and death and
realise our own latent Buddha Nature. It is perfect and natural
to go, stay, sit and lie down; to see, hear, understand and know
are natural manifestations of the True Self; between first mind
and last mind there is no difference and none can make an argument about either knowledge or ignorance. Do Zazen with
your whole being, never forget, and lose, it.

ANNOTATIONS.

1. E.A. Burtt, ed., *The Teachings of the Compassionate Buddha* (New York: New American Library, Mentor Books, 1955), p. 147. Paraphrased slightly.

2. A better description for this nowadays might be Buddha Nature.

3. From "Ultimate Reality is Absolute Mind," in Burtt, ed., *Teachings of the Compassionate Buddha*, pp. 193–194. Slightly paraphrased. Emphasis added.

4. From "Ultimate Reality Transcends What Can Be Expressed in Words," in Burtt, ed., *Teachings of the Compassionate Buddha*, pp. 198–201. Paraphrased.

5. *Ibid*, p. 203.

6. The *Shushōgi* is not mentioned as one of Dōgen's major works because it is, strictly speaking, not a text by Dōgen. Rather, it is a composite of Dōgen statements compiled in 1900 by the chief abbots of Eiheiji and Sōjiji, the two main temples of the Japanese branch of Sōtō Zen Buddhism. Their aim was to distill Dōgen's essential teachings in as concise a form as possible.

[Hōun Hubert]

7. From "The Ten Oxherding Pictures," by Kaku-an Shi-en, in D.T. Suzuki, *Manual of Zen Buddhism*, (New York: Grove Press, Evergreen Books, 1960), p. 134.

8. Dōgen Zenji uses the words Mind, Mind that seeks the Way, Mind of the Buddhas, Way Seeking Mind, Buddha Mind, own Original Face, True Mind and True Body and Mind of the Buddhas and Ancestors to refer to the same thing. They are not different concepts but rather different ways of pointing towards one indescribable Reality which Keizan Zenji has called the Lord of the House and others have called the Buddha Nature.

9. When "I" appears in italics in this chapter only it refers to the non-egocentric state.

GLOSSARY.

The following abbreviations are used:
- J—Japanese
- C—Chinese
- S—Sanskrit
- P—Pali

ABHIDHARMA (S), higher teaching.

ACARYA (S), ajari (J). A master or teacher; a senior of five years standing.

AKSAYAMATI BODHISATTVA (S), Mujinni Bosatsu (J), That which exhibits and expresses devotion.

AMIDA (J), see AMITABHA BUDDHA.

AMITABHA BUDDHA (S), Amida Butsu (J), O-mi-t'o-fo (C). The Buddha of Fathomless Light, or Amitayus, the Buddha of Immeasurable Life. His is another name for the Cosmic Buddha. See also COSMIC BUDDHA, NEMBUTSU, PURE LAND BUDDHISM.

AMITABHA SCRIPTURE, Amida-kyo (J), Sukhavati-vyuha (S). One of the three most important Scriptures of the Pure Land Church.

ANANDA (S). The Buddha's personal jiisha.

ANATTA (P), anatman (S), no separate self or soul.

ANCESTOR. Refers to any teacher, male or female, who has fully understood Buddhism and who is in the line of succession.

ANCESTRAL LINE. The unbroken line of teachers from the Seven Buddhas.

ANGEL, see DEVA.

ANICCA (P), anitya (S), impermanence. Transience.

ANIRUDDHA (S). The cousin of Shakyamuni Buddha and one of His ten chief disciples.

ANJA (J). An assistant to the Abbot's personal jiisha, q.v.

ARADA KALAMA. The future Shakyamuni Buddha's first teacher.

ARHAT (S), arahant (J), lo-han (C). One who has cleansed his or her heart of all greed, hatred and ignorance and, knowing the Unborn, Undying, Uncreated and Unchanging in life, becomes completely at one with It in death.

ARUPA JHANA (P). The four formless meditations:– Meditation on the realm of Infinite Space; Meditation on the realm of Infinite Consciousness; Meditation on the realm of Infinite Nothingness; Meditation on the realm of Neither Perception nor Non-perception.

ASANGA (S), 310–390, Mujaku (J). An Indian Master of the Yogacara church of Mahayana.

ASITA (S). An Indian ascetic who visited the future Shakyamuni Buddha at the time of His birth and foresaw His destiny.

ASOKA (S). King Asoka Maurya, ruler of India from 269 to 232 B.C.

ASURA (S), those who do not shine, i.e. Titan.

ASVAGHOSHA (S), c. 100, Anabotei Memyō (J). An Indian Buddhist Master, the twelfth Ancestor in the Zen tradition and the reputed author of the *Buddhacarita* and *The Awakening of Faith*.

AVALOKITESVARA BODHISATTVA (S), Kanzeon Bosatsu, Kannon (J), Kuan-shi-yin, Kuan Yin (C). He who hears the cries of the world. Avalokitesvara is the Bodhisattva who exhibits Great Compassion and Mercy.

AVALOKITESVARA BODHISATTVA, SCRIPTURE OF, Kanzeon Bosatsu Fumonbon, Kannon-gyo (J). The twenty-fifth chapter of the *Lotus Scripture* (Saddharma Pundarika—S) in which the Buddha explains the activity of Avalokitesvara in the world. See also AVALOKITESVARA BODHISATTVA.

AVATAMSAKA SCRIPTURE (S), see KEGON-KYO.

AYUWAN-SHAN (C). A large Chinese Buddhist temple, visited by Dōgen, named after King Asoka, q.v.

BA (J), see BASO DŌITSU.

BADARABOSATSU (J), Bhadrapala Bodhisattva (S). A trainee who attained enlightenment whilst bathing. In Zen temples, there is a small altar dedicated to him in the bathroom. His story is told in the *Surangama Scripture*.

BASHYUBANZU (J), see VASUBANDHU.

BASO DŌITSU (J), 709–788, Ma-tsu Tao-i (C). A Chinese Zen Master, the disciple of Nangaku Ejō and the grand-disciple of Daikan Enō, the Sixth Ancestor.

BHADDIYA (P). The son of one of the seven Brahmins who were invited to Prince Siddhartha's naming ceremony. He became one of Shakyamuni Buddha's first five disciples.

BIMBISARA (P). The ruler of Magadha during Shakyamuni Buddha's life and a strong supporter of Buddhism.

BISHARI, Vaisali (S). The place where the Second Buddhist Council was held one hundred years after Shakyamuni Buddha's death.

BODAIDARUMA (J), see BODHIDHARMA.

BODAISHIN (J), Bodhicitta (S). The will to supreme enlightenment.

BODH-GAYA (S), see BUDDHA GAYA.

BODHI (S). Understanding, enlightenment, wisdom.

BODHI TREE (S), also called bo or pipal tree. The Indian fig tree under which Shakyamuni Buddha sat when He found His enlightenment. Place of enlightenment.

BODHICITTA (S), see BODAISHIN.

BODHIDHARMA (S), c. 530, Bodaidaruma or Daruma (J). The Indian Ancestor who brought Zen teaching to China; known to the Chinese as the First Ancestor.

BODHISATTVA (S), bosatsu (J), pu-sa (C), enlightened being.

BODHISATTVA PRECEPTS, see TEN PRECEPTS.

BODHISATTVA VOW, see FOUR VOWS.

BOMPU ZEN (J). Sitting in meditation simply for physical advantages. The first stage of Zen training.

BONTEN (J). (1) Brahma Deva, the Hindu God and Creator; (2) the lowest of the Four Dhyana Heavens in the world of form where beings have no desire.

BOSATSU (J), see BODHISATTVA.

BOW. An act of respect and gratitude. "As long as bowing lasts, Buddhism will last. When bowing ceases, Buddhism is destroyed"—Manzan Dōhaku.

BRAHMA (S), see BONTEN.

BRAHMIN (P). The highest of the four Indian castes:– Brahmin, priest caste; Kshatriya, warrior caste; Vaisya, merchant caste; Sudra, common caste.

BUDDHA (S), Butsu (J). Enlightened One, Awakened One. (1) A person with direct understanding of the Truth. A completely awakened person. (2) The historical Shakyamuni Buddha.

BUDDHA GAYA (S), or Bodh-gaya (S). The place in India where Shakyamuni Buddha sat beneath the Bodhi Tree and gained enlightenment.

BUDDHA MIND. The mind without attachment and discrimination which is the real mind of all beings, although they themselves may not recognise it: another name for the Buddha Nature.

BUDDHA NATURE, Busshō (J), Buddhata (S). One's own true nature, True Self. Buddha Nature should not be misunderstood as a separate soul.

BUDDHISM. A religion, founded by Shakyamuni Buddha in the sixth century B.C., in India, which teaches the path to enlightenment.

BURMESE POSITION. A form of sitting in which the feet are not placed over the thighs but rest on the sitting surface.

BUSSHŌ (J), see BUDDHA NATURE.

BUTSU (J), see BUDDHA.

BUTSUDANDA RYO-Ō (J). One of the dragon kings, deities who bring rain. One of the eight types of beings who protect the Dharma. See also DRAGON.

BUTSUDEN (J). Buddha Hall. A hall enshrining the statue of either a Buddha or Bodhisattva. In Zen temples the main religious image is enshrined in the Butsuden.

CAKRAVARTI RAJA (S), Tenrinnō (J), Wheel rolling King. A universal monarch whose chariot wheels roll everywhere without hindrance.

CH'AN (C), see ZEN.

CHANDAKA (S), Channa (P). The future Shakyamuni Buddha's favourite attendant before leaving home. Chandaka later became one of Shakyamuni's disciples.

CHIDORON, or Daichidoron (J), Ta-chih-tu-lun (C), the Maha-prajnaparamita-shastra (S). Discourses on the Great Wisdom Scriptures written by the Buddhist Ancestor Nagyaarajyuna. It was translated from Sanskrit into Chinese by Kumarajiva and is studied by many churches of Mahayana Buddhism.

CHIEF JUNIOR, Shusōshō (J). A trainee selected by the Abbot for a training term of one hundred days to lead all trainees in the monastery.

CHIJI (J). The officers, under the Abbot, who are in charge of running a temple: The Chief Junior (Shusōshō—J), Chief Administrator (Kanin), Treasurer (Fusu), Disciplinarian (Inō), Chief Cook (Tenzo) and Head of Maintenance (Shissui).

COMPASSION, daiji (J), mahakaruna (S). Loving kindness towards all living things which arises naturally out of meditation.

CONTRITION, see SANGE.

COSMIC BUDDHA. THAT which appears in every place and time and in all beings; also called by various other names such as Vairocana Buddha, Amitabha Buddha, Dharmakaya, Buddha Nature and Lord of the House. IT can be revealed through genuine training but cannot be explained as existing or not existing being beyond dualism.

CUCKOO, kalavinka (S). Indian cuckoo. A bird with a wondrously beautiful voice, said to be found in the Himalayan valleys.

DAI HON ZAN (J). Great head temple. The main temples of a Buddhist church.

DAIAN (J), 793–883, also Chōkei Daian (J), Ch'ang-Ch'ing Ta-an (C). Disciple of Hyakujō Ekai.

DAIBAIJŌ ZENJI, also known as Daibai Hōjō (J), 752–839, Tamei Fa-ch'ang (C). A Chinese Zen Master of the Rinzai Church and a disciple of Baso Dōitsu.

DAIBUTSUJI (J), Great Buddha Temple. The original name of Eiheiji. See also EIHEIJI.

DAIE SŌKŌ (J), 1089–1163, Ta-hui Tsung-kao (C). A Chinese Zen Master of the Rinzai Church. He was famous for advocating the use of kōans in meditation practice. He was posthumously known as Fukaku Zenji.

DAII DŌSHIN (J), 580–651, Tao-hsin (C). A fourth century Chinese Zen Ancestor and a disciple of Kanchi Sōsan. His teaching emphasised the unity of daily life and meditation. His chief disciple was Daiman Kōnin, the Fifth Ancestor and master of Daikan Enō.

DAIJŌJI (J). A temple, situated in Ishikawa Prefecture, Japan, which originally belonged to the Shingon Church but later became Sōtō. Keizan was Chief Abbot there for ten years. See also KEIZAN JŌKIN.

DAIKAN ENŌ (J), 638–713, Hui-nêng (C). The Sixth Ancestor of Chinese Zen. While still a layman, he received the Transmission from Daiman Kōnin becoming a monk sometime later. His teaching is referred to as the "Southern Church of Zen" and all surviving Zen traditions are descended from him. He was responsible for the great spread of Zen in the T'ang dynasty and two of his most famous disciples are Seigen Gyoshi and Nangaku Ejō. He was posthumously known as Sōkei Daishi or Daikan Zenji. His lectures were recorded by one of his disciples and are known as *The Platform Scripture.*

DAIMAN KŌNIN (J), 601–674, Hung-Jen (C). The Fifth Ancestor of Chinese Zen and teacher of Daikan Enō. He is also known as Goso Gunin or Ōbai Gunin since he lived on Mt. Ōbaisan for many years.

DAIOSHŌ (J). A Japanese term meaning Great Priest. See also OSHŌ.

DAISHI (J). A title given posthumously meaning Great Teacher or Master. For example, Keizan is known as Jōsai Daishi.

DANDOKUSEN (J), Dandaka or Dandaloka (S). A mountain in Gandhara, India, where the future Shakyamuni Buddha trained Himself prior to His enlightenment.

DARUMA (J), see BODHIDHARMA.

DASABHUMIKA (S), Ten stages. A chapter of the *Kegon Scripture* concerning the ten stages of the Bodhisattva's training.

DELIBERATE THOUGHT, see THOUGHT, NATURAL AND DELIBERATE.

DENKŌROKU (J), "The book of the Transmission of the Light." The *Denkōroku* was written by Keizan as fifty-two biographical chapters showing how the Truth was passed down from Shakyamuni Buddha to Dōgen. See also KEIZAN JŌKIN.

DENTŌROKU (J), "The Record of the Transmission of the Lamp." The *Keitoku Dentōroku* was written by the Chinese priest Tao-hsuan in 1004. It presents the biographies of 1701 priests and teachers from the time of the Seven Buddhas.

DEPENDENT ORIGINATION, Paticca Samuppada (P). One of the earliest Buddhist teachings which explains the law of causal relationships. It describes the wheel of becoming which consists of twelve steps or stages, each stage giving rise to the next:– (1) Avijja—ignorance; (2) Sankhara—volitional formations (pre-dispositions); (3) Vinnana—consciousness; (4) Nama-rupa—name and form; (5) Salayatana—sense organs; (6) Phassa—contact; (7) Vedana—feeling or emotion; (8) Tanha—craving; (9) Upadana—clinging or attachment; (10) Bhava—becoming; (11) Jati—birth; (12) Jaramarana—decay and death.

DEVA (S), ten (J). (1) Gods; heavenly beings; beings in possession of supernatural powers. (2) A great person who, having understood the Truth, leads others to it.

DEVILS. (1) Beings from hell. (2) The personifications of the egocentric self, greed, hate and delusion. See also HELL, MARA.

DHAMMAPADA (P), The Way of Truth. An early Buddhist Scripture emphasising good moral conduct, meditation and self-discipline.

DHARANI (S). Litany, hymn; a brief Buddhist Scripture similar to the even-shorter Mantras. Often used as a religious invocation or as the core of a Scripture to encourage a religious attitude of mind, such as compassion, gratitude or faith. A Dharani must not be understood as a magical formula.

DHARMA (S), hō (J), fa (C). (1) Law, Truth, the Teachings of the Buddhas and Ancestors. (2) The second of the Three Treasures and Refuges:– "I take refuge in the Dharma." The Dharma is the medicine for all suffering as it teaches the way to transcend greed, hate and delusion.

DHARMA HEIR. A senior priest who has been named by his Master as a Master in his own right with permission to teach. In the Sōtō tradition a teacher may transmit the Dharma to any number of people but name only one or two of his worthiest disciples to be his heirs.

DHARMA LOTUS SCRIPTURE, see LOTUS SCRIPTURE.

DHARMACHAKRA (S), hōrin (J), The Wheel of the Law. An eight-spoked wheel symbolising the eightfold path. Often a tomoe is depicted in the center. See also MANJI, TOMOE.

DHARMAKAYA (S), Hosshin (J), Law Body. The highest of the Three Bodies (Trikaya) of the Buddha, representing Absolute Truth, Buddha Mind. The Dharmakaya is one's own True Nature and can be realised directly for oneself through one's own training. See also THREE BODIES.

DHYANA (S), jhana (P), Zen (J), ch'an (C), Meditation.

DIAMOND SCRIPTURE, Vajracchedika Prajnaparamita Sutra (S), Kōngo-kyo (J). One of the Great Wisdom Scriptures which succinctly deals with the training of the Bodhisattva especially relating to the awakening of True Wisdom and to the practice of the Six Paramitas. The *Diamond Scripture* is widely used in all Mahayana traditions and it was this Scripture which Daikan Enō used to teach his disciples. See also PRAJNAPARAMITA.

DISCRIMINATORY MIND. The mind of duality.

DŌ (J), see WAY.

DŌAN (J). A disciplinarian's monitor in a Zen temple. See also SAMANTABHADRA BODHISATTVA.

DŌGEN KIGEN (J), 1200–1253. Founder of the Sōtō Zen Church in Japan. He was of noble birth and was orphaned as a child. He entered the priesthood at the age of twelve, studied Tendai on Mt. Hiei and then went on to study under Myoan Eisai at Kenninji Temple. In 1223 he journeyed to China with Eisai's disciple, Myozen, in order to study Zen, eventually entering Tendōzan Keitokuji where he became the disciple of Tendō Nyojō Zenji, one of the great Sōtō Zen teachers then alive: he became Nyojō Zenji's Dharma Heir receiving the Transmission from him. He returned to Japan in 1227; he was at first Abbot of Kenninji, then Abbot of Kōshōji and later founded Eiheiji in 1244. His chief disciple was Koun Ejō. His major works are the *Shōbōgenzō,* the *Eihei-kōroku,* the *Eihei-shingi* and the *Kyōjukaimon.* He was given the posthumous title of Kōsō Jōyō Daishi. He is widely acknowledged to be Japan's greatest religious thinker. See also NYOJŌ, TENDŌZAN KEITOKUJI.

DOKUSAN (J). Spiritual counseling with a Rinzai Zen Master. Another term for sanzen.

DRAGON, ryu (J), naga (S). (1) The Buddhist symbol of the Defender of the Faith. The term can refer to either people who aid and protect Buddhism or to heavenly beings who safeguard the Dharma. (2) Supernatural beings (Ryuten—J). See also BUTSUDANDA RYO-Ō.

DUKKHA (P), suffering. The first of the Four Noble Truths.

ECHŪ, Nanyo Echū (J), c. 776, Nan-yang Hui-chang (C). A Chinese Zen Master and a disciple of the Sixth Ancestor, Daikan Enō. He was the teacher of two emperors. His chief disciple was Tangen Ōshin. Echū was also known as Chū Kokushi, Ryotei Kokushi and Daishō Zenji.

EIGHT MISERIES. Eight types of human suffering:– (1) birth, (2) old age, (3) decay, (4) death, (5) being apart from loved ones, (6) being together with those one hates, (7) being unable to get what one wants, (8) being attached to a false notion of self and being attached to existence itself.

EIGHTFOLD PATH. The way to transcend suffering as taught by Shakyamuni Buddha in the fourth Noble Truth. The eight stages are right understanding, right thought, right speech, right action, right livelihood, right effort, right mindfulness and right concentration. See also FOUR NOBLE TRUTHS.

EIGHTY-EIGHT OPINIONS. The various false views that arise as a result of desire and attachment.

EIGHTY MINOR MARKS, see THIRTY-TWO MARKS OF A BUDDHA.

EIHEI (J). Refers to Eihei Temple.

EIHEI KAISAN (J), founder of Eihei, i.e. Dōgen, q.v.

EIHEIJI (J). Eihei Temple, one of the two head temples of the Sotō Zen Church, founded in Echizen in Fukui Prefecture in 1244, by Dōgen. Its original name was Daibutsuji.

EISAI, Myoan Eisai (J), 1141–1215. A Japanese Zen Master considered to be the founder of Rinzai Zen in Japan. Eisai first studied Tendai on Mt. Hiei, visiting China for a year in 1168 in order to deepen his Tendai training; he returned to China in 1186 this time to study Zen. He became the disciple of Kian Eshō of the Ōryo lineage of the Rinzai tradition. Eisai returned to Japan in 1191. In 1194 he founded Shōfukuji, the first Rinzai Zen temple in Japan and later became Abbot of Kenninji in Kyoto. Eisai's chief disciple was Ryonen Myozen. Dōgen studied Rinzai Zen under Eisai and, later, under Myozen with whom he went to China. Eisai's teaching was a combination of Rinzai, Tendai and Pure Land. See also DŌGEN KIGEN, MYOZEN, TENDAI.

EKA, see TAISŌ EKA.

EMPTINESS, see SUNYATA.

ENAN (J), see ŌRYO ENAN.

ENDLESS TRAINING. Spiritual training without end or limit; the flowing and going on which embodies the highest Truth.

ENGAKU (J), see PRATYEKABUDDHA.

ENGAKU DAISHI (J), Fully Enlightened Great Teacher. Refers to Bodhidharma.

ENGO KOKUGON (J), 1063–1135, Yuan-wu K'o-ch'in (C). A Chinese Zen Master. He was the disciple of Goso Hōyen and the master of Daie Sōkō. Engo wrote the commentary on the *Hekiganroku.*

ENLIGHTENMENT, Nirvana, Bodhi (S). Religious realisation or understanding.

ENŌ (J), see DAIKAN ENŌ.

ESHI (J), 515–577, Hui-ssu (C). The Second Ancestor of the Chinese Tendai Church and the teacher of Chigi (Chih-i—C). See also TENDAI.

ESOTERIC BUDDHISM. Refers to Zen and some churches of Tibetan Buddhism.

FAITH. In Sōtō Zen faith is of the greatest importance since it is the entrance to training. Faith gives rise to true conviction, to humility and eventually to true wisdom and certain knowledge.

FIRE DRAGON, see DRAGON.

FIRST MIND. The mind of the sincere beginner; open, naïve, determined and willing to bow.

FIVE BUDDHAS. Buddhas found in esoteric Buddhism.

FIVE DHYANAS. The Five Wisdoms of esoteric Buddhism which correspond to the Five Buddhas. See also FIVE BUDDHAS.

FIVE DISCOMFORTS. Discomforts said to be felt by heavenly beings (devas) when their good karma runs out and decay sets in.

FIVE LAWS OF THE UNIVERSE. The five laws by which the universe operates are:– 1) the laws of the physical world—the world is not answerable to one's personal will; (2) the laws of the organic world—all things flow; (3) the laws of morality—karma is inexorable; (4) the laws of the Dharma—evil is vanquished and good prevails; (5) the laws of mind—the will to enlightenment: the intuitive knowledge of the Buddha Nature occurs to all men.

FIVE SCHOOLS (CHURCHES). During the late T'ang dynasty in China, there were five Zen traditions, all of which had descended from the Sixth Ancestor; the five were Sōtō, Rinzai, Igyo, Ummon and Hōgen.

FIVE THOUGHTS. The Five Thoughts, which are part of the mealtime ceremonial, encourage trainees to reflect carefully on their attitude of mind. In Chinese temples the Dining Hall is called the "Hall of the Five Thoughts."

FOUNDER'S HALL, kaisandō (J). A hall where the relics of the priest who founded the temple are enshrined.

FOUR BENEFACTORS. They are:– (1) the Buddha, (2) the head of state (President, King or Queen), (3) one's parents and (4) all people.

FOUR ELEMENTS. Fire, air, water and earth; the four classical elements that combine to produce existence. Sometimes five elements are named, wind, ether, or consciousness, being the fifth.

FOUR EXISTENCES, or Lives. The four categories of Buddhists (Fourfold Pure Assembly):– male priests, female priests, laymen and laywomen.

FOUR GUARDIAN KINGS, Shitennō (J). The four deities in the lowest heaven who guard the four directions:– Bishamon-ten (Vaisravana—S) who guards the north; Zōjō-ten (Virudhaka—S) who guards the south; Jikoku-ten (Dhrtarastra—S) who guards the east and Kōmoku-ten (Virupaksa—S) who guards the west.

FOUR LIVES, see FOUR EXISTENCES.

FOUR NOBLE TRUTHS. These are:– (1) suffering exists; (2) suffering's cause; (3) suffering's end; (4) the Eightfold Path. See the EIGHTFOLD PATH.

FOUR TYPES OF ACTION. Sitting, walking, lying down and standing still.

FOUR VIEWS. (1) There is impurity of body; (2) there is pain in sensation; (3) mind is transient; (4) things have no ego.

FOUR VOWS. The four Bodhisattva vows. (1) However innumerable beings are, I vow to save them; (2) However inexhaustible the passions are, I vow to transform them; (3) However limitless the Dharma is, I vow to understand it completely; (4) However infinite the Buddha's Truth is, I vow to attain it.

FOUR WISDOMS. Charity, tenderness, benevolence and sympathy.

FOURFOLD ASSEMBLY, see FOUR EXISTENCES.

FUGEN BOSATSU (J), see SAMANTABHADRA BODHISATTVA.

FUKANZAZENGI (J). Dōgen's Rules for Meditation.

FULL-LOTUS. The form of cross-legged sitting in which each foot is placed over the opposite thigh.

FUNZOE (J). The seven types of rags used in making the kesa.

FUTŌROKU (J), Record of the Lamp compiled in 1204 by the Chinese priest Lei-an Cheng-shou.

GAITAN (J), outside sitting place. The meditation platform outside the Meditation Hall.

GASAN, Kassan Zene (J), 805–881, Chia-shan-hui (C). A Chinese Zen Master. He was a disciple of the famous Boatman Priest, Sensu Tokujō, and a contemporary of Tōzan Ryokai.

GASSAN JOSEKI (J), 1275–1365. A disciple of Keizan, Gassan was installed as Abbot of Sōjiji one year before Keizan's death.

GASSHŌ (J). The Buddhist mudra which expresses gratitude and humility.

GAUTAMA (S). Shakyamuni Buddha's name prior to enlightenment.

GEDŌ ZEN (J), wrong way. Training done solely to gain power, unusual experiences, visions, etc.

GENII, plural of genius. Refers to the people considered to be the most brilliant in India.

GENJŌ-KŌAN (J). The kōan that appears naturally in daily life.

GHEE (S). Clarified butter; considered to be a great delicacy in India.

GOI THEORY (J). Tōzan's Five Ranks.

GREAT DOUBT. Great questioning or probing.

GREAT GRIEF, Kokoro Kanashiku (J), the grief of the heart.

GUNIN, see DAIMAN KŌNIN.

GYOJI (J). Endless training.

HAISEKI (J), Bowing seat.

HAKAMA (J). A skirt-like garment worn in Japan.

HALF-LOTUS. A form of cross-legged sitting in which one foot is placed on the opposite thigh whilst the other rests on the sitting place.

HAN (J). The wooden board which is struck with a mallet to signal various events in a temple.

HAN PERIOD. A Chinese dynasty; 25–225 A.D.

HARA (J). The triangular region of the front of the body formed from the base of the sternum and reaching down the sides of the rib cage to just below the navel.

HARANA (J), Varanasi (P). The place in India where Shakyamuni Buddha first began to teach after His enlightenment.

HEART SCRIPTURE, see SCRIPTURE OF GREAT WISDOM.

HEAVEN, ten (J). One of the Six Worlds, or Lokas, inhabited by devas (angels or gods).

HELL, niraya (S). One of the Six Lokas or Worlds.

HERESY. In Buddhism, the term heresy implies wrong understanding, delusion or not seeing clearly: it does NOT imply a violation of doctrine.

HIEI, MOUNT, or HIEI-ZAN (J). The headquarters of the Japanese Tendai Church is located on Mt. Hiei.

HINAYANA (S), the small vehicle as contrasted with Mahayana or the large vehicle.

HIPARAKUTSU (J). A cave near Rajagrha where it is believed Makakashyo was meditating when Shakyamuni Buddha entered Parinirvana.

HŌGEN BUNEKI (J), 855–958, Fa-yen Wen-i (C). Founder of the Hōgen (Fa-yen—C) Church of Chinese Buddhism and a disciple of Rakan Keishin.

HOKEKYO (J), see LOTUS SCRIPTURE.

HONDŌ (J). Hall of a temple where ceremonies are held and lectures given.

HONSHI (J). True Master; the master by whom a trainee is Transmitted.

HOSSEN (J). The name of the ceremony in which a trainee is given the rank of Chief Junior; one of the four ceremonies of Kessei.

HUANG-PO (C), see ŌBAKU KIUN.

HUI-NÊNG (C), see DAIKAN ENŌ.

HUNGRY GHOST, gaki (J), preta (S). An occupant of one of the Six Worlds depicted with a tiny throat and bloated stomach.

HYAKUJŌ EKAI (J), 720–814, Pai-chang Huai-hai (C). One of the great Chinese Zen Masters of the T'ang dynasty. He was one of Baso's Dharma Heirs and the master of Ōbaku Kiun (Huang-Po) and Isan Reiyu. He established the first formal rules of Zen training called *Hyakujō-shingi*, or the *Zen Temple Regulations*. He was famous for his teaching, "A day without work is a day without eating." He is known for the famous kōan "Hyakujō's Fox." See also ZEN TEMPLE REGULATIONS.

HYAKUJŌ, RULES OF, see ZEN TEMPLE REGULATIONS.

IGYO ZEN (J), Kuei-yang (C). One of the five schools (churches) of Zen in China, founded by Isan Reiyu in the eighth century. It was quickly absorbed into the Rinzai Church. See ISAN REIYU.

INDRA, also Sakra (S). The Hindu creator of the world. According to Buddhist Scriptures, Indra was converted to the Dharma and is often portrayed as asking questions. See also HEAVEN.

INŌ (J). The Chief Disciplinarian in a Zen temple.

IRON MAN, tetsugen (J), Vajrasattva (S). The immovable, imperturbable and indestructible Buddha Nature within one.

ISAN REIYU (J), 771–853, Kuei-shan Ling-yu (C). A Chinese Zen Master, a disciple of Hyakujō. His two main students were Reiun Shigon and Gyozan Ejaku. He established the Igyo Church of Zen, the name coming from the first syllables of Isan and Gyozan.

JATAKA TALES. Tales of the Buddha's previous lives, used to express aspects of the Buddha's teaching.

-JI (J), -ssu (C). A suffix used to indicate a temple, as in Eiheiji (Eihei Temple). Sometimes a temple is known by the name of the mountain it is situated on as in Tendōzan (Mt. Tendō).

JIISHA (J). A priest constantly with the Abbot, or constantly with a priest who is his senior: he is not a servant although he may help the Abbot in many ways. The post of jiisha is much sought after; this is because a jiisha is not only constantly with his teacher, thus having the advantage of constant teaching, but also since the future Abbot of a temple is frequently the former Abbot's jiisha— Makakshyo was jiisha to Shakyamuni Buddha; Ananda was second jiisha to Shakyamuni and first jiisha to Makakashyo.

JIKIDŌ (J). The Meditation Hall monitor.

JIKKŌ (J). An assistant jiisha.

JINSHŪ JŌZA (J), 605–706, Shen-hsui (C). He was the foremost and most learned disciple of the Fifth Chinese Ancestor, Daiman Kōnin. It was assumed that he would become the Sixth Ancestor but Daikan Enō had the <u>True</u> understanding and was given the Transmission. Later Jinshū received the Transmission and formed what was known as the "Northern Church of Zen" as opposed to Enō's "Southern Church." Jinshū taught gradual, while Enō taught sudden, enlightenment. They were referred to as the "Ancestors of South and North."

JŌDŌ (J), Pure Land. The Western Paradise of Shin Buddhism. See also AMITABHA and PURE LAND BUDDHISM.

JŌDŌ (J). (1) The festival of the attainment of Buddhahood held on December 8th. (2) A Zen ceremony in which the Abbot ascends the high altar to be tested in mondo (question and answer) on his realisation of the Truth. One of the Kessei ceremonies.

JŌDŌ SHINSHU (J), see SHIN BUDDHISM.

JOGŌ-TEN (J). (1) Fourth heaven in the world of form. (2) The personification of the world.

JŌSHŪ JŪSHIN (J), 788–897, Chao-chou Ts'ung-shen (C). One of the most famous of the Chinese Zen Masters. He was a disciple of Nansen Fugan and was posthumously known as Shinsai Zenji. He is most famous for the kōan "Mu."

JŪ (J), stage. Refers to the ten stages of the Bodhisattva.

JŪKAI (J). The festival at the time of the taking of the Precepts by all trainees and lay Buddhists.

JŪKAI SESSHIN (J). The week retreat during which lay trainees receive the Precepts and formally become Buddhists.

JŪKAI TOKUDŌ (J). Lay ordination; becoming a lay Buddhist.

KAISAN (J). The founder of a temple, as in Eihei Kaisan (the founder of Eiheiji, i.e. Dōgen) and Sōji Kaisan (the founder of Sōjiji, i.e. Keizan). A posthumous title of a temple's founder.

KALEIDOSCOPIC MIND. That state of mind that flows, adapting to every situation, responding accordingly and holding on to, and discriminating against, nothing.

KALPA (S). An aeon.

KANADAIBA (J), Kanadeva (S). The chief disciple of the Indian Ancestor Nagyaarajyuna and the fifteenth Ancestor after Shakyamuni Buddha.

KANCHI SŌSAN (J), d. 606, Seng-ts'an (C). The Third Chinese Ancestor, a disciple of Taisō Eka and grand-disciple of Bodhidharma. The famous Zen poem "On Trust in the Heart" (Shinjinmei—J) is attributed to him. His chief disciple was Daii Dōshin, the Fourth Chinese Ancestor.

KANIN (J). The Chief Administrator, under the Abbot and Vice Abbot, of a Zen training temple; one of the Chiji.

KANNON (J), see AVALOKITESVARA BODHISATTVA.

KANTHAKA (P). Prince Siddhartha Gautama's horse.

KANZEON BOSATSU (J), see AVALOKITESVARA BODHI-SATTVA.

KAPILAVASTU (P), see KABIRA.

KARMA (S), kamma (P). Action, resulting from cause, and its effect. The Law of Cause and Effect; the third of the Five Laws of the Universe.

KAROKU PERIOD. Around 1227, the year in which Dōgen wrote the *Fukanzazengi*.

KASHIKOKU (J). That area of India just north of Magadha.

KASYAPA (S), see MAKAKASHYO.

KEGON (J), Hua-yen (C), Avatamsaka (S). A Chinese church of Buddhism based upon the teachings of the *Avatamsaka Scripture*. It was founded by Tojun (557–640) and flourished under Hōzō (643–712). Much of the Kegon teaching was influenced by Zen and many Zen teachers adopted some of the Kegon teaching for use in training their students. Kegon was introduced to Japan by Dōsen (702–760) in 736. It is a relatively small church with only thirty temples in Japan today. See also KEGON-KYO.

KEGON-KYO (J), Hua-yen-ching (C), Avatamsaka Sutra (S), Garland Scripture. The teaching of Shakyamuni Buddha during the three weeks immediately after His enlightenment while He was still in a deep state of meditation. The *Gandavyuha* and *Dasabhumika Scripture* are sections of this Scripture.

KEIZAN JŌKIN (J), 1267–1325. One of the two famous Ancestors of Japanese Sōtō Zen and the founder of Sōjiji. He entered the priesthood at the age of twelve under Koun Ejō, the successor to Dōgen and second Abbot of Eiheiji. He later studied with Tetsū Gikai under whom he attained enlightenment. He was Abbot of Daijōji for ten years thereafter establishing Sōjiji. Dōgen is regarded as the father of Sōtō Zen in Japan whilst Keizan is thought of as its mother. Keizan is responsible for the wide spread of Sōtō Zen in Japan. His writings include the *Denkōroku*, *Zazen-yojink*i and most of the Sōtō Zen ceremonial. See also SŌJIJI, DENKŌROKU.

KENNINJI (J). One of the head temples of the Rinzai Church in Kyoto founded in 1202 by Myoan Eisai. Dōgen trained there under Eisai and later under Myozen. On his return from China, Dogen was appointed Abbot of Kenninji. See also DŌGEN KIGEN.

KENSHŌ (J), to see into one's own nature. The experience of enlightenment, satori (J).

KENTAN (J). A tour of the Meditation Hall either performed by the Abbot or the Chief Junior.

KESA (J), kasaya (S). The Buddhist priest's robe.

KESSEI (J). That series of ceremonies performed whenever a new Abbot has a trainee whom he feels is ready for the rank of Chief Junior.

KINHIN (J), mindful walking. Walking meditation.

KINMEI (J). Emperor Kinmei ruled over Japan in the sixth century A.D. During his reign (552) the first Buddha statue was brought to Japan from Korea.

KŌAN (J), kung-an (C), public case. A statement or story, used usually by a Rinzai Zen Master, as a teaching device.

KOHŌ KEIDŌ CHISAN ZENJI (J), 1879–1967. Former Chief Abbot of Sōjiji who received Rōshi P.T.N.H. Jiyu-Kennett as disciple in 1962 and Transmitted, i.e. gave higher ordination to, her in 1963. See also SŌJIJI.

KOKORO (J), see SHIN.

KONDANNA (P). The Brahmin invited to the naming ceremony of the future Shakyamuni Buddha who predicted that the child would renounce the world to seek Nirvana. Kondanna later became one of the Buddha's followers and attained enlightenment under Him.

KOROMO (J). A priest's robe.

KŌSEI (J). Refers to Baso Dōitsu.

KŌSHŌJI (J). A temple in Uji, in Japan, established by Dōgen in 1236. He was Abbot there until he established Eiheiji in 1244.

KŌSŌ (J), Great Monk. Dōgen is referred to as Eihei Kōsō, Great Monk of Eihei.

KOUN EJŌ (J), 1198–1280. Dōgen's chief disciple and the second Abbot of Eiheiji. His chief work is the *Shōbōgenzō Zuimonki*. His successor was Tetsū Gikai, Keizan's master.

KŌYA, MOUNT (J). A mountain in Japan, the location of the headquarters of the Shingon Church. In 816, Kōbō Daishi founded a temple there.

KSHATRIYA (S). The warrior caste; one of the four Indian castes. See BRAHMIN.

KUAN-YIN (C), see AVALOKITESVARA BODHISATTVA.

KUKKUTAPADA (S), Mount Keisoku (J). The mountain in Magadha where Makakashyo died.

KŪŌ BUDDHA (J), Dharmagahana bhyudgata Raja (S). A Buddha mentioned in the *Lotus Scripture* as having taught the understanding of the Absolute.

KUTSUJUN (J). A fine-textured cloth resembling cotton. Bodhidharma's kesa was of blue-black kutsujun.

KYŌJUKAIMON (J). Dōgen's explanation of the Buddhist Precepts.

KYOSAKU (J), awakening stick.

KYOSHI (J). A word used to indicate a Japanese teaching of divinity degree. It is received from a licensed seminary temple where the priest has undergone training.

LANKAVATARA SUTRA (S), Ryogikyo (J), The Lanka Entering Scripture. A Mahayana Scripture widely studied by Zen trainees from the time of Bodhidharma until Daikan Enō.

LAY ORDINATION, see JŪKAI TOKUDŌ.

LAW, see DHARMA.

LIGHT. Another word for Dharma, Truth and Wisdom.

LITANY OF THE GREAT COMPASSIONATE ONE, Daihishin Dharani (J). An Indian Buddhist Scripture addressed to Avalokitesvara.

LOKA (S), world. The Six Lokas represent the states of being produced by the three fires of greed, hate, and delusion.

LORD. Refers to Buddha and that which shows Buddha.

LORD OF THE HOUSE. Buddha in each being, Buddha Nature, Cosmic Buddha; That which is not explicable in terms of existence and non-existence or self and other. Another term for Buddha Mind, Iron Man, True Heart.

LOTUS BLOSSOM, renge (J), padma, pundarika (S). A Buddhist symbol for training, enlightenment, compassion and purity.

LOTUS POSITION, see FULL-LOTUS, HALF-LOTUS, BURMESE POSITION.

LOTUS SCRIPTURE, Hoke-kyo or Myo-hō-renge-kyo (J), Saddharma Pundarika (S). *The Lotus of the Good Law Scripture*. A

Mahayana Buddhist Scripture which teaches that all living things have the Buddha Nature and can attain Buddhahood.

LUMBINI (P). The grove of trees at Kabira where Shakyamuna Buddha was born.

MAGADHA (S), Makada (J). The area in northern India where the Bodhi Tree was located and where Shakyamuni Buddha began His teaching. King Bimbisara, a follower of the Dharma, ruled Magadha during the Buddha's life.

MAHA MAYA (S). The mother of Prince Siddhartha Gautama, the future Shakyamuni Buddha. She died seven days after His birth.

MAHA PRAJAPATI (S). Aunt of Prince Siddhartha Gautama, the future Shakyamuni Buddha. She took care of the new-born prince after His mother's death. Later, she became the first female member of the priesthood.

MAHAKASYAPA (S), see MAKAKASHYO.

MAHAPRAJNAPARAMITA (S), see PRAJNAPARAMITA.

MAHASATTVA (S), great being. Avalokitesvara is referred to as a Bodhisattva-Mahasattva.

MAHAYANA (S), large vehicle. One of the two major divisions of Buddhism. See HINAYANA.

MAITREYA (S), Miroku (J), also called Jushi (J), Loving One. The Buddha who is to come. He is waiting, as a Bodhisattva, in the Tushita heaven. To realise one's own Buddha Nature is to bring Maitreya here.

MAKADA (J), see MAGADHA.

MAKAKASHYO (J), Mahakasyapa (S), also called Kasyapa, Kashō. One of the ten great disciples of Shakyamuni Buddha. Born into a Brahmin family, he became a disciple of the Buddha and reached Understanding in only eight days.

MAKYO (J). Hallucinations, which must be distinguished from genuine religious visions, which may arise during meditation; usually due to incorrect breathing, posture or physical or mental stress.

MANDA-RYU-Ō (J). Dragon. See BUTSUDANDA RYO-Ō.

MANDALA (S), mandara (J). A diagram which expresses a religious view of the universe by means of symbols or portraits of
Buddhas and Bodhisattvas.

MANDARA BLOSSOMS (J). Heavenly red flowers.

MANGALAMA (S), see MOKKENREN.

MANJI (J), swastika (S). The ancient symbol of Indian Buddhism.
See also TOMOE.

MANJUSRI BODHISATTVA (S), Monju Bosatsu (J). Manjusri
personifies great wisdom (prajna).

MANTRA (S), shingon (J), True Word. A very short Scripture comprised of a few Sanskrit words. Mantras are not magical spells;
they rather express the essence of a Scripture.

MANZAN DŌHAKU (J), 1635–1714. A great Japanese Sōtō
Zen Master who lived twenty-two generations after Dōgen. He
was the Chief Abbot of Eiheiji and later became the Abbot of
Daijōji.

MARA (S). The personification of all temptations to evil and distractions from training.

MAT, zagu (J). A priest's rectangular bowing mat used during meditation and ceremonies.

MEDITATION, see SHIKAN-TAZA, ZAZEN.

MERIT. The Buddhist teaching that positive spiritual good arises
from training and the keeping of the Precepts.

MIAO-HSIN (C), Myoshin (J). A famous female Chinese Zen
priest and a disciple of Gyozan Ejaku. She became well known
for instructing seventeen priests on the meaning of the "Wind
and Flag" kōan (*Mumonkan*, twenty-ninth chapter).

MIDDLE EXISTENCE. The time between death and the next rebirth. In traditional Buddhism, it is believed to take a maximum
of forty-nine days.

MIDDLE WAY. Another term for the Dharma which teaches the
middle way between over-indulgence and asceticism. The way
of non-attachment.

MIROKU (J), see MAITREYA.

MO SHAN (C), Massan Ryonen (J). A famous female Chinese Zen Master during the late T'ang dynasty. She was a disciple of Kōan Daigu (Kao-an Ta-yu) and a contemporary of Rinzai. Little about her has survived.

MOKKENREN (J), Maudgalyayana or Mangalama (S). One of the Buddha's ten great disciples and a friend of Shariputra.

MONDO (J), question and answer. A verbal, spiritual interchange between master and disciple, or between Zen priests, used to deepen spiritual training and clarify understanding. It is not an intellectual or philosophical exercise but arises naturally from heart to heart. In Zen, True mondo is like "two arrows in mid-air that meet."

MONJU (J), see MANJUSRI.

MOST EXCELLENT MIRROR—SAMADHI, Hōkyo-Zammai (J). Scripture written by Tōzan Ryokai, one of the founders of the Sōtō Zen Church.

MOUNT RYOJU (J), see RYOJU.

MU (J), wu (C), no, not, nothing. Immaculacy, Buddha Mind.

MUDRA (S). Gestures used in Buddhist ceremonies and iconography.

MYOZEN, Ryonen Myozen (J), 1184–1225. The chief disciple of Eisai, founder of the Rinzai Church in Japan. He taught Dōgen for nine years after Eisai's death and, in 1223, went with Dōgen to China where he died in 1225.

NAGYAARAJYUNA (J), Nagarjuna (S), c. 200 A.D. One of the great Buddhist teachers and writers of India. He is in the Madhyamika (Middle Way) tradition. His commentaries on the Great Wisdom Scriptures are studied by many churches of Buddhism. He is the fourteenth Ancestor in the Zen tradition.

NANGAKU EJŌ (J), 677–744, Nan-yueh Huai-jang (C). A Chinese Zen Master and one of the great disciples of the Sixth Ancestor, Daikan Enō. He and his brother disciple Seigen head the two great lines of Chinese Zen which later spread into the five schools (churches).

NANSEN FUGAN (J), 748–835, Nan-ch'uan P'u-yuan (C). A Chinese Zen Master, disciple of Baso Dōitsu. Nansen is known for a number of famous kōans, including "the cutting of the cat."

NATURAL THOUGHT, see THOUGHT.

NEMBUTSU (J), nien-fo (C), to think on Buddha. The repetition of the Buddha's name. The term generally refers to the Pure Land, or Jōdō Shinshu, practice of reciting Namu Amida Butsu (Homage to Amitabha Buddha).

NERANJARA RIVER (P). The river by which the future Shakyamuni Buddha sat in order to realise His enlightenment.

NI-OSHŌ (J), female (ni) priest (oshō). A woman priest; a priestess.

NIRMANAKAYA (S), ōjin (J), transformation body. The first of the Three Bodies (Trikaya) of the Buddha. This is the physical Shakyamuni Who is seen in the world. See also THREE BODIES.

NIRVANA (S), nehan (J). That which is realised at the time of enlightenment.

NOVICE MASTER. A senior priest in charge of the instruction of priest trainees.

NYOI (J). A sceptre carried by a celebrant during ceremonies.

NYOI JEWEL (J), cintamani (S). A jewel capable of removing all suffering. A symbol of the Dharma and the Three Treasures united into one jewel.

NYOJŌ, Tendō Nyojō (J), 1163–1228, T'ien-t'ung Ju-ching (C). Chinese Zen Master, Abbot of Tendōzan Keitokuji and Dōgen's master. Nyojō advocated a strong Zazen practice and strict training. See also DŌGEN KIGEN, TENDŌZAN KEITOKUJI.

NYORAI (J), see TATHAGATA.

NYUDO-NO-HAI (J). (1) The ceremony during which a new trainee enters the Meditation Hall for the first time. (2) Refers to the induction ceremony of a new Chief Junior. See also CHIEF JUNIOR.

ŌBAI (J), see DAIMAN KŌNIN.

ŌBAKU KIUN (J), d. 850, Huang-po Hsi-yün (C). A Chinese Zen Master, the chief disciple of Hyakujō Ekai, and Rinzai's master.

One of the Japanese Zen churches bears his name. See also ŌBAKU ZEN.

ŌBAKU ZEN (J). One of the three Zen churches in Japan. It was brought to Japan by Ingen Ryuki (1592–1673) a Chinese Zen priest. Ōbaku Zen is actually a mixture of Zen and Pure Land practices and has a relatively small following in Japan. Its head temple is Mampukuji at Uji in Kyoto. Ōbaku was not a separate Zen church in China but arose out of the amalgamation of Zen and Pure Land during the Ming dynasty.

OFFICERS, TEMPLE, see CHIJI.

OHIGAN (J), crossing over. The Japanese festival held at the equinox.

OM (S). A word often used as the invocation of a mantra or dharani and also as a mantra by itself. It originally came from Hinduism.

ONE MIND. A word referring to Nirvana, Buddha Mind and Dharmakaya.

ONE VEHICLE, ichijō (J), Ekayana (S). The One Way; the Buddha Path.

ŌRYO ENAN (J), 1002–1069, Huang-lung Hui-nan (C). A Chinese Zen Master of the Rinzai Church who lived on Mt. Ōryu.

ŌRYUNAN, see ŌRYO ENAN.

ŌRYUZAN (J), yellow dragon mountain. Ōryo Enan lived there for many years. See also ŌRYO ENAN.

OSHŌ (J), upadhyaya (S). A Buddhist priest.

OX-HERDING PICTURES. A series of ten pictures depicting Zen training. These drawings are attributed to Kaku-an Shi-en, a Chinese Zen priest of the twelfth century.

PARAMITA (S), reaching the other shore. The Paramitas are the qualities that arise from meditation and training and are the signs of enlightenment. The Six Paramitas are (1) giving (dana—S), (2) keeping of the Precepts (sila), (3) patience (kshanti), (4) vigour (virya), (5) meditation (dhyana) and (6) wisdom (prajna). Other Paramitas sometimes included are (7) skilful means (upaya), (8) commitment (pranidhana), (9) strength (bala) and (10) knowledge and understanding (jnana). The Paramitas are fully discussed in the Diamond and Great Wisdom Scriptures. See also FOUR WISDOMS.

PARINIRVANA (S), complete, all, round (pari) Nirvana. Parinirvana means complete and final extinction of greed, hate and delusion; rest, eternal meditation.

PARINIRVANA SCRIPTURE. The scripture of the last words of Shakyamuni Buddha before His Parinirvana (passing into eternal meditation).

PARYANKA (S), kekka-fuza (J), see FULL-LOTUS.

PIPAL TREE, see BODHI TREE.

PLATFORM SCRIPTURE. A collection of sermons delivered by Daikan Enō, the Sixth Ancestor of Chinese Zen. They were compiled by his disciple Fa-hai.

PRAJNA (S), hannya (J), wisdom. Seeing clearly. The Wisdom that is beyond discriminatory thought that arises naturally from meditation and diligent training.

PRAJNAPARAMITA (S), Hannya haramita (J), the perfecting of wisdom.

PRATYEKABUDDHA (S), dokkaku, engaku (J), self-enlightened. A general term referring to one who is enlightened as a result of his own efforts but does not share his understanding with others.

PRECENTOR. The priest who intones and leads Scriptural recitations. See INŌ.

PRECEPTOR. The priest who gives the Precepts to new priesttrainees.

PRECEPTS, kai (J), sila (S). The ways of living that are in accordance with the Dharma.

PURE LAND BUDDHISM. The Mahayana church based on faith in Amitabha Buddha. It arose in fourth century China never having existed in India.

PYTHON. As used by Keizan it refers to those trainees who cling to solitude and their own enlightenment, refusing to help others.

QUIETISM. A spiritual disease caused by a grave misunderstanding of karma.

RAHULA (P), impediment. The son of Prince Siddhartha Gautama, the future Shakyamuni Buddha.

RAKHUSU (J). A small kesa (priest's robe) worn around the neck.

RASAN DŌKAN (J), Lo-shan Tao-hsien (C). A Chinese Zen Master of the late T'ang dynasty.

REIUN SHIGON (J), Ling-yun Chih-ch'in (C). A Chinese Zen Master, disciple of Isan Reiyu. He was enlightened, after many years of training, on seeing peach blossoms.

RENGESHIKI (J), Utpalavarna (P). A female priest during the time of Shakyamuni Buddha. Originally she was a prostitute who entertained her clientele by wearing different costumes. Someone suggested she put on a kesa; she did so and was at once converted to the Three Treasures. She was taught by Maha Prajapati.

RI (J), li (C). A measure of distance, approximately one-third of a mile.

RINZAI KIGEN (J), d. 866, Lin-chi I-hsuan (C). A Chinese Zen Master, founder of the Rinzai Church of Zen.

RINZAI ZEN (J), Lin-Chi (C). One of the five schools (churches) of Zen in China and one of the three present-day Zen traditions in Japan. It was founded by the Chinese Zen Master Rinzai Kigen and is known for its use of kōans. It was brought to Japan by Eisai in 1191.

RŌSHI (J), reverend master.

RULES FOR MEDITATION, see FUKANZAZENGI.

RULES OF HYAKUJŌ, see ZEN TEMPLE REGULATIONS.

RUPA (S), form or matter. Used to express body, matter, statue or portrait; i.e. Buddha-rupa = Buddha form.

RYO, EMPEROR OF, Butei (J), Wu-ti of the Liang dynasty (C). The Chinese emperor who questioned Bodhidharma on Buddhism.

RYOGIKYO (J), see LANKAVATARA SUTRA.

RYOGONKYO (J), see SURANGAMA SUTRA.

RYOJU, MOUNT, Ryozen (J), Grdhrakuta (S). A mountain in India known as Vulture Peak.

RYOKAI PERIOD (J). The Liang dynasty in China, 502–557 A.D.

RYOZEN (J), see RYOJU.

SACRISTAN. The temple officer in charge of the ceremony halls.

SALA TREES. Shakyamuni Buddha passed into Parinirvana while lying in a grove of sala trees.

SAMADHI (S), zammai (J), Meditation.

SAMANTABHADRA BODHISATTVA (S), Fugen Bosatsu (J), Full of Virtue.

SAMBHOGAKAYA (S), Hōjin (J), reward body. The second of the Three Bodies of the Trikaya representing the reward of training.

SAMMYAKU-SAMBODAI (J), Samyak-sambodhi (S). The supreme, perfect and complete enlightenment of the Buddha.

SAMSARA (S), shōji (J), this world of life and death.

SANDŌKAI (J), Ts'an-t'ung-chi (C), the harmonising of the all is one and the all is different. A Zen Scripture written by Sekitō Kisen.

SANGE (J), contrition, confession, repentence. The sincere recognition of all that is wrong within one and the acceptance of one's past karma. Sange is the true source of religious humility and a principal gateway to enlightenment.

SANGHA (S), sō (J). The community of those who follow the Buddha's Teaching: male priests, female priests, laymen, laywomen.

SANZEN (J). Spiritual direction under a Zen Master.

SARIRA (S), shari (J). The relics of the Buddhas, or of any priest, after cremation.

SATORI (J). Sudden understanding.

SATTVA (S), sentient being.

SCRIPTURE OF AVALOKITESVARA BODHISATTVA, see AVALOKITESVARA BODHISATTVA, SCRIPTURE OF.

SCRIPTURE OF GREAT WISDOM; Hannya-Shingyo; full name:– Makahannya haramita shingyo (J); Mahaprajna paramita hrdaya sutra (S). Sometimes called the *Heart Scripture* since it is considered to be the essence, or heart, of the Great Wisdom Scripture.

SCRIPTURE OF THREE THOUSAND MANNERS. A Scripture that is concerned with the conduct of priests. One of several extensions of the Vinaya.

SEAL, or Mind Seal. A term used to refer to the Transmission.

SECK KIM SENG (C), 1913–1980. Former Abbot of Cheng Hoon Teng Temple in Malacca, Malaysia, and Rōshi P.T.N.H. Jiyu-Kennett's ordination master.

SEIGEN GYOSHI (J), d. 740, Ch'ing-yuan Hsing-ssu (C). A Chinese Zen Master, one of the great disciples of the Sixth Ancestor, Daikan Enō.

SEKITŌ KISEN (J), 700–790, Shih-t'ou Hsi-ch'ien (C). A Chinese Zen Master. At first a disciple of the Sixth Ancestor, Daikan Enō, he trained under Seigen Gyoshi after Daikan Enō's death.

SEKKŌ (J). A Zen Master.

SELF. Refers to the worldly mind that is dominated by self-interest.

SENSEI (J), teacher. A term sometimes used to address Zen priests in Japan.

SENSU TOKUJŌ (J), Ch'uan-tzu Te-ch'eng (C). A Chinese Zen Master and disciple of Yakusan Igen. He was called Sensu, the Boatman Priest, since he worked as a ferryman. His disciple was Kassan Zene (Gasan).

SEPPŌ GIZON (J), 822–908, Hsueh-feng I-ts'un (C). A Chinese Zen Master, disciple of Tokusan Senkan. Seppō was the master of Ummon Bun'en, the founder of the Ummon Church of Zen.

SESSHIN (J), searching the heart.

SEVEN BUDDHAS, Kakoshichibutsu (J). The historical Shakyamuni Buddha and the six Buddhas preceding Him.

SEVEN TREASURES. They are:– (1) faith (sraddha—S); (2) keeping the Precepts (sila); (3) humility (hri); (4) renouncing evil (apatrapya); (5) learning (sruta); (6) self-training and self-control (tyaga); and (7) wisdom (prajna). The term can also refer to the seven prerequisites for awakening wisdom:– (1) mindfulness; (2) investigating the Dharma; (3) vigour, exertion; (4) joy, bliss; (5) calmness; (6) meditation (samadhi), and (7) equanimity.

SHAKU (J). A unit of measure; one shaku is a little over one foot in length.

SHAKYA (S). The caste into which Shakyamuni Buddha was born.

SHAKYAMUNI (J), sage of the Shakyas. Refers to the historical Buddha after His enlightenment.

SHAMON (J), sramana, sramanera (S), novice. A wanderer, Buddhist monk or priest.

SHARIHOTSU (J), see SHARIPUTRA.

SHARIPUTRA (S), Sharihotsu (J). One of the Buddha's chief disciples. *The Scripture of Great Wisdom* is addressed to him.

SHASHU (J). A position in which the hands are held clasped on the chest.

SHIKAN-TAZA (J), just sitting. The form of Zazen done in Sōtō Zen temples.

SHIN, kokoro (J), hsin (C), citta (S), heart, mind, will. True Self or Buddha Nature. See also BODAISHIN, BUDDHA NATURE.

SHIN BUDDHISM, see PURE LAND BUDDHISM.

SHINGI (J), pure training rules, see ZEN TEMPLE REGULATIONS.

SHINTŌ (J). Japanese folk religion primarily concerned with ancestor worship and nationalism.

SHŌBŌGENZŌ (J), The Treasury Eye of the True Teaching.

SHŌMON (J), see SHRAVAKA.

SHŌRINJI (J), Shao-lin-ssu (C). The temple in China where Bodhidharma sat facing a wall for nine years. See also BODHIDHARMA.

SHRAVAKA (S), Shōmon (J), one who hears. A disciple. The term originally applied to those who heard the Buddha's teaching and became Arhats.

SHU (J). Suffix meaning church or school.

SHŪRA (J), Buddha curl. A small tuft of hair on the crown of the head which is the last to be shaved at the ordination ceremony.

SHŪRYO, Sōdō (J), Trainees' Hall.

SHURYOGON-SAMMAI (J), Surangama-samadhi (S), meditation in the heroic way. (1) A samadhi in which all illusions are transcended and one dwells in Nirvana in the midst of everyday life. (2) The name of a Buddhist Scripture, *Surangama-samadhi Scripture*, which discusses this samadhi in great detail.

SHUSHŌGI (J), What is Truly Meant by Training and Enlightenment. The most basic text of Sōtō Zen compiled from extracts of Dōgen's essential teachings by two Sōtō teachers, Rozan Takushū and Hōun Fugai. It is carefully studied by both priests and lay people as it provides the most basic guide to Zen training.

SHUSŌSHŌ (J), see CHIEF JUNIOR.

SHUZAN SHŌNEN (J), 926–993, Shou-shan Sheng-nien (C). A Chinese Zen Master of the Rinzai tradition. He was the disciple of Fuketsu Enshō; among his disciples was Fun-yō Zensho.

SIDDHARTHA GAUTAMA (S). The given name of Shakyamuni Buddha.

SIX LOKAS, see LOKA.

SIX PARAMITAS, see PARAMITA.

SIX STAGES OF ENLIGHTENMENT. A Tendai doctrine concerning Bodhisattva training.

SIX SUPERNATURAL POWERS. (1) Extraordinary sight, (2) extraordinary hearing, (3) ability to know the thoughts of others, (4) remembrances of past lives, (5) extraordinary activity and (6) eradication of defilements.

SIX TASTES. Food has six tastes:– bitter, sour, sweet, hot, salty and bland.

SIX WORLDS, see LOKA.

SKANDHAS (S), heaps, aggregates. The psycho/physical existence of a human being is categorised into five aggregates. They are:– (1) form or matter; (2) sensations or feelings; (3) thoughts and perceptions; (4) mental activity or impulses; (5) consciousness. When the skandhas are viewed through ignorance, a false notion of a self is created.

SŌJI KAISAN (J), Founder of Sōjiji. Refers to Keizan.

SŌJIJI (J). One of the two head temples of the Sōtō Zen Church now located in Yokohama, Japan. It was originally a Shingon temple, established by Gyogi (668–749), but was later given to Keizan in 1321. In 1898 it was moved from Ishikawa Prefecture to its present site. The Very Reverend Kohō Keidō Chisan Zenji, Rōshi P.T.N.H. Jiyu-Kennett's teacher, was Chief Abbot of Sōjiji from 1957 until his death in 1967.

SŌKEI (J), Ts'ao-ch'i (C). The name of the place where Daikan Enō, the Sixth Ancestor, had his monastery; the name is also used to refer to the Sixth Ancestor himself.

SŌTŌ ZEN (J), Ts'ao-Tung (C). The oldest of the five schools (churches) of Zen in China. It was established by Tōzan Ryokai and his disciple Sōzan Honjaku. The name Sōtō is derived from the Sō in Sōzan and the Tō in Tōzan.

SŌZAN HONJAKU (J), 840–901, Ts'ao-shan Pen-chi (C). A Chinese Zen Master, one of Tōzan Ryokai's main disciples.

SRAMANERA (S), see SHAMON.

SRENIKA VATSAGOTRA (P). A non-Buddhist wanderer at the time of Shakyamuni Buddha who questioned Him on points of doctrine. Srenika believed that there was a constant self within the skandhas and this became known as the Srenika heresy.

STAFF, shakujō (J). A Buddhist priest's staff made of wood and metal.

STUPA (S). A mound or monument, usually made of earth or stone, erected over the relics of a Buddha or saint to mark the place as consecrated.

SUBHUTI (S). One of the ten great disciples of Shakyamuni Buddha.

SUDDHODANA (S). The father of Prince Siddhartha Gautama, the future Shakyamuni Buddha, and King of the Shakyas. He later became a disciple of Shakyamuni Buddha and attained Arhatship.

SUJATA (S). The woman who offered food to Shakyamuni Buddha just before His enlightenment.

SUMERU (S). Mount Sumeru is the symbol for the Buddhist universe; all the worlds are located upon it.

SUNG DYNASTY (C). Chinese dynasty from 960–1279.

SUNYATA (S), ku (J), emptiness, void, immaculacy.

SURANGAMA SUTRA (S), Ryogonkyo (J). A Mahayana Buddhist Scripture which discusses many of the obstacles that arise in training as well as the various states into which one can fall as a result of confusion and attachment.

SUTRA (S), kyo (J), sutta (P). A Buddhist Scripture. The first division of the *Tripitaka*.

TAIKO (J). A senior member of the priesthood who has undergone at least five years of training.

TAISŌ (J). A title meaning Great Ancestor.

TAISŌ EKA (J), 487–593, Hui-k'o (C). The Second Ancestor in Chinese Zen and Bodhidharma's principal disciple. Eka studied both Hinayana and Mahayana before becoming Bodhidharma's disciple at the age of forty.

TAN (J). The raised platform in the Meditation Hall upon which trainees sit, eat and sleep.

T'ANG DYNASTY. Chinese dynasty from 618–907.

TAO (C), see WAY.

TATHAGATA (S), Nyorai (J), Thus come One, Thus gone One. A title for a Buddha.

TEACHING, see DHARMA.

TEIJŌ (J). A famous Chinese priestess who began her training at the age of twelve under Isan Reiyu.

TEN BENEFITS. The ten benefits received from food. They are:–
(1) physical strength; (2) substance; (3) long life; (4) pleasure; (5) maintenance of training; (6) cleansing of the body; (7) settling of the mind; (8) satisfaction of hunger; (9) satisfaction of thirst and (10) improvement of health.

TEN DIRECTIONS. The Ten Directions or Quarters:– north, south, east, west, northeast, northwest, southeast, southwest, zenith and nadir.

TEN FORCES. The ten powers of understanding belonging to a Buddha.

TEN GOOD ACTIONS, see TEN GREATER PRECEPTS.

TEN GREATER PRECEPTS. The Precepts that are taken by both priests and laymen at Jūkai.

TEN STAGES OF BODHISATTVA TRAINING, see DASA-BHUMIKA.

TEN WORLDS. The Six Worlds plus those of the Buddhas, Bodhisattvas, Pratyekabuddhas and Shravakas.

TENDAI (J), T'ien T'ai (C). A Mahayana Buddhist church established in China by Chigi (Chih-i—C) in the sixth century. The name is derived from Mt. Tendai, heavenly terrace, where he founded Kokusei Temple; it held approximately four thousand trainees.

TENDŌ NYOJŌ (J), see NYOJŌ.

TENDŌZAN KEITOKUJI (J), T'ien T'ung-ssu (C). A Chinese Zen monastery founded in 300 by Gikō. In 1129 Wanshi Sōgaku, one of the great Sōtō Masters, became Abbot there and turned it into one of the greatest training monasteries of China. Dōgen studied there under Tendō Nyojō from 1223 until 1227. Tendōzan still flourished up to the 1960's with as many as five hundred trainees in residence. It was one of the first temples to be rebuilt in the 1970's after being severely damaged by the Red Guard.

TENGETSU (J). Clear, penetrating vision. The ability to see what the ordinary human eye cannot see. See SIX SUPERNATURAL POWERS.

TENKIEN (J). The senior priest on night duty in a Zen training temple.

TENNITSU (J). Clear, penetrating hearing. The ability to hear what the normal ear cannot hear. See SIX SUPERNATURAL POWERS.

TENZO (J). The Chief Cook of a Zen temple.

THERAVADA (S), teaching of the elders. The only surviving church of Hinayana Buddhism found primarily in Ceylon, Burma and Thailand. See HINAYANA.

THIRTY-TWO MARKS OF A BUDDHA, Good Aspects. Early Buddhist Scriptures speak of the Buddha as possessing thirty-two good aspects and eighty minor marks.

THOUGHT, NATURAL AND DELIBERATE. Terms used to assist trainees during meditation.

THREE BASKETS, see TRIPITAKA.

THREE BODIES, Trikaya (S), Sanshin (J). See NIRMANA-KAYA, SAMBHOGAKAYA and DHARMAKAYA.

THREE FIRES. The Three Hindrances; greed, hate and delusion.

THREE PURE PRECEPTS. Cease from evil, Do only good, Do good for others.

THREE REFUGES. I take refuge in the Buddha (Namu kie Butsu—J); I take refuge in the Dharma (Namu kie Hō); I take refuge in the Sangha (Namu kie Sō). All traditions of Buddhism have the Three Refuges as the basis of their teaching.

THREE STYLES OF TRAINING. A reference to Tendai doctrine.

THREE THOUSAND WORLDS, sanzen (J). The teaching that there are three thousand realms or worlds:– the ten worlds, each of which contains within it the other nine, multiplied by ten characteristics and three factors.

THREE TREASURES, Sambō (J). The Buddha, the Dharma and the Sangha; they are also referred to as the Three Jewels.

THREE TREASURES PRECEPTS, see THREE REFUGES.

THREE VEHICLES, triyana (S). (1) Hinayana, or small vehicle (also called Shravakayana), by means of which one becomes an Arhat through the understanding of the Four Noble Truths. (2) Pratyekabuddha-yana by means of which one reaches understanding through one's own efforts but does not teach others. (3) Mahayana, or great vehicle, by means of which one becomes a Bodhisattva.

THREE WISDOMS. (1) Insight into the mortal conditions of self and others in past existences as well as this one, (2) insight into possible future mortal conditions and (3) comprehension of the wisdom in, and experience of, that wisdom in the Four Noble Truths.

THREE WORLDS. (1) The past, present and future worlds. (2) The formless realm, the realm of form where there is no desire and the realm of form where there is desire. One of the ways of classifying sentient existence.

T'IEN-T'UNG-SSU (C), see TENDŌZAN KEITOKUJI.

TOKUDŌ (J). Ordination.

TOMOE (J). A Buddhist symbol. See MANJI.

TOSOTSUTEN (J), Tushita Heaven (S). The fourth heaven in the Buddhist cosmology.

TŌZAN RYOKAI (J), 807–869, Tung-shan Liang-chieh (C). A Chinese Zen Master and principal founder of the Sōtō Zen Church. The second syllable of the word "Sōtō" comes from his name. He was the disciple of Ungan Donjō and his two main disciples are Sōzan Honjaku and Ungo Dōyō.

TŌZAN SHUSHŌ (J), 910–990, Tung-shan Shou-chu (C). A Chinese Zen Master and disciple of Ummon Bun'en.

TREASURE HOUSE. Another term for Buddha Nature.

TRIKAYA (S), see THREE BODIES, NIRMANAKAYA, SAMBHOGAKAYA and DHARMAKAYA.

TRIPITAKA (S), three baskets. Collection of canonical Buddhist Scriptures consisting of the *Vinaya* (monastic rules), *Sutras* (teaching Scriptures) and *Abhidharma* (philosophical analyses). See ABHIDHARMA, SUTRA and VINAYA.

TWELVE ASPECTS, see DEPENDENT ORIGINATION.

TWENTY-FIVE WORLDS, Nijugo-u (J). Twenty-five abodes:– four evil worlds of hell, asuras, hungry ghosts and animals; four continents in the human world; six heavens in the realm of desire; seven heavens in the world of form without desire and four heavens of the formless realm. See LOKA.

TWO VEHICLES. Mahayana and Hinayana.

UDAYAMA (P). King Udayama was the ruler of Kosambi in India

at the time of Shakyamuni Buddha. The first statue of the Buddha is said to have been made by him.

UDRAKA RAMAPUTRA (S). One of the ascetic teachers under whom the future Shakyamuni Buddha studied before His enlightenment.

UDUMBARA (S). A tree which is said to flower only when a Buddha is born.

UJI (J), existence, time, flow.

UMMON BUN'EN (J), 863–949, Yun-men Wen-yen (C). A Chinese Zen Master and founder of the Ummon Church, one of the five schools (churches) of Chinese Zen. Ummon Zen was absorbed into Rinzai in the thirteenth century.

UMPAN (J), cloud plate. A flat metal plate in the shape of a cloud.

UNGAN DONJŌ (J), 780–841, Yun-yen T'an-sheng (C). A Chinese Zen Master, disciple of Yakusan Igen and master of Tōzan Ryokai, the founder of the Sōtō tradition.

UNSUI (J), cloud and water. A priest trainee, male or female.

UPADHYAYA (S). A senior priest of ten years standing.

URUVELA (P). A town in India where Shakyamuni Buddha practiced asceticism prior to His enlightenment.

VAIROCANA BUDDHA (S), Birushanofū, Bironshanubutsu, Birushana or Dainichi Nyorai (J). The Illuminator; He represents the Dharmakaya, Pure Buddha Mind.

VAJRASATTVA (S), Diamond Being. The Iron Man; the Indestructible Buddha within.

VASUBANDHU (S), c. fourth century A.D., Bashyubanzu (J). A Master of the Yogacara church in India and the younger brother of Asanga. He is the author of the *Abhidharma-kosa* and many other works.

VIMALAKIRTI (S), Yuima (J), Spotless Reputation. A layman, living during the time of Shakyamuni Buddha, who was highly enlightened.

VIMALAKIRTI SCRIPTURE (S), Yuimakyo (J). A Scripture consisting of the discourses of Vimalakirti.

VINAYA (S). The collection of the monastic rules formulated in India during and after the life of Shakyamuni Buddha; a section of the *Tripitaka* or Three Baskets.

VIPAKA (S). The karmic results of our thoughts, words and deeds.

VISHNU (S). The Preserver, a Hindu deity, also known as Narayana. He represents life having the power to manifest in many forms.

WANSHI SŌGAKU (J), 1090–1157, Hung-chih Cheng-chueh (C). One of the great Sōtō Zen Masters of Sung China and a disciple of Tanka Shijyun (d. 1119). Wanshi was Abbot of Tendōzan from 1129 until his death. He rebuilt Tendōzan and, under his direction, the Meditation Hall held over twelve hundred trainees. In the twelfth century, Wanshi was the major advocate of Shikan-taza or just sitting.

WAY, dō (J), tao (C). A synonym for Buddha Mind, True Self.

WESTERN PARADISE, see PURE LAND.

WHEEL, see DHARMACHAKRA.

YAJNADATTA (S), Enyadatta (J). The subject of a parable from the *Surangama Scripture*.

YAKUSAN IGEN (J), 745–828, Yueh-shan Wei-yen (C). A Chinese Zen Master and disciple of Sekitō Kisen; also known as Kōdō Daishi (J). His two chief disciples were brothers, Ungan Donjō and Dōgo Enichi.

YAMA (S). The king of hell.

YASHODHARA (S). The wife of Prince Siddhartha Gautama, the future Shakyamuni Buddha, and the mother of His son, Rahula. She entered the priesthood five years after Shakyamuni Buddha's enlightenment.

YŌFU, SEAL OF, (J). Refers to the Chinese legend of Chiang K'ang's rescue of a suffering tortoise.

YOGA (S), union. An Indian teaching system using physical

postures, forms of mantric meditation and special diet to achieve various meditational states.

YŌKA GENKAKU (J), 665–713, Yang-ch'i (C). A Chinese Zen Master and disciple of Daikan Enō, the Sixth Ancestor. He is the author of the *Shōdōka*.

YUIMA (J), see VIMALAKIRTI.

ZAFU (J), sitting cushion.

ZAMMAI (J), see SAMADHI.

ZAZEN (J), sitting meditation. Zen meditation done in the formal seated position.

ZAZEN RULES, see FUKANZAZENGI.

ZEN (J), dhyana (S), ch'an (C), Meditation.

ZEN MASTER, see DHARMA HEIR, RŌSHI.

ZEN TEMPLE REGULATIONS, or Rules of Hyakujō, Hyakujō-shingi (J). The *Zen Temple Regulations* established in the eighth century by the Chinese Zen Master Hyakujō Ekai.

ZENDŌ (J), Meditation Hall.

ZENJI (J), ch'an-shih (C), Zen Master.

ZUDA (J), Dhutaguna (S). Twelve practices, originating in early Hinayana Buddhism, which were considered of great benefit. They are:– (1) living in the forest; (2) begging food; (3) wearing clothes made from rags; (4) eating only before noon; (5) eating a meal in one sitting; (6) living on alms; (7) living in cemeteries; (8) living in an open place; (9) dwelling at the foot of trees; (10) remaining in the meditation position even during sleep; (11) sleeping at night wherever one is; (12) having no more than three robes.

INDEX.

ABOUT THE AUTHOR.

Born in England in 1924, Reverend Master P.T.N.H. Jiyu-Kennett became a Buddhist at an early age, studying Theravada Buddhism. She was later introduced to Rinzai Zen Buddhism by D.T. Suzuki in London, where she held membership in, and lectured at, the London Buddhist Society. She studied at Trinity College of Music, London, and Durham University, and pursued a career as a professional musician before meeting her future master, the Very Reverend Keidō Chisan Kohō Zenji.

Rev. Master Jiyu-Kennett began her priest training in 1962, with her ordination into the Chinese Buddhist Sangha in Malaysia by the Very Reverend Seck Kim Seng, Archbishop of Malacca. She then continued her training in Japan under Kohō Zenji, who was then Chief Abbot of Dai Hon Zan Sōjiji, one of the two head temples of Sōtō Zen Buddhism in Japan. In 1963 she received Dharma Transmission from him and was later certified by him as a Rōshi (Zen Master). She held several positions during her years in Japan including that of Foreign Guestmaster of Dai Hon Zan Sōjiji and Abbess of her own temple in Mie Prefecture.

It had always been Kohō Zenji's wish that Sōtō Zen Buddhism be successfully transmitted to the West by a Westerner. He worked very hard to make it possible for Rev.

Master Jiyu-Kennett to train in Japan and, after his death, she left Japan in order to carry out this task. In November 1969, Rev. Master Jiyu-Kennett came to San Francisco on a lecture tour, and as her following of disciples grew rapidly, the Zen Mission Society was founded and moved to Mount Shasta, where Shasta Abbey was founded in November 1970. The "Zen Mission Society" was reorganized as "The Order of Buddhist Contemplatives" in 1978.

Rev. Master Jiyu-Kennett served twenty-six years as Abbess and spiritual director of Shasta Abbey, ordaining and teaching monks and laypeople. She founded Throssel Hole Buddhist Abbey in England in 1972 and was Head of the Order of Buddhist Contemplatives. Her written legacy as a Zen Master includes the books *Zen is Eternal Life; How to Grow a Lotus Blossom; The Wild, White Goose; The Book of Life* and *The Liturgy of the Order of Buddhist Contemplatives for the Laity.* She died on November 6, 1996.

ABOUT THE ORDER
OF BUDDHIST CONTEMPLATIVES.

The Order of Buddhist Contemplatives is a religious order practicing Serene Reflection Meditation (J. Sōtō Zen) as transmitted from the Very Reverend Keidō Chisan Kohō Zenji, Abbot of Dai Hon Zan Sōjiji in Yokohama, Japan, to Reverend Master P.T.N.H. Jiyu-Kennett. Rev. Master Jiyu-Kennett came to the United States in 1969 and established Shasta Abbey in 1970. She founded the Order of Buddhist Contemplatives in 1978, serving as Head of the Order until her death in 1996. In North America, the Order now has Priories (congregational temples) in Albany and Santa Barbara, California; Eugene and Portland, Oregon; McKenna and Seattle, Washington; and Vancouver B.C., Canada. In Europe, Throssel Hole Buddhist Abbey in northern England was founded in 1972, and O.B.C. Priories are located in Edinburgh, Scotland, and Reading and Telford, England. There are also meditation groups affiliated with the Order in Great Britain, Canada, the United States, the Netherlands, and Germany. The Order has male and female monks; women and men have equal status and recognition and train together in the Buddhist priesthood; they are referred to as both monks and priests. The monastic order is celibate and vegetarian. In addition to monastics, the Order includes lay ministers throughout the world. The Head of the Order is Rev. Master Daizui MacPhillamy; its international headquarters are at Shasta Abbey. The Order publishes *The Journal of the Order of Buddhist Contemplatives* quarterly.

ABOUT THE MONASTERIES
OF THE ORDER.

Shasta Abbey, located on sixteen forested acres near Mount Shasta city in northern California, is a seminary for the Buddhist priesthood and training monastery for both lay and monastic Buddhists and visitors. It was established in 1970 by Rev. Master P.T.N.H. Jiyu-Kennett, who was Abbess and spiritual director until her death in 1996. Buddhist training at Shasta Abbey is based on the practice of Serene Reflection Meditation and the keeping of the Buddhist Precepts. The monastery is home to over 30 ordained male and female monks and its Abbot is Rev. Master Ekō Little, a senior disciple of Rev. Master Jiyu-Kennett.

Guests and visitors follow a schedule that is similar to that of the monastic community, providing a balance of sitting meditation, work, ceremonial, and instruction in Buddhism. The schedule allows the mind of meditation to be cultivated and maintained throughout all aspects of daily life. Retreat guests stay at the Abbey's guest house, which accommodates about 40 people. All meals are vegetarian and are prepared in the Abbey kitchen. A stay at Shasta Abbey allows visitors to set aside their usual daily concerns so that they may participate wholeheartedly in the spiritual life of the monastery.

In addition to its monastic and lay training programs, Shasta Abbey offers a Buddhist Supply service and publishes books through Shasta Abbey Press. For more information, call or write Shasta Abbey, 3724 Summit Drive, Mt. Shasta, California, 96067-9102; phone: (530) 926-4208; fax: (530) 926-0428; e-mail: shastaabbey@obcon.org.

Throssel Hole Buddhist Abbey is situated in a quiet valley in the north of England. It was founded in 1972 by Rev. Master P.T.N.H. Jiyu-Kennett as Throssel Hole Priory, and over the years has become a monastery and seminary for training priests of the Order, as well as a retreat and training center for a large European congregation. Its Abbot is Rev. Master Daishin Morgan, a senior disciple of the late Rev. Kennett.

The Abbey offers for lay guests a full and varied program, to which all are warmly invited. Experienced senior priests teach both meditation and how to use the Buddhist Precepts in establishing a daily practice. Through these means one can find the Truth, or Buddha Nature, at the heart of oneself and all beings. Training shows how to let go of the clinging that causes suffering, thus allowing this inner compassion and wisdom to enrich our lives. Guests meditate in the bright and spacious ceremony hall, and sleep there at night, dormitory-style, with complete privacy between men and women maintained. A large dining hall includes a small library and common room area for guests. By following the monastery's daily schedule, guests experience how it is that all activities of life—working, relaxing, reading, eating, and sleeping—have true spiritual depth and value. For more information, call or write Throssel Hole Buddhist Abbey, Carrshield, nr. Hexham, Northumberland NE47 8AL, United Kingdom; phone: +44 (0) 1434 345204 or fax: +44 (0) 1434 345216.

O.B.C. website: www.obcon.org